BOBB

FISCHER

GOES TO

WAR

ALSO BY DAVID EDMONDS AND JOHN EIDINOW

Wittgenstein's Poker

DAVID EDMONDS

AND

JOHN EIDINOW

ecco

An Imprint of HarperCollins*Publishers*

BOBBY FISCHER GOES TO WAR

HOW THE

SOVIETS LOST

THE MOST

EXTRAORDINARY

CHESS MATCH

OF ALL TIME

The lyrics from *Chess* by Benny Andersson, Tim Rice, and Bjorn Ulvaeus are reprinted with the kind permission of 3 Knights Ltd. The Prefab Sprout lyrics are reprinted with the kind permission of Kitchenware Management. The lines from *Selected Poems of Evgeny Rein* are reprinted by kind permission of Bloodaxe Books.

BOBBY FISCHER GOES TO WAR. Copyright © 2004 by David Edmonds and John Eidinow. All rights reserved. Printed in the United States of America. No part of this book may be used or reproduced in any manner whatsoever without written permission except in the case of brief quotations embodied in critical articles and reviews. For information, address HarperCollins Publishers Inc., 10 East 53rd Street, New York, NY 10022.

HarperCollins books may be purchased for educational, business, or sales promotional use. For information, please write: Special Markets Department, HarperCollins Publishers Inc., 10 East 53rd Street, New York, NY 10022.

FIRST EDITION

Designed by Jessica Shatan Heslin

Library of Congress Cataloging-in-Publication Data is available upon request.
ISBN 0-06-051024-2

04 05 06 07 08 BVG/FFG 10 9 8 7 6 5 4 3 2 1

TO ELISABETH EIDINOW

AND

TO THREE EDMONDS SIBLINGS,
PHILIP, RICHARD, AND JULIA

CONTENTS

NOTE ON THE TRANSLITERATION OF RUSSIAN

In general, we have transliterated Russian names and other words in accordance with the Library of Congress system. However, where we feel an established version of a name is so familiar that changing it might disturb a reader, we have retained that version—for instance, Spassky and Dostoyevsky. We have similarly made changes to assist readers' pronunciation.

DRAMATIS PERSONAE

THE AMERICANS

Bobby Fischer	World championship contender
Pal Benko	Grandmaster, enabled Fischer to enter world championship rounds
Robert Byrne	Grandmaster, coauthor with Ivo Nei of book on match
Fred Cramer	Chief assistant to Fischer in Reykjavik
Brad Darrach	*Life* reporter and member of Fischer's Reykjavik team
Andrew Davis	Attorney to Fischer
Ed Edmondson	Executive director of the U.S. Chess Federation and mentor to Fischer
Larry Evans	American grandmaster and former second to Fischer
Regina Fischer	Bobby's mother
Chester Fox	TV producer with exclusive rights to film the match
Victor Jackovich	Junior diplomat in U.S. Icelandic embassy
Henry Kissinger	U.S. national security adviser

William Lombardy	Roman Catholic priest, grandmaster, and second to Fischer
Paul Marshall	Attorney to Fischer
Paul Nemenyi	Allegedly Fischer's biological father
Richard Nixon	U.S. president
Anthony Saidy	Chess player, gave sanctuary to Fischer
Don Schultz	Fischer aide and future president of the U.S. Chess Federation
Frank Skoff	Fischer aide and president of U.S. Chess Federation from August 1972
Ken "Top Hat" Smith	American chess and poker player, helped Fischer prepare
Theodore Tremblay	U.S. chargé d'affaires in Iceland

Various attorneys, journalists, chess players, commentators, and acquaintances of Fischer

THE SOVIETS

Boris Spassky	World champion
Lev Abramov	Former head of Chess Department, USSR Council of Ministers Committee for Physical Training and Sport
Sergei Astavin	Soviet ambassador to Iceland
Yuri Averbakh	President of the USSR Chess Federation and of the Trainers' Council, grandmaster
Viktor Baturinskii	Director of the Central Chess Club; head of the Chess Department, chief trainer, and inspector of the USSR Council of Ministers Committee for Physical Training and Sport; former colonel and deputy chief military prosecutor

Yevgeni Bebchuk	Journalist and former president of the Chess Federation of the Russian Federation (a republic of the USSR)
Mikhail Beilin	Former head of the Chess Department, USSR Council of Ministers Committee for Physical Training and Sport
Isaac Boleslavskii	Grandmaster
Igor Bondarevskii	Grandmaster and trainer to the world champion
Mikhail Botvinnik	Former world chess champion
Valeri Chamanin	Soviet embassy interpreter
Piotr Demichev	Communist Party of the Soviet Union Central Committee secretary responsible for ideology
Anatoli Dobrynin	Soviet ambassador to Washington, D.C.
Efim Geller	Grandmaster, second, and trainer to the world champion
Viktor Ivonin	Deputy chairman of the USSR Council of Ministers Committee for Physical Training and Sport, in charge inter alia of chess (deputy sports minister)
Anatoli Karpov	Future world chess champion
Nikolai Krogius	Psychologist, grandmaster, second, and trainer to the world champion, future head of the USSR state chess organization
Ivo Nei	Second and tennis partner to the world champion
Sergei Pavlov	Chairman of the USSR Council of Ministers Committee for Physical Training and Sport (sports minister)
Tigran Petrosian	Former world chess champion, defeated by Fischer in Candidates
Larisa Spasskaia	Second wife of world champion

Mark Taimanov	Grandmaster, defeated by Fischer in Candidates, concert pianist
Dmitri Vasil'iev	Second secretary, Icelandic embassy
Aleksandr Yakovlev	Acting head of the Propaganda and Agitation Department of the Party Central Committee

Various apparatchiks, psychiatrists, journalists, and shadowy figures from the KGB

THE ICELANDERS

Gissli Gestsson	Cameraman
Freysteinn Johannsson	Icelandic Chess Federation press officer
Olafur Johannesson	Prime minister
Fridrik Olafsson	Icelandic grandmaster, later clerk to the Icelandic Parliament
Saemundur "Saemi-Rock" Palsson	Fischer's police bodyguard
Gudmundur Thorarinsson	President of the Icelandic Chess Federation, chief match organizer, and responsible for gaining match for Iceland

Various car dealers, salmon fishers, technicians, scientists, doctors, stonemasons, and blond dancers

MATCH OFFICIALS

Gudmundur Arnlaugsson	Assistant arbiter (referee)
Max Euwe	Dutch president of the Fédération Internationale des Échecs (FIDE) and former world chess champion
Harry Golombek	British chess master and vice president of FIDE, *The Times* correspondent

Lothar Schmid	German grandmaster and chief arbiter (referee)

OTHERS

Leonard Barden	British chess player and journalist, friend of James Slater
Dimitri Bjelica	Yugoslav journalist
Svetozar Gligoric	Yugoslav grandmaster and commentator on match
Bent Larsen	Danish grandmaster, defeated by Fischer in Candidates
James Slater	Multimillionaire British financier
Bob Wade	New Zealand international master, helped Fischer prepare

GLOSSARY

a1 ... b1 ... g1 ... h1 ... a2 ... h2, and so on—Each of the sixty-four squares on the chessboard has a unique coordinate, from a1 to h8. a1 to a8 runs down a "file," from white to black; a1 to h1 runs down a "rank," from one side of the board to the other. This is the algebraic notation for identifying squares on the board. Thus, "Re3," means the rook moves to the "e3" square. In 1972, most people operated with another language. A white move of the pawn to e4—the pawn to the fourth square of the king file—was written down as "P-K4." When black moved, his/her moves were seen from his/her side: thus, if black moved his/her king's pawn two squares (to e5), this was also jotted down as "P-K4."

Castle A maneuver in chess in which the king moves two squares and the rook jumps over it to the adjacent square. Each side can perform this maneuver only once per game. This is the only maneuver in chess in which two pieces are moved simultaneously. It is allowed under the following conditions: 1) there can be no pieces between the king and rook; 2) neither the king nor the rook can previously have moved; 3) the king cannot be in check; 4) nor can the king pass over a square that is under attack by an opposing piece.

Central Committee of the Communist Party of the Soviet Union (CPSU) The governing body of the Communist Party. The general secretary (or first secretary) was the true leader of the USSR.

Checkmate The king is attacked and cannot escape; the end of the chess game.

Federal Bureau of Investigation (FBI) Founded in 1908 as the Bureau of Investigation, it is the investigative arm of the U.S. Department of Justice and answerable to the U.S. attorney general. Broadly, it investigates cases where a federal interest is involved. At the period of this story, its name was inseparable from that of J. Edgar Hoover, who had been director since 1924.

Fédération Internationale des Échecs (FIDE) Formed in 1924, it has responsibility for the organization of chess at the international level, including the rules of play and international championships. The membership is of national chess federations.

Grandmaster The highest international ranking of a player. The title is earned through a complex rating system but essentially requires several strong results in top-class tournaments. "International master" is the next highest ranking. In 1972, there were approximately ninety grandmasters; there are now six times that number.

Icelandic Chess Federation (ICF) Responsible for organized chess in Iceland.

Komitet Gosudarstvennoi Bezopasnosti (KGB) Committee for State Security, successor to the secret police, the NKVD.

Komsomol The Youth League of the Communist Party.

Narodnyi Komissariat Vnutrennikh Del (NKVD) People's Commissariat for Internal Affairs, the state security organization until 1943. With its own armed force and control over the penal system, it answered directly to Stalin and included the political police, ordinary police, and border troops.

Opening There are no fixed frontiers separating the three phases of chess—the opening, the middle game, and the ending—but the opening covers the first moves of the game, often well known to the players from their experience and from study to the players; in the middle game, the majority of the pieces will still be on the board, but the game will have entered virgin territory; and the ending is usually marked by the disappearance of the queens.

Politburo The policy-making body or cabinet of the CPSU Central Committee and center of Soviet political power.

Second A chess player who supports another player, in a tournament or a match, with opening preparation and, when unfinished games were adjourned, with adjournment analysis.

United States Chess Federation (USCF) Responsible for organized chess in the United States.

USSR Council of Ministers Committee for Physical Training and Sport (GosKomSport) In effect, the Sports Ministry, coming under the jurisdiction of the Council of Ministers. Constitutionally, GosKomSport was part of the government but in practice was answerable to the corresponding Central Committee department. It ran chess through its chess committee, the Central Chess Club, and the USSR Chess Federation. (Referred to here as the Sports Committee.)

WORLD CHESS
CHAMPIONS TO 1969

1886	Steinitz
1894	Lasker
1921	Capablanca
1927	Alekhine
1935	Euwe
1937	Alekhine
1948	Botvinnik
1957	Smyslov
1958	Botvinnik
1960	Tal
1961	Botvinnik
1963	Petrosian
1969	Spassky

BOBBY

FISCHER

GOES TO

WAR

MATCH OF
THE CENTURY

Funny to be a war correspondent again after all these years.
— ARTHUR KOESTLER

When you play Bobby, it is not a question of whether you win or lose. It is a question of whether you survive.

— BORIS SPASSKY

It is five o'clock in the evening of Tuesday, 11 July 1972. The seats filling the arena of the sports hall, the Laugardalsholl, in Reykjavik's featureless leisure complex are sold out. On the platform, the world chess champion, thirty-five-year-old Boris Vasilievich Spassky, sits alone at the chessboard. He is playing white. Precisely on the hour, the German chief arbiter, Lothar Schmid, starts the clock. Spassky picks up his queen's pawn and moves it forward two squares. The Soviet Union's king of chess has begun the defense of the title that has been his since 1969, and his country's without interruption since World War II. He glances up at the other side of the board. The expensive, low-slung, black leather, swivel chair, specially provided for his opponent, is empty.

Six minutes later, the American challenger, Bobby Fischer, arrives. A communal sigh of relief gusts through the hall. Because of his refusal to leave New York in time for the match's opening, the first game has already been postponed and many had feared that he might not appear at all: with Fischer, one can never be sure. Now a large hand reaches across the chessboard, plucks up the black king's knight, and places it on f6.

In the provincial and normally tranquil Icelandic capital, what is already being called "the Match of the Century" is at last under way.

The World Chess Championship has existed since 1886. But with this final, it is a front-page story for the first time; at $250,000, the prize money is nearly twenty times more than in the last title contest, when Boris Spassky triumphed over his fellow Soviet, the then champion Tigran Petrosian.

Why do the games make news on television and stars of commentators? Already a people's sport in the communist bloc, why does chess now become the rage in the West, the pastime of the moment, like the Charleston, canasta, or the Hula Hoop; what you talk about in the bar with strangers and over the dinner table with friends? The 1972 championship will become immortalized in film, on the stage, in song. It will remain incontrovertibly the most notorious chess duel in history. There will never be another like it.

This has little to do with the games themselves. If it had, the Reykjavik tale could be left to the existing books and myriad reports in chess volumes and articles that analyze the chess, game by game, in every detail. There are scores of them—for the most part, instant works. What turned this championship into a unique and compelling confrontation was off the chessboard, beginning with the conviction that history was being made.

To Western commentators, the meaning of the confrontation seemed clear. A lone American star was challenging the long Soviet grip on the world title. His success would dispose of the Soviets' claim that their chess hegemony reflected the superiority of their political system. The board was a cold war arena where the champion of the free world fought for democracy against the apparatchiks of the Soviet socialist machine. Here was the *High Noon* of chess, coming to you from a concrete auditorium in Iceland.

Given the mutual hostility of the two great power blocs of the cold war, such a reading of the encounter was inevitable. But the story can now be retold from a new perspective, stripped of cold war distortions, a story more nuanced and surprising than could be seen in 1972. The end of the cold war has allowed access to people and records that reveal the individuals inside the Soviet monolith. White House, State Department, and FBI sources offer remarkable insights on official attitudes to the match and to Fischer. Far from being a simple ideological confrontation, the championship was played out on many levels, of which chess itself was only one. Reykjavik was the setting for a collision of personalities, of moral and legal obligations, of social and political beliefs.

However, in large measure, the sheer notoriety of the event was due to the presence of Bobby Fischer, a volatile genius, enthralling and shocking, appealing yet repellent.

In 1972, Fischer was still only twenty-nine, but he had already been at the summit of international chess for over a decade and the subject of increasing public fascination since he was a boy.

BROOKLYN BOY

Fischer wants to enter history alone. —MIGUEL NAJDORF

Robert J. Fischer was born to a life of chess in Chicago at 2:39 P.M. on 9 March 1943. He grew up in a bustling, hustling society that to a great extent saw itself in the image of a Norman Rockwell *Saturday Evening Post* cover—the self-portrait of Middle America, prosperous, warmhearted, gainfully employed, family centered, community minded.

The Fischer family's life would not have made the cover of the *Saturday Evening Post*. Bobby never knew the person named as his father on his birth certificate, Gerhardt, a German biophysicist. His mother, Regina, of Polish-Jewish descent, was a remarkable woman, clever and domineering. As well as Bobby, there was his sister, Joan, older by five years, to support. Throughout Bobby's infancy, Regina was constantly short of money, struggling to feed and clothe her children, leading an itinerant existence.

However, in those early years of worry, she was nothing if not resourceful. There were jobs to be had: this was boom time for the American worker. Fueled by federal spending on the military, the combination of manufacturing technology and "can do" attitude was transforming the nation into the most powerful and productive in history. The U.S. economy had long outperformed Europe's and now per capita income in America was twice as high as in the most developed of Western European countries, only slowly recovering from World War II despite massive injections of American money. Demobilized troops returned from Europe and the Pacific to full employment, high wages, and record growth, to diners and hot-dog stands, to homes with labor-saving machines and Main Street bursting with consumer goods. Television was starting its march through the nation; it was a time of cultural optimism.

The soldiers came back to a government under President Truman that was infused with a sense of mission—a determination to contain Soviet expansionist tendencies and to make the world safe for democracy.

During the war, Regina had gone from Chicago to Washington, D.C., to visit a Hungarian close friend, Paul Nemenyi, then to Idaho for a few months of study (she majored in chemistry and languages), before taking a job as a stenographer in Oregon and then as a shipyard welder. After that the family transferred south to Arizona, where she taught in elementary schools. Then a move east was undertaken so she could study for a master's degree in nursing and subsequently enter a career as a nurse. They came to rest in Brooklyn, apartment Q, 560 Lincoln Place, small, basic, but habitable. It was in Brooklyn that Bobby spent his formative years. That was fortunate: in so far as America had a chess capital, it was undoubtedly New York.

When Fischer was six, Joan brought him home a chess set—he was a taciturn child, fascinated by board games and puzzles. Together they learned the moves from the instructions. Fischer soon became so engrossed in the game that Regina feared he was spending too much time alone. She sent an advertisement to the local paper, the *Brooklyn Eagle*, appealing for chess playmates for her son. The ad was never published because the editorial staff could not decide under what category to place it. What they did instead gives them a cameo part in chess history: they forwarded it to veteran chess journalist and official Hermann Helms. He wrote to Regina in January 1951, suggesting she bring Bobby along to the Brooklyn Chess Club.

Over the next few years, Fischer would spend many hours there being coached by the president of the club, Carmine Nigro. Frustrated by his own son's stubborn resistance to the charms of the game, Nigro was elated by the enthusiasm of his recruit. On nights when the club was closed, Bobby pestered his mother to take him to Manhattan's Washington Square Park, where the game was a unique leveler of class distinctions; the square acted as a magnet for New York's social gamut, from wealthy Wall Street stockbrokers to the beer-drinking homeless. To his mother's distress, Bobby's obsession showed no sign of abating; she took him to the Children's Psychiatric Division of the Brooklyn Jewish Hospital. There, he was seen by Dr. Harold Kline. He told her there were worse preoccupations. As Fischer got older, he began to make the trip to Manhattan unaccompanied. His mother traveled into town late into the evening to drag him away.

Fischer was no instant prodigy. Clearly talented, with a deep intuitive grasp of the game, he performed well in club games and tournaments, though not spectacularly. It was not until 1954, at the age of eleven, that Fischer, in his own words, "just got good." In 1955, he joined the Manhattan Chess Club and rose quickly through its divisions. It was the establishment club; according to the American player Jim Sherwin, the atmosphere "was rather staid—full of old white men." A year later, Fischer joined the Hawthorne Chess Club, an informal gathering of chess masters who met at least biweekly at the home of Jack Collins. Wheelchair bound, Collins lived with his sister, Ethel, a nurse, and was mentor to several promising players, including the future grandmasters William Lombardy and Robert Byrne. Collins would have a major influence on Fischer's life. He had built an enormous chess library for himself, and it was here that young Fischer had his first taste of chess literature, for which his appetite became limitless. He would go to other chess clubs, too;

there were several to choose from in Manhattan, such as the Marshall Club, which was in Greenwich Village and attracted a younger crowd, and the Flea House on 42nd Street. Games at these clubs were sometimes played for small amounts of money. At the Flea House, "Sam the Rabbi" was the easiest target if one wished to supplement one's income.

Rumors about the arrival of a new wunderkind slowly spread through the chess community. A boy of such potential had not been seen since 1920, when the nine-year-old Polish-born Samuel Reshevsky first toured the United States. At thirteen, Fischer was already receiving invitations to give simultaneous displays, in which he would compete against many players at once. He gave one exhibition in Cuba; his mother chaperoned her little boy. In July 1956, he won the U.S. Junior Chess Championship, the youngest to do so. That same year, he was offered a place in the elite Rosenwald competition, a round-robin (in which each contestant plays all the others) of the nation's top players, considered the most prestigious event in the U.S. chess calendar. His tactical masterpiece against Donald Byrne (brother of Robert) was instantly, if exaggeratedly, branded the best individual game of the century. A dazzling work of art, multilayered in its complexity, and demonstrating audacious vision, it was pored over across the world. According to international master Bob Wade, the seventeenth move, in which Fischer (black) retreated a bishop, Be6, ignoring the attack on his queen, raised this game to "an immortal level." In fact, Fischer had no rational alternatives to Be6; all other moves would have led to his defeat—but the swiftness with which his opponent's position subsequently disintegrated was still a marvel for chess enthusiasts to behold. By move twenty-five, it was already apparent that Byrne's pieces were in wretched disarray. Soviet grandmaster Yuri Averbakh says that it was after this game that he realized the Soviets faced a threat to their hegemony.

Physically, Fischer was now shooting up into a tall, gangly adolescent—while his chess was evolving and maturing with still greater rapidity. Over the new year of 1957–1958, he once again competed in the Rosenwald tournament. This time the result carried added significance: it served to determine both the U.S.

Fischer at fourteen. Already the youngest ever junior U.S. champion, within months he will become the youngest ever U.S. champion. ASSOCIATED PRESS

champion and which American players qualified for the next round of the World Chess Championship cycle. Fischer did not lose a single game. Still three months short of his fifteenth birthday, he emerged as U.S. champion. He was to win the U.S. title eight times.

Now he was capturing headlines. In rapt tones, it was reported how this youngster had the opening knowledge, technical skills, and intuitive judgment of a veteran grandmaster. In 1957, Regina wrote directly to the Soviet leader, Nikita Khrushchev, requesting an invitation for her son to participate in the World Youth and Student Festival. The reply—affirmative—came too late for him to go. Fischer was already convinced of his destiny as world champion; he was still determined to reach Moscow, the Mecca of chess, where he could test himself against the world's best. A year later, he went. (This time his sister kept him company.)

The quest proved a disaster. It was not that his hosts treated him badly. On the contrary, the Soviets regarded him as an honored guest, putting him up at a showcase hotel and giving him a car, a driver, and an interpreter. They offered to show him the Kremlin and take him to the Bolshoi. Fischer declined all distractions; he was there to play chess. He went to the Moscow Central Chess Club in the morning, returned to the hotel for lunch, then was back in the club until evening, where his opponents included the young Russian masters Aleksandr Nikitin and Yevgeni Vasiukov. He told the head of the Chess Department of the State Sports Committee, Lev Abramov, who had arranged his welcome, that he wished to take on some Soviet grandmasters. Abramov claims that he approached a number of grandmasters, whereupon the teenage American champion inquired how much he was to be paid. Abramov replied that it was not the Soviet custom to pay guests. In the end, Fischer managed only a few speed games with future world champion Tigran Petrosian. Even at that age, Fischer's demand for recognition was clear. His feeling slighted seems to have been the origin of his life-long antipathy toward all things Soviet, no doubt heavily influenced by the pervasive anticommunist climate in the United States. Fischer's interpreter complained to the authorities that Fischer was discourteous—the pilgrimage was aborted. American government documents contain reports that in the Moscow Chess Club, Fischer had called the Russians "a bunch of pigs" and that he had written an insulting postcard that the censor might have passed to the Soviet chess authorities.

The next decade and a half of Fischer's career was a protracted, bumpy, meandering trail, maddening for his supporters, toward the destination that he cared most about—a seat at the world championship table. To become a challenger in that period, three chess hurdles had to be surmounted. First came the regional tournament, the Zonal. Then came an international tournament, the Interzonal. Finally, the highest-scoring players in the Interzonal would square off in a tournament known as the Candidates. The winner of the Candidates would challenge the world champion in a one-to-one match for the title. This cycle, Zonals, Interzonal, Candidates, would repeat itself roughly every three years.

Having won the U.S. Chess Championship, Fischer had automatically qualified for the 1958 Interzonal, which was to take place in the resort town of Portoroz, Yugoslavia. He announced confidently, to anybody who would listen, that his strategy for making it through to the Candidates was to draw with the strong grandmasters and hammer the weaklings, predictions that were dismissed as youthful bravado. In the event, Fischer did pretty much as he had pledged, winning six games, losing only two, and coming in joint fifth. He thus became an international grandmaster, the youngest in history. It was hailed, rightly, as a staggering performance, as was his fifth place the following year in the Candidates tournament—also held in Yugoslavia.

The contrast between his star status in international chess and his mundane status as a high school student would have been difficult for any fifteen-year-old to manage, even one with the happy background which Fischer lacked. Fischer was now arguing incessantly with his domineering mother. There was much of the mother in the son: for instance, high intelligence. She was a brilliant linguist—in addition to English, she spoke French, German, Russian, Spanish, and Portuguese. Her master's degree in nursing from New York University was obtained, it is said (probably apocryphally), with the best marks ever recorded. Like Bobby, she was also instinctively antiauthority and a nonconformist. Difficult and uncompromising, she had few friends and little social life. She often behaved as though the primary function of the United States Chess Federation (USCF) and the U.S. government was to nurture the talent of her precocious Bobby. Regina became a regular at USCF meetings, a bundle of outraged energy, forcibly putting the case for more financial backing for her boy. In short, to an awkward, withdrawn, obsessive, and independent-minded teenager, she must have been the mother of all embarrassments.

At the local school, Erasmus Hall, Fischer was sullen and uninterested; he did little work and ignored authority. He did not see how a high school diploma could advance his true career and his real calling. The teachers understood that in Fischer they had a singular mind, but he proved impossible for them to teach. Sometimes he was caught in lessons playing chess on a pocket set. And even though they could confiscate the set, they could not control the insatiable journeyings of his mind around the sixty-four squares. Perhaps they could not empathize with how insecure he felt in the world beyond the board. As soon as he could, he abandoned his formal education.

From inside his chess isolation ward, Fischer showed no interest in that external world. America was on the verge of social upheaval; the Norman Rockwell *Saturday Evening Post* cover was being ripped apart. Race was the deepest fissure: the demand for civil rights had moved onto the streets. In 1963, Martin Luther King Jr. led 250,000 marchers through Washington to hear him make his historic declaration: "I have a dream..." In 1964, Cassius Clay rejected his "slave name" to become Muhammad Ali. In the 1968 Mexico Olympics, sprinter Tommie Smith gave a Black Power salute from the gold medalist's podium. There were riots in the black ghettos across the nation. King's doctrine of peaceful protest was challenged by the militant Black Power demands of Malcolm X and Stokely Carmichael.

Lyndon Johnson's government plunged deeper and deeper into debt, drawn on not only by the cost of the war on inequality, discrimination, and poverty, but by the steadily increasing commitment to Vietnam that would see 58,000 Americans killed and another 300,000 wounded. The "body bag" count entered the language of public debate and private anguish; antiwar demonstrations on the streets and campuses battered American confidence. The antiwar movement joined hands with the campaign for equal rights. Students played a significant role in both.

Esmond Wright remarks in *The American Dream* how "parents watched in bewilderment as their children dropped out of college, burned their draft cards, grew their hair long and joined free-living communes where drink, drugs and sex were readily available." "Turn on, tune in, drop out" was the mantra of Harvard LSD guru Timothy Leary. (He used chess sets as visual props in his lectures on the drug: "Life is a chess game of experiences we play.") But in some neighborhoods where the counterculture flourished, drugs and guns, gangs and violence fell in behind. Inner-city crime in particular rocketed—as did the prison population.

President Nixon contrasted student "bums blowing up the campuses" with the young men who were "just doing their duty. . . . They stand tall, and they are proud." On 4 May 1970, part-time soldiers of the National Guard fired into demonstrators at Kent State University in Ohio, killing four students and wounding eleven. In the turmoil that followed, state governors, alarmed at the breakdown of order, sent the National Guard into colleges across the nation. However, an older America remained the bedrock of society. As the 1970s opened, troops were withdrawn from Vietnam in increasing numbers. The "trillion-dollar economy" blossomed. By 1972, the "silent majority" was ready to return Richard Nixon to the White House.

⸪

By his mid-teen years, Fischer was showing signs of the personality that would make him forever dreaded as well as respected. In this period, the government documents contain a report that "the State Department did not want him overseas as a representative of the U.S. anymore." To obsession with chess and the belief that he was the best in the world was added an insistence on total control that brooked no compromise. His tempestuous relationship with his mother deteriorated to such an extent that *she* moved out of their apartment, going to stay with a friend on Longfellow Avenue in the Bronx, leaving him alone. Visitors found him living amid chaos, clothes strewn across the floor, chess books and magazines everywhere. There were four rooms and three beds. He is reported to have slept in a different bed each night; a chessboard stood by each one.

He met Boris Spassky for the first time in 1960 at a tournament in Mar del Plata in Argentina. The two men shared first prize, fully two points ahead of the Soviet grandmaster David Bronstein, who took third place. In their individual match, Spassky, with the white pieces, played the King's Gambit, a fierce opening in which white gives up a pawn in order to dominate the center of the board and rapidly develop his major pieces. (The opening has become largely discredited: accurate play by black leaves white with next-to-no compensation for the loss of the pawn.) Fischer analyzes this game in his book *My 60 Memorable*

Games. His big mistake, he admits, was not to exchange queens on move twenty-three, when he would have gone into an ending with his pawn advantage still intact. On move twenty-five, "I started to feel uncomfortable, but little did I imagine that Black's game would collapse in four short moves!" Three of these short moves later, it was clear his bishop could no longer be defended. "I knew I was losing a piece, but just couldn't believe it. I had to play one more move to see if it was really true!" Resignation came on move twenty-nine. That same year, Fischer won a small tournament in Iceland, his first visit there.

In 1962, Fischer, not yet twenty, came top by a large margin in the Stockholm Interzonal. He was the first non-Soviet to win an Interzonal, and in so doing he qualified for the Candidates tournament, held later that year in the island of Curaçao in the Dutch West Indies. He was now one of the favorites; certainly that is how he regarded himself. In the event, he got off to a terrible start, and although he managed to claw back some ground, he finished only in fourth place, several points behind the leaders, Tigran Petrosian, Paul Keres, and Efim Geller. Commentators were divided: either Fischer had not achieved full chess maturity or he was simply off form. The would-be champion had an alternative explanation, one that revealed his belief in his chess invincibility: If he had not won, he must have been the victim of a conspiracy.

In an article in the American weekly *Sports Illustrated,* he raged against the Soviet players, charging them with collusion. All twelve games between Petrosian, Keres, and Geller, he pointed out, had been drawn; many were quick draws. They had settled these games, he wrote, to conserve their intellectual and physical energies for struggles against the non-Soviets—Fischer himself in particular. And he concluded, "Russian control of chess has reached a point where there can be no honest competition for the World Championship."

Even if it was true that the Soviet players went easy on one another (grandmaster Viktor Korchnoi—then a Soviet—says it is true), they were able to do so only because Fischer lagged behind on points. Otherwise, to finish ahead of him, they would have had to press for victories. The American player Arthur Bisguier, in

Curaçao to act as chess aide to both Fischer and Pal Benko, is dismissive. "It's absurd to say [the Soviets] were cheating. Of course they agreed draws; they were ahead in the tournament. Fischer's complaint was just sour grapes."

The need for control was incompatible with respect for the rights of others. Anger lay just below the surface. In Curaçao, Bisguier, who says his principal job was "to calm Fischer's ruffled feathers when he had a bad result," was himself caught up in the teenager's dark moodiness. Fischer maintained that as he was America's best prospect in the tournament, Bisguier should be there to support him alone, not Benko as well. Just before midnight on 9 May, the thirty-three-year-old Benko came looking for Bisguier in Fischer's room; he needed some help in analyzing his adjourned game with Petrosian. Fischer and Benko started scrapping—what Bisguier calls "fisticuffs." The following day, Fischer wrote to the tournament organizing committee, saying Benko should be fined and/or expelled from the tournament. It was a letter they chose to ignore.

Bisguier has a more disturbing memory of Curaçao. During a break in the tournament, they went to stay on the beautiful tropical island of St. Martin. "I used to look in on him every day to try to cheer him up. And I saw that there was a door open and he had a shoe in his hand. I said, 'Why do you leave the door open? You get all these tropical bugs in here.' And he said, 'That's what I want.' And it turned out he had captured some poor creature and was banging on each one of its legs. There were other things of this sort. And it was scary. If he wasn't a chess player, he might have been a dangerous psychopath."

Tigran Petrosian went on to win the tournament and then to become world champion in 1963. Considered a strong bet for the 1966 title, Fischer stated that he would stay away from future Interzonals and Candidates tournaments unless the system was reformed to prevent collusion. He got his way: it was subsequently announced that, henceforth, the round-robin Candidates tournament would be replaced by a series of knockout matches.

Fischer's difficulties with competition organizers had already begun to escalate. His attendance at tournaments became conditional upon high appearance fees, which the sponsors reluctantly found—they understood that the participation of the American added glamour to any lineup and stimulated public interest. But money was only part of it. Playing conditions had to be up to Fischer's rigorous standards. The lighting had to be just right, the crowd had to be kept far enough back to limit noise. Less unusual, the rounds had to be prearranged so as to accommodate his religious practices. (Reshevsky, an Orthodox Jew, had the same requirement.)

In the mid-1960s, Fischer had become involved in the Worldwide Church of God, though he never formally joined. Based in Pasadena in Southern California, it was a rapidly growing fundamentalist sect, with over 75,000 members in 300 congregations across the country and abroad. The founder was an erstwhile newspaper advertising designer turned charismatic radio preacher, Herbert Armstrong. He served a Bible-based theological cocktail, part Judaism, with salvation through Jesus Christ, and a strict moral life. Followers were ordered to observe the Jewish Sabbath and such festivals as Passover and to adopt a kosher diet. With one exception, Fischer fitted in with the Church's religious practices, broadly observing its dietary code as well as more strictly following its Sabbath injunctions. Even so, one has the sense that the American imposed his personalized interpretation on the rules of his Church, just as he did on competition rules. Yevgeni Vasiukov records seeing Fischer on the Sabbath at a tournament: "I have no wish to cast doubt on Fischer's religious beliefs, but it was somewhat strange to see him come to the hall and analyze the games that had ended." The pronouncement Fischer chose to ignore entirely was the Church's doctrinal prohibition on board games, anathematized as "frivolous."

In December 1963, Fischer entered the U.S. Chess Championship. He had already won it five times, but nobody could have foreseen the outcome. Against eleven of the highest-ranked players in the country, he won every game. It was an awesome performance; "historic" was the adjective used, rightly, in the press. To win a national tournament is one thing, to win it several years in succession is another, but to win it without losing or even drawing a single game is staggering. He had proved himself in a different league.

On such form, Fischer posed a real threat to Soviet supremacy, and the chess world buzzed in anticipation of his participating in the Amsterdam Interzonal of 1964. Not to participate—missing this world championship cycle—would mean that he could not hope to become world champion until the end of the following cycle, in 1969. Surely this was a chance he would not pass up.

But still raging against the "Soviet swindlers," Fischer did indeed pass it up. His fury was turned in on himself, in the rejection of what he wanted most. He did not play competitive chess again for a year and a half. Offers came in, but Fischer turned them all down or asked for appearance fees beyond even the most munificent of sponsors. At the age of twenty-one, he staged his first retirement.

The tournament that brought him back was the Capablanca Memorial in Havana, which opened in August 1965—Fischer's first international event since what he regarded as the catastrophe of Curaçao. For an American, participation was a diplomatic challenge. This was only a few years since the Bay of Pigs fiasco and the Cuban missile crisis. Contact between Cuba and the United States was severely curtailed—when Fischer applied to the U.S. State Department for a permit to visit Cuba, they flatly turned him down.

Rather than fight the bureaucracy, Fischer's ingenious solution was to offer to play by telex. (Some claim the idea originated with the Cuban chess organizer José Luis Barreras.) He would make his moves in New York while his opponents made theirs in Cuba. The solution would set the Cubans back $10,000. In the meantime, his lust for control was undiminished. Before the tournament began, Fischer read that Castro was proclaiming his, Fischer's, involvement a propaganda victory. Fischer reacted with a cable to the Cuban leader withdrawing from the tournament unless "you immediately [send] me a telegram declaring that neither you, nor your government, will attempt to make political capital out of my participation."

To students of Fischer's psychology, Castro's choice of riposte carried an interesting lesson, as the Cuban leader stood his ground. Scornful counterattack was the mode. Cuba, he wrote back, had no need of propaganda victories. "If you are frightened . . . then it would be better to find another excuse." Fischer agreed to play. He came joint second.

In January 1966, Fischer took his seventh U.S. title, qualifying him for the 1967 Interzonal in Sousse, Tunisia. He was again on his way to another shot at his ultimate goal, the world title. In the meantime, there was a tournament in Santa Monica, in which the then world champion Tigran Pertrosian would participate, together with his recently defeated challenger Boris Spassky. Fischer had a disastrous first half, losing his individual game against Spaasky. As so often, however, he somehow stepped up a level, gathered momentum, and began cruising through the field. In the penultimate round, he faced Spassky again (all players played each other twice). This time he secured a draw—he had still not managed to beat the Russian—and Spassky went on to take the top prize, with Fischer finishing second.

Fischer and Spassky were to square off once more, in the chess Olympiad in Cuba in November 1966. There was almost a diplomatic incident when the Soviets initially refused to adjust the game times to fit in with Fischer's Sabbath. Eventually the entire U.S.-USSR match was rescheduled, and hundreds watched Fischer and Spassky eke out a long draw. Castro and Fischer were later seen in amicable conversation as though no cross words between them had ever been exchanged. By now, Spassky and Fischer had played four times, with Spassky drawing two and winning two.

The following year, the Interzonal was held in the Sousse-Palace hotel. What happened there continues to stimulate comment. Fischer was the favorite, and the organizers had done what they could to accommodate his wishes, including placing additional lamps by his table, so that the lighting met with his approval, and scheduling the matches in such a way that both Fischer and Reshevsky would be free of chess for twenty-four hours from Friday night as well as on religious holidays.

Nevertheless, the tournament was beset by problems. Fischer was acutely sensitive to offstage noise and commotion, demanding on one occasion that a cameraman be removed from the hall.

More important, as a result of the rescheduling, he had to play a number of games in succession—which he claimed put him under unreasonable strain. Although he was way ahead on points, halfway through he summarily departed his hotel and the tournament—and set off for Tunis.

Soviet international master Aivar Gipslis was his scheduled opponent the following day: Fischer was defaulted for failing to appear. A representative of the U.S. embassy went to see him, as did one of the organizers, begging him to return. In the next game, he was pitted against his old adversary and compatriot Samuel Reshevsky. Reshevsky watched Fischer's clock slowly tick down and must have expected not to have to make a move. With only five minutes to go before the automatic forfeit, Fischer strolled in and began to make accurate moves with extraordinary speed. Emotionally drained, Reshevsky capitulated quickly despite his time advantage. The veteran American then went around the other players with a petition objecting to Fischer's behavior.

Now the issue was the lost Gipslis game. Fischer said it must be replayed. The organizers discussed it, but they knew that if they complied, the other players would regard this as too great a concession—there would be mutiny. On the authorities' considered refusal, Fischer finally walked out, for good measure ripping up the hotel bill for "extras" that he was handed at reception.

Apparently at the peak of his powers, Fischer now disappeared from chess for two years. It appeared that in forfeiting the Gipslis game, he might forever have forfeited his chance of winning the world title. As the Sousse Interzonal had testified, Fischer had become the enfant terrible of chess, his antics attracting global attention to the normally sedate, dignified, inside-page, down-column Royal Game. But some of those who suffered at his hands would have thought "enfant terrible" too kind, believing that there was something demonic about him. Beyond the antics, what must be accounted for is how he lacked concern for others' feelings while retaining the loyalty of rejected supporters, how he aroused fear as well as reverence, and why he was willing to risk the highest prize to get his way.

MIMOPHANT

. . . a complete pain in the fundament.

— *LOS ANGELES FREE PRESS*

A BBC journalist once asked Fischer whether it bothered him that he had chosen to focus so single-mindedly on the game. It was a problem, Fischer admitted, "because you're kind of out of touch with real life being a chess player—not having to go to work and deal with people on that level. I've thought of giving it up, off and on, but I always considered: What else could I do?" It was a reply that showed more insight than is normally credited to him.

Even to other grandmasters, Fischer's total absorption in chess was incomprehensible. The Soviet grandmaster Yuri Averbakh describes meeting him for the first time in 1958 at the Interzonal tournament in Portoroz. The newly crowned U.S. champion, all of fifteen years old, was still in his scruffy presuit period, dressed in jumper and jeans. Averbakh says he was "something of a savage in communicating with people. He gazed without interest at the beautiful scenery of the Adriatic Côte d'Azur, never once went to the beach, never took a swim." Perhaps the Brooklyn boy felt a stranger to the richness of the Yugoslav coast, but there is a similar anecdote from 1971, when Fischer, then twenty-eight, was preparing for his confrontation with Petrosian and stayed at the exclusive New York Park Sheraton hotel. The management reserved a plush suite for him, as befitted a celebrity. He turned it down because the view was distracting. He ended up in a modest room at the back.

Admittedly, he had other interests. He liked listening to music (particularly the Temptations and the Four Tops, but also jazz and heavy rock), he read comics into adulthood (*Tarzan* and *Superman*), and he watched a few movies (he was a big fan of James Dean). He liked spaceships and cars. He also enjoyed swimming and table tennis. He once tested himself against a table tennis hustler, Marty "the Needle" Reisman, who wrote, "Fischer played table tennis the way he played chess: fiercely, ferociously, going for his opponent's jugular. He was a killer, a remorseless, conscienceless, ice-blooded castrator. . . ."

But all these activities were never more than temporary distractions from his all-consuming passion. His lack of social graces was striking—sometimes when he was spoken to, he did not bother to turn his head in response. Former president of the U.S. Chess Federation Don Schultz remembers sharing meals with Fischer and other chess players. If the conversation strayed from chess, "you would look over to him and he'd be hunched over the side of the table, running through moves on a pocket set." When not showing indifference to those around him, he was often suspicious of them. A journalist wrote that Fischer was likely to greet even an old friend as if he were expecting a subpoena.

Fischer was notoriously insensitive to other people, as was demonstrated constantly by his conduct in tournaments. Lateness might upset an opponent, as it did Reshevsky in Sousse, but it never produced an apology from the offender. The only objects Fischer appeared to feel an emotional affinity for were his chess pieces. His biographer, Frank Brady, put it well: "He empathizes with the position of the moment with such intensity that one feels that a defect in his game, such as a backward pawn or an ill-placed knight, causes him almost physical, and certainly psychical, pain. Fischer would become the pawn if he could, or if it would help his position, marching himself rank-by-rank to the ultimate promotion square. In these moments at the board, Fischer is chess."

He had an inexhaustible appetite for chess work. When the Dane Bent Larsen, eight years Fischer's senior, acted as his second (supporting Fischer with his chess preparation and analysis) in the Candidates tournament in Yugoslavia in 1959, the sixteen-year-old Fischer would not give him time off, insisting that every spare moment, evenings included, be spent studying openings.

How does a man who lives for chess take defeat? Among Fischer watchers there are, broadly, two schools of thought. One school maintains that he was petrified of losing, that this was his deepest dread, and that his incessant demands about the playing conditions were conscious or subconscious strategies to avoid appearing. This view of Fischer was common in Soviet circles. Lev Abramov, the former head of the Sports Committee Chess Department, wrote an article called "The Tragedy of Bobby Fischer." Why "tragedy"?

A tragedy in that Fischer was scared to sit next to the chessboard. The most paradoxical thing was that this outstanding, amazing chess player sometimes couldn't force himself to come to the game, and if he managed to overcome this "disease" he still lacked confidence until he got a good result. I think it was a disease.

Soviet grandmaster and psychologist Nikolai Krogius agrees: "As a psychological type, Fischer resembles the French marshal [Masséna], who was unable to pull himself together before a battle, but who was transformed when the battle began. Napoleon said that [Masséna] demonstrated his talent as a military leader only from the moment 'when the cannons began to fire.'"

A linked but divergent interpretation is that Fischer was so utterly convinced of his superiority that failure became inconceivable. Thus even the occasional defeat tended to have a shattering impact on his self-esteem. Certainly there is empirical evidence to back up such a claim. The records show that on those rare occasions on which he lost in tournaments, he would perform below par in the following game, too, with his percentage of victories not as high as normal. Recovery from knocks was easier for players whose worldview included their own fallibility. As a boy, if Fischer lost a speed game—in which there is no pause for thought and moves are bashed out rapidly, often in split seconds—he would invariably reset the pieces and demand another; it hinted at a deep psychic need to reconstruct his self-image, the self-image of a winner. Tears often accompanied defeat. He cried in the Candidates tournament in 1959 when Mikhail Tal defeated him. He was seen crying again when he lost to Spassky at the Mar del Plata tournament the following year. When goaded by reporters before his match with Petrosian—"Do you cry after losing?"—the twenty-eight-year-old Fischer countered like a petulant schoolboy, "Well, if I cry, the Russians get sick after losing."

The most interesting phenomenon about Fischer, however, is not the effect chess had on him, but the effect his chess had on his opponents, destroying their morale, making them feel that they were in the grip of an alien hostile force to whose powers there was no earthly answer. "He's a chess computer" was a compliment often paid by his admirers. "He's nothing but a computer" was the disparaging comment of his detractors.

What did they mean? Well, computers do not suffer nerves. They lack a psychological attachment to particular rules or styles of play, and they calculate with both speed and precision. In all these regards, Fischer appeared to his opponents to function like a microchip-driven automaton. He analyzed positions with amazing rapidity; his opponent always lagged behind on the clock. Referring to the future chess computer, Jim Sherwin, an American player who knew Fischer well, described him as "a prototype Deep Blue." The Soviet analysis showed that even when faced with an unexpected position, Fischer took not longer than fifteen or twenty minutes to make his move; other grandmasters might take twice as long. Nor did Fischer appear to be governed by any psychologically predetermined system or technique. Take just one example, the twenty-second move of game seven against Tigran Petrosian in the 1971 Candidates match. Who else but Fischer would have exchanged his knight for the bishop? To give up an active knight for a weak bishop was inconceivable; it seemed to violate a basic axiom of the game, to defy all experience. Yet, as Fischer proved, it was absolutely the right decision, transforming an edge into another ultimately winning advantage.

Human chess players can often feel insecure in open, complex positions because a part of them dreads the unknown. Thus they avoid exposing their king because they worry that, like a general trapped in no-man's-land, this most vital of pieces will inevitably be caught in the crossfire. Common sense and knowledge born of history tells them that this is so. An innate pessimism harries them, nagging away, warning them off the potentially hazardous move. Not Fischer. If he believed his opponent could not capitalize on an unshielded king, if he could foresee no danger, then he would permit it to stand brazenly, provocatively unguarded.

Faced with Fischer's extraordinary coolness, his opponents assurance would begin to disintegrate. A Fischer move, which at first glance looked weak, would be reassessed. It must have a deep master plan behind it, undetectable by mere mortals (more often than not they were right, it did). The U.S. grandmaster Robert Byrne labeled the phenomenon "Fischer-fear." Grandmasters would wilt, their suits would crumple, sweat would glisten on their brows, panic would overwhelm their nervous systems. Errors would creep in. Calculations would go awry. There was talk among grandmasters that Fischer hypnotized his opponents, that he undermined their intellectual powers with a dark, mystic, insidious force. Time after time, in long matches especially, Fischer's opponents would suffer a psychosomatic collapse. Fischer managed to induce migraines, the common cold, flu, high blood pressure, and exhaustion, to which he himself was mostly resistant. He liked to joke that he had never beaten a healthy opponent.

Part of Fischer's destructive impact lay in his demeanor during the game. Tall (six feet two) and confident, he cut an imposing figure. Don Schultz, the former president of the U.S. Chess Federation, says that "just watching him sitting at the board you'd think, Gee, that guy's going to win." The fact that Fischer never looked for a draw and rarely agreed to a draw while there was still some uncertainty in the position, increased the mental exertion required to play him.

In Reykjavik to cover the match, the novelist Arthur Koestler famously coined the neologism "mimophant" to describe Fischer. "A mimophant is a hybrid species: a cross between a mimosa and an elephant. A member of this species is sensitive like a mimosa where his own feelings are concerned and thick-skinned like an elephant trampling over the feelings of others."

There is no doubt that, like a psychopath, Fischer enjoyed that feeling of complete power over his opponent. Like a psychopath, he had no moral compunction about using his power. In a letter to a chess-playing acquaintance about the 1962 Olympiad in Bulgaria, he describes a game he played against the great Mikhail Botvinnik. Ultimately the game was drawn when Fischer fell for a Botvinnik trap (after which, according to Fischer, Botvinnik puffed out his chest, and strode away from the table like a giant). But Fischer had held the initiative for much of the game, and in the letter he is gleeful about the discomfort Botvinnik appeared to suffer, mocking the Soviet for changing color and looking about to expire.

Yet here was a paradox. Chess players are often described as either objective or subjective, those who play the board and those who play the opponent. In the thin air at the summit of grandmaster chess, where each player's style and opening repertoire are familiar to all, there can be no such precise division; a mixture of the two approaches is inevitable. Within this spectrum, however, Fischer certainly occupied the board end. Fischer relished his opponent's suffering but did not require it to take pleasure in the game. Indeed, some gibed that from his perspective the only thing wrong with chess was the necessity of having another human being on the other side of the board to play the moves.

According to his biographer, Frank Brady, Fischer's intelligence quotient was estimated at Erasmus Hall High School to be in the 180s, and clearly he was capable of great mental feats in chess.

He had a prodigious memory. He could remember all his games, even most of the speed games he had played. He would amaze fellow grandmasters by reminding them of some casual speed game they had played more than a decade earlier. This recall could be applied beyond chess. There are anecdotes about how he could listen to a foreign language with which he was completely unfamiliar and then repeat an entire conversation.

It was an intelligence distinct from knowledge or wisdom. He was not "educated," he was not well-informed about current events, he was not "cultured"—and showed no desire to be. Nobody would describe him as mature. Indeed, those who knew him best were struck by his lack of social and emotional development.

He had little sense of humor in any of its forms; he never deployed irony or sarcasm or games with language such as punning. He appeared always to take remarks literally. The Yugoslav chess journalist Dimitri Bjelica remembers once traveling in a car with Fischer and the future world champion Mikhail Tal in Zurich in 1959. The driver was speeding along in a reckless fashion. "Fischer said, 'Careful, we could crash.' And I joked, if we died now, the world headlines tomorrow would say, 'Dimitri Bjelica killed in an automobile with two passengers.' Tal laughed, but Fischer said, 'No, Dimitri, I am more famous and popular than you in America.' "

Many of Fischer's views seemed to be locked in to his adolescence—for instance, his attitude to women: "They are all weak, all women. They are stupid compared to men." His lifelong awkwardness with the opposite sex was legendary, his natural gaucheness particularly pronounced in the company of those women who knew little and cared less about the sixty-four squares. He believed women were a terrible distraction and that Spassky should have remained single: "Spassky has committed an enormous error in getting married."

Fischer never had girlfriends, though he did express a crude preference. "I like vivacious girls with big tits," he once said. *Playboy* magazine was favorite reading material. At the Bulgaria Olympiad in 1962, he told Mikhail Tal that he found Asian girls attractive—especially those from Hong Kong or Taiwan; American girls were too vain, they thought only of their looks. Mind you, he had to think about the economic costs of bringing over an Asian bride. He estimated it at $700, roughly the same as a secondhand car; if the bride did not meet with his approval, he could always send her back.

In 1971, Fischer went to Yugoslavia, where he stayed with Bjelica, who was directing a series of television programs on great chess players of the past. Bjelica used Fischer to analyze some of their games. On a day off, they decided to go and watch a beauty pageant in Sarajevo, for which they had been offered front-row seats. As Bjelica recalls, halfway through the event "Fischer suddenly whipped out his pocket set: 'What do you think of queen to g6?' "

Hate was among Fischer's mechanisms for dealing with the world beyond the board; indeed, he was capable of being a grandmaster of hate. This hate could spring from the most trivial personal slight or from a worldview most would find bizarre. Once formed, it was unshakable; he had no concept of forgiveness.

After the Curaçao tournament, his wariness and dislike of the Soviet Union slowly and inexorably descended into a state of delusion. He said his aim for the world championship match against Spassky was to teach the Soviets "a little humility." Soviet players were not only "cheats" who were unfairly privileged by the support they received from the state, but they were out to get him personally. This conviction took Fischer into a land of fantasy. He had to be vigilant in case they tried to poison his food. He worried about flying in case the Soviets had tampered with the engine.

Fischer also hated Jews. Long before Reykjavik, he made anti-Semitic remarks and expressed his admiration for Adolf Hitler to Lina Grumette, a chess player who had arranged a simultaneous match in Los Angeles, when Fischer was seventeen, and in 1967 put him up for a couple of months after he had moved to the West coast. As his mother was Jewish, under Jewish law he was Jewish himself, although this was a label he always rejected. When he discovered that he had been included in a list of famous Jews in the *Encyclopedia Judaica,* he wrote to the editor to declare how distressed this mistake had made him and to demand that it not be repeated. He was not and never had been Jewish, he said. And in what he must have regarded as confirmation of his status, he revealed that he was uncircumcised.

Perhaps his rejection of his Jewishness was part of his rejection of his mother, though she appears to have been religiously unobservant (while turning to Jewish charities for help in looking after her children). However, Fischer was able to separate his hatred for Judaism as a religion and Jews as an ethnic group from Jewish people as individuals. He was on perfectly amicable terms with Jewish chess masters in the United States and the USSR.

We have already touched on a final aspect of Fischer's personality. Naturally, all grandmasters want the playing environment in tournaments to be as good as it can possibly be. But in the history of chess competition, nobody had ever imposed the preconditions insisted upon by Fischer, or risked all to gain them.

He was acutely sensitive to noise, light, the color of the board, and the proximity of the audience. Noise or disturbance in the audience was not, as for most players, a mere irritant; it could, and increasingly did, cause what seemed a searing distress. (Fischer would, no doubt, have approved of a German book, *Instructions to Spectators at Chess Tournaments,* containing three hundred blank pages followed by the words "SHUT UP.") As for the lighting, Fischer required the glare off the squares to be neither too bright nor too dim. Otherwise, he said, he could not concentrate.

And yet, Fischer's powers of concentration were legendary. Sometimes he would stare angrily when there was a whisper or rustle of a sweet wrapping. But on other occasions, a door would slam or there would be a commotion in the hall and he would be oblivious. At restaurants, he would take his pocket set to the table, shutting out the rest of the world entirely. In tournaments, other players might stretch their legs between moves, perhaps wander over to observe another game, engage in small talk with a fellow competitor. Fischer would for the most part remain seated, hunched forward over the board, or assume his alternative pose, leaning back, head cocked to one side, with his long legs and his size fourteen feet stretched out under the table, but always with his eyes boring deep into the squares, pieces, and patterns.

If it was pointed out, as often it was, that other competitors in a tournament had to play under identical conditions to Fischer's, he would reply, justifiably, that it was he who attracted the most attention: Unless the audience were held back, they would jostle around his table. The press wanted pictures not of Smyslov or Geller or Petrosian or Larsen or Olafsson or Portisch, but of Fischer—photographers were constantly snapping away at him as he arrived at and left a tournament or match location.

Yet it is tempting to see his demands over lighting and noise, in part, as a means to another end. It appeared that Fischer always needed to be in control. Forcing concessions on the part of organizers was an affirmation of his power, that play was going ahead under his terms, not theirs. Even when tournament organizers did their best to preempt Fischer's objections by pledging conditions in advance such as that the audience would be so many feet from the stage and the like, Fischer would still manage to identify a fault or two. Every now and again he would test the patience of the organizers to the limit, and then, when they were on the brink of despair, he would suddenly, and without explanation, have a change of heart and either impose an additional condition or pass over his original complaint as though it had never been made.

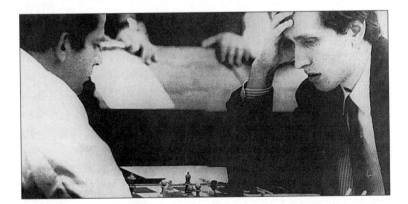

Fischer in 1970: the will to win. UNITED PRESS INTERNATIONAL

His attitude to money was equally mysterious. At one level, his insistence on high fees was straightforward. He believed he should be paid at appropriate rates, appropriate rates being those on a par with sporting superstars such as Arnold Palmer or Joe Frazier. Never mind that chess had never been in the same league as table tennis, let alone golf or heavyweight boxing. Never mind that, with few spectators and little sponsorship, chess had no secure financial foundations outside the Soviet Union.

Fischer always maintained that his ambition was to get rich. He would say so repeatedly and unabashedly, in a way that made even Americans blanch. "I am only interested in chess and money," he told a journalist from the Italian newspaper *Corriere della Sera*. His incessant financial demands came across still worse in Europe, where emphasis on money was considered embarrassing, even vulgar. In weighing up the bids for the Taimanov, Larsen, and Petrosian Candidates matches, Fischer declared that one consideration should outweigh all others: which city paid the most. In a letter to the up-and-coming chess prodigy Walter Browne in January 1971, inviting Browne to become his full-time manager and chess second, Fischer says he believes chess is merely a means of making money. Without any evident irony, he remarks that chess players did not become rich because their egocentric nature led them to work alone. But the moneymaking possibilities were limitless. In what he calls the chess business, he could make $100,000 in the first year and double that in the next.

But what, apart from his expensive taste in suits, did Fischer want money for? He had no dependants, he did not yearn for luxuries, such as going to the opera or collecting art. He did not own a car, he never traveled for the sake of travel, and as far as food was concerned, his preference was for quantity over quality. One has the impression with Fischer that money was not about material possession. He was always reluctant to allow any marketing of himself, whatever the financial windfall. He was appalled by the notion that anyone else might make money out of his name. When his mother wanted to market purses with his signature, he furiously jumped on the idea.

Cash itself was about status and again about control and domination: if he was offered five, he wanted ten; if he was offered twenty, he wanted fifty. Perhaps his unwillingness even to put his signature on a contract stemmed from the same need; an agreement took his control away. Somehow, the actual amounts were immaterial.

In the media, Fischer was routinely portrayed with a range of derogatory adjectives. He was insolent, arrogant, rude, uncouth, spoiled, self-centered, abusive, offensive, vain, greedy, vulgar, disrespectful, boastful, cocky, bigoted, fanatical, cruel, paranoid, obsessive, and monomaniacal. But what is so intriguing is that those who knew him best rarely had a bad word to say about him. "Oh, that's just Bobby," they'd say, smiling indulgently, when discussing one or other bizarre episode. Something in Fischer spoke to his friends as the perpetual lost teenager, to be helped, not punished; to be assisted in realizing his potential for stardom, not hindered. Even allowing for the natural desire to be part of the celebrity's entourage, it is striking how they chorus, "He was a wonderful kid," when they are talking about him as a man.

American chess player Jim Sherwin says Fischer was just a "rough kid" from Brooklyn. Lothar Schmid, the chief arbiter in Reykjavik, tried to understand the American as he tried to understand his children: "He was not a bad boy." Boris Spassky saw him as "always seventeen." "He was a boy all the time," says the former captain of the U.S. Olympic team, Eliot Hearst. "I don't want you to paint a negative image of him; he was very nice." And they also all point out that Fischer was capable of great kindness. As a child he would play opponents for a dollar a game and would give twenty-five cents of each dollar to his wheelchair-bound mentor, Jack Collins. In Curaçao, Fischer was the only competitor to visit Mikhail Tal when Tal fell ill and was hospitalized.

In his biography of Fischer, Brady points out that Fischer's tantrums at tournaments were aimed always at organizers, not at players. Nobody has a single complaint to make about Fischer's behavior once he finally sat down at the board. He was the perfect gentleman. There was no gamesmanship, he never deliberately tried to distract or disturb his opponent. He followed the rules strictly and demanded the same of others. On one well-known occasion, when Fischer was playing Wolfgang Unzicker in Buenos Aires in 1960, he touched a pawn, intending to move it; his fingers then hovered as he suddenly spotted that the move was disastrous. Another less upright player might have announced, "J'adoube" ("I adjust"), a legitimate way of touching a piece when one merely wants to reposition it in the middle of a square. Fischer moved the pawn—and rapidly lost the game. Unzicker, who observed the whole thing, though he was away from the board, says, "If Fischer had moved another piece, I was determined not to protest. But ever since this moment I have known that Fischer is a gentleman at the chessboard."

Perhaps the most curious insight into what drove Fischer—curious to the point of being uncanny—comes in Elias Canetti's masterpiece of obsession, *Die Blendung (The Blinding)*, in English entitled *Auto-da-Fé*, published eight years before Fischer was born.

A central character is a hunchback Jewish dwarf and chess fanatic—Fischerle. Fischerle is a thief who lives off his wife's earnings from prostitution and who dreams of defeating the world chess champion Capablanca, reducing him to tears. He introduces himself with, "Do you play chess? A person who can't play chess isn't a person." Fischerle passes half his life at the chessboard, and it is only there that people treat him as normal, or perhaps normally abnormal, with his potent memory for games and rampaging play.

During his games his partners were far too much afraid of him to interrupt him with objections. . . . He dreamed of a life in which eating and sleeping could be got through while his opponent was making his moves.

Fischerle has unusually long arms and total recall of any chess game he has studied. He imagines becoming world champion and changing his name to Fischer. "He'll have new suits made at the best possible tailor. . . . A gigantic palace will be built with real castles, knights, pawns, just as it ought to be." Bobby, who had long arms and total recall of his games, once said he wanted to hire an architect to build a house in the shape of a rook. Canetti wrote *Auto-da-Fé* in the turmoil of 1930s Vienna. The prophetic similarities between the fictional Fischerle and the real Fischer have their roots in the young Canetti's attempt to make sense of the apparent chaos of human actions. Thus each of his characters holds a completely personal perspective—and, indifferent to externalities, is driven down one path, like a live one-man rocket. Fischerle's/Fischer's view of the world is unidirectional, expressing itself through chess, governed only by the game and the power and rewards it could bring.

Commentators have made much of the similarities between Fischer and Spassky, pointing out that Spassky too was a second child, had a single-parent upbringing, and spent his early years in poverty. In fact, challenger and champion could scarcely have had more contrasting personalities and attitudes to life. Nor were America's prosperity and democracy remotely comparable with the Stalinist horrors among which Spassky grew up and where the chessboard provided protection, fame, and, in Soviet terms, a fortune.

CHILD OF
DESTRUCTION

Chess provides indisputable proof of the superiority of socialist culture over the declining culture of capitalist societies.

—ALEKSANDR KOTOV AND MIKHAIL YUDOVICH,
THE SOVIET SCHOOL OF CHESS

Spassky was born in Leningrad on 30 January 1937 into the maelstrom of suspicion, denunciation, arrest, torture, confession, and death known as the Great Terror—Stalin's liquidation of a wholly fantastic conspiracy against the Soviet state. Such was the upheaval that in the year of Spassky's birth, each of the most senior positions in the provincial Party and state apparatus was vacated and refilled, on average, five times. The Great Terror cost between two million and seven million lives. So frenzied was the destruction that an exact total will never be known.

Stalin placed Spassky's home city, Leningrad, at the center of the imagined plots against which he directed his savagery. The Leningrad poet Yevgeni Rein, unpublished during the Soviet era, conjured up the deadly effect, writing of the Vitebsk Canal in his home city: ". . . malodorous and sticky, / like a poisoner palming cyanide, / creeping into union with the river."

This I have seen and cannot unremember;
The war, which destroyed and delivered me,
And this canal of mine, while I have breath, will
Companion me until my dying day.

On 22 June 1941, Adolf Hitler launched Operation Barbarossa, a massive ground and air attack on the Soviet Union. The German leader attached particular significance to the taking of Leningrad, a city he despised as "the cradle of Bolshevism." On 8 September 1941, Leningrad came under heavy assault from the Luftwaffe; incendiary bombs wiped out the food warehouses. Faced with the threat of starvation, the city authorities ordered the evacuation of thousands of children. With his seven-year-old brother, Georgi, four-year-old Boris Spassky was sent to the Kirov district, in the shadow of the Ural Mountains well to the east of Moscow. "Fortunately our train wasn't bombed," he says. It was there that he learned the rudiments of chess, watching the other inhabitants of the children's home where they had been placed. In 1943, his parents escaped the siege and took their two children to Sverdlovka, forty kilometers from Moscow, saving them from starvation.

Behind him in Leningrad, the agony of the German siege was prolonged for nine hundred days, until January 1944. Over a million of those left behind died, 200,000 directly from German shelling and air raids, but the majority from starvation and cold: in the winter the temperature fell to minus twenty degrees centigrade. The living were too exhausted to bury the dead or fell into the grave after them. Cannibalism was endemic, the bodies of children preferred because their flesh was tender; for a long time afterward, Leningraders could not bring themselves to buy meat pies on the street. Spassky's future rival Viktor Korchnoi survived only because so many in his family perished, leaving behind their ration cards. "Were we stronger chess players—tougher—because of our background?" Korchnoi asked the authors rhetorically. "On the contrary; imagine what my generation would have produced without this trauma."

Returning to Leningrad in 1946, the nine-year-old Spassky would have passed through a lunar landscape of destruction wrought by the retreating German army. The suburbs had been demolished. Scarcely a tree was standing where thousands had stood before. Just outside the city, the Tsar's Village, renamed for Aleksandr Pushkin in the year of Spassky's birth, was dominated by fresh graves, Catherine the Great's breathtaking Baroque palace reduced to a devastated shell. The writer Ilya Ehrenburg noted that not a building in the city was without a wound or scar.

Amid the ruins of his city, chess provided the near destitute young Spassky with a connection to society, subsistence, and a much needed sense of order.

In no other country would chess have bestowed on a child the financial support Spassky received. But in no other country was chess seen as part of the state system and its players' success as a symbol of that system's superiority. In the Soviet Union, chess stars were lauded and privileged, the top players revered household names, their results followed in the newspapers, their faces recognized in the streets.

Official encouragement of chess had not begun with the revolution in 1917. Some Tsars approved of chess: Nicholas II conferred the original "grandmaster" title on five players of legendary skill during the great St. Petersburg tournament of 1914: Emanuel Lasker, José Capablanca, Alexander Alekhine, Frank Marshall, and Siegbert Tarrasch.

But with the revolution came the idea of the game as a *socialist* sport. Three years after the revolution, a strong chess master, an old Bolshevik who had played chess in exile with Lenin, Aleksandr Fiodorvich Iliin-Zhenevskii, was appointed chief commissar at the General Reservists' Organization in Moscow, responsible for preparing young men for conscription into the factory workers' militia, the Red Guard, and later the Red Army, providing them with both physical and military training. The physical training included a range of sporting activities, ball games, athletics, swimming, boxing, and so on.

Iliin-Zhenevskii believed that chess could take on a political role and purpose and that it should be subordinated to the ideological struggle. In the USSR, he wrote, "chess cannot be apolitical as in capitalist countries." Sport improved discipline; it taught patience, composure, and determination; it enhanced concentration, endurance, and willpower; it sharpened and focused the mind. Chess in particular could help educate the proletariat and sharpen the minds of the workers, offering an ideologically sound activity after the rigors of a hard day's toil in the factory or on the collective farm.

In 1924, the All-Union Chess Section was established, answering to the Supreme Council for Physical Education. The chairman of this Chess Section was Nikolai Krylenko, short, bald, and burly, an old Bolshevik who shared a platform with Lenin, rousing the masses during the October revolution. Lenin appointed him supreme commander and commissar for war. Later he became public prosecutor for the revolutionary tribunals, terrifying defendants and sending thousands to their deaths before he himself became one of the victims in 1938. To the British agent Bruce Lockhart, he was a "degenerate epileptic."

In the previous fourteen years, working alongside Iliin-Zhenevskii, Krylenko had created a Soviet chess production line. "We must for once and all put an end to the neutrality of chess. . . . We must organize shock brigades of chess players and immediately begin fulfilling the five-year plan for chess," he proclaimed. Hundreds of experts began to receive a stipend from the state. They were dispatched to the far-flung corners of the Soviet empire to evangelize and proselytize. Krylenko founded and edited a chess magazine, 64, still going today. Major newspapers such as *Pravda* and *Izvestia* began to carry regular chess columns.

The results were spectacular. It is estimated that there were only 1,000 registered chess players in 1923. By 1929, the number had risen to 150,000. In 1949, four years before Stalin's death, 130,000 people entered a tournament for collective farm workers. By 1951, there were 1 million registered players; by the end of that decade, almost two million; by the mid-1960s, three million.

At the end of World War II, much to Stalin's pleasure (he telegraphed them, "Well done lads"), a Soviet team twice beat one from the United States, but the ultimate prize—the world championship—still awaited capture. In the interwar years, the Soviet Union had fought shy of such international competitions. In 1945, the title was held by the Russian exile Alexander Alekhine. He was not someone the Soviets wanted to claim as their own, having (in their eyes) the temerity to rail continuously against the Bolshevik takeover.

During the war, Alekhine (then living in France) had been discredited by allowing himself to be used by the Nazis to propagate their racialist worldview. With his reputation in tatters, this peerless champion died alone in a hotel in the Portuguese resort of Estoril. A picture taken after his death shows him still in his overcoat, slumped over a desk. There in front of him is a chessboard.

In 1948, the International Chess Federation arranged a tournament to decide Alekhine's successor. It involved five of the top players in the world—Mikhail Botvinnik, Vasili Smyslov, and Paul Keres from the USSR, Samuel Reshevsky from the United States, and, from Holland, the former world champion Max Euwe.

The winner was Mikhail Botvinnik, an exemplar of Stalinist model citizenry—apart from his Jewishness, though in common with so many Soviet chess players, that was a matter of descent, not practice. He said, "By blood I am Jewish, by culture Russian, by education Soviet." (At the age of nine, he had determined that he would be a Communist Party member.) For the state, successful Jewish competitors brought a double benefit: they proclaimed the triumph of the system and the absence of anti-Semitism in the Soviet Union.

During the quarter of a century after Botvinnik emerged as the world's number one player, the championship shifted back and forth among a cohort of Soviets. Twice he lost the title; twice he regained it. He was really primus inter pares in a generation of unprecedented talent drawn from the length and breadth of the enlarged postwar Union of Soviet Socialist Republics.

Chess was governed by the state through the State Committee for Physical Training and Sport (GosKomSport) and, more powerful still, the Ideology Department of the Communist Party Central Committee. Lev Abramov, who ran the Chess Department of the USSR Sports Committee for eleven years during the 1950s and 1960s, credits Botvinnik with cementing the ideological significance of chess within the Soviet system: "We had chess achievements before any other achievements. And chess came to be seen as tangible proof that the system worked, something completely reliable. Something that wouldn't let the state down." According to grandmaster Mark Taimanov, the Soviets would construct their propaganda edifice on three main pillars, "chess, the circus, and ballet. In all three the Soviet Union could be shown to be far ahead of the West."

While ballerinas and clowns enchanted audiences worldwide, verification of superiority in chess was the retention of the world championship. Botvinnik was defeated the first time by the solid and intensely musical Vasili Smyslov, famed for his beautiful baritone voice. Then there was Mikhail Tal, a tactical wizard whose games overflowed with pyrotechnics. He was followed by Tigran Petrosian, whose style relied on a profound, if unspectacular, conception of strategy. Petrosian's successor was Boris Spassky, the first Soviet world champion to have to defend the title against a challenger not from his motherland.

After war and evacuation, how had he found his future in chess?

Like Fischer, Spassky was a second child and brought up in a family with an absent father. In the brief autobiography the world champion contributed to Jan van Reek's *Grand Strategy*, he describes his mother, Ekaterina Petrovna, as coming from peasant stock, illegitimate, and nurtured by her godfather. She was a poorly educated, deeply religious woman—though when in a good mood, says Spassky, she sang a post–civil war song with "an optimistic tune. I preferred her Russian songs." Spassky records how, in despair over sustaining her family, she sought support from the famous saintly monk Seraphim of Viriza. "The old man looked at my mother and said, 'Be calm. Very soon everything will be alright.'" Spassky's father, Vasili Vladimirovich, was from a family of priests—a source of pride for Spassky. His grandfather, a priest, had been elected from the Kursk region to the Fourth Duma in 1916. Nicholas II personally presented him with a golden cross. Vasili was a builder by trade: he began work as a laborer on a construction site but earned promotion first to the equivalent of foreman and then to supervisor. Boris Spassky has been widely described as half Jewish. He told the present authors that there was no truth in this; he was mystified as to how it came to be reported.

In 1944, Spassky's parents divorced. Vasili left his wife and three children, Georgi and Boris, and the youngest, Iraida, who was born in the year the marriage ended and who would later become a checkers champion, winning the USSR Women's Championship several times. Back in Leningrad, Ekaterina embarked on a lonely struggle for survival, digging potatoes until the forty-kilogram sacks she had to carry damaged her back. His father gave what help he could and stayed in touch with the children.

In the summer of 1946, Spassky passed his days watching the players in a chess pavilion "with a black knight on top" on an island in the Leningrad river, the Neva. "Long queen moves fascinated me. I fell in love with the white queen. I dreamed about caressing her in my pocket, but I did not dare to steal her. Chess is pure for me." He had thirteen kopecks for his fare and a glass of water with syrup to see him through until the last streetcar carried him home. His feet were bare. "Soldiers' boots were my worst enemy."

When the pavilion closed, he remembers, "it was a tragedy. Life without chess was like dying." He searched the city "like a hungry dog" for a chess club. The Palace of Young Pioneers, the center run by the junior section of the Komsomol, the Communist Party Youth League, became the scene of his epiphany. Facing the Neva, the grandly pillared, marbled building was the former Anichkov Palace, home to a number of imperial favorites, including Catherine the Great's lover Prince Potemkin, and to Tsar Aleksandr III. When not receiving ideological instruction or singing paeans to waving fields of collective wheat, the pioneers could play games, chess among them. The chess club met in the Tsar's walnut-paneled former study, sitting under an enormous crystal chandelier and inspired by a painting of Lenin playing Gorky in sunlit Capri. (Gorky could not play chess.) Spassky borrowed his mother's boots and went off to join the chess section. To this day he remembers a lecture given by grandmaster Grigori Levenfish on a 1925 game between Alekhine and the British player Frederick Yates: "A pawn majority attack, starting with b2–b4, was very instructive."

The club was the making of him. Leading players such as Mikhail Botvinnik, David Bronstein, and Igor Bondarevskii paid visits; its members included future grandmasters Mark Taimanov, Aleksandr Tolush, and Semion Furman. In *Grand Strategy*, Spassky compares Levenfish and Botvinnik in terms that say much about his prejudices. In Leningrad, "Levenfish was treated as a man of Russian culture and intelligence. . . . Botvinnik was regarded as a representative of the Komsomol, a thirties man of Soviet culture."

Among such stars present and future, the senior chess coach, Vladimir Zak, spotted the little boy's huge talent immediately. The thirty-three-year-old Zak took on the role of guardian and tutor. As well as chess, Zak insisted on swimming and skating and on visits to the opera and ballet. According to Spassky, Zak looked at

The sun shines down on socialist chess. Left to right: Maxim Gorky, Nadezhda Krupskaia (Lenin's wife), Vladimir Lenin.

him "as if I were a miracle or boy prodigy." And so he must have seemed: the others in his class were at least five years older. At eleven, Spassky gave a simultaneous display at the Minsk House of Officers. (Play had to be adjourned for fifteen minutes when the prodigy became upset after losing to an officer whom he had allowed to take back a move—never so generous again, he vowed.) He bought his first winter coat with his fee. Under Zak's tutelage, Boris's chess evolved quickly—so quickly that in 1948 he was given a monthly state stipend of 1,200 roubles—only 400 roubles less than his father and higher than the average salary of an engineer. (This was before the ten-to-one revaluation in the 1960s.) He was his family's salvation. At this stage of his life, the preteen breadwinner was a tumult of emotions that he would learn later to suppress; a defeat meant storms of angry tears.

Through the 1940s and into the 1950s, Spassky's career was one of effortless success, groomed by the chess authorities for the grandmaster status that such natural ability made his for the taking. In 1952, he parted from Vladimir Zak. His coach, tutor, and friend had realized that he had given all he could. To develop, his protégé needed a heavier hitter. The replacement was Aleksandr Kasimirovich Tolush. In chess terms, Tolush, a master of attack, was exactly the right man. Spassky "watched with delight how K. [Kasimirovich] mobilized reserves, manoeuvred, and created threats." Tolush continued Spassky's wider education, "teaching me how to eat with a knife and fork, how to knot and wear a tie, how to use a serviette and handkerchief, things like that."

In 1953, in a Bucharest tournament, he justified splitting from his first coach with a sensational win in thirty-four moves over the world championship challenger Vasili Smyslov. But in Romania he learned about more than high-level chess. This was not long before the death of Stalin in March of that year, and the tremors of his latest, and last, purge—the "doctors' plot"—were shaking Party and government. Laszlo Szabo, a Hungarian grandmaster, was in the lead, and in a Soviet team meeting, the "commissar" in charge of them read a telegram from the Sports Committee: "Stop fighting each other. Make draws. Stop Szabo." The committee's anxieties were unnecessary, says Spassky. "Szabo was stopped because he wasn't strong enough. Even I won against him."

Two years later, Spassky won the World Junior Chess Championship in Antwerp, and a year after that he tied for first place as Soviet champion and became the youngest player ever to qualify for the Candidates round. He finished third at the

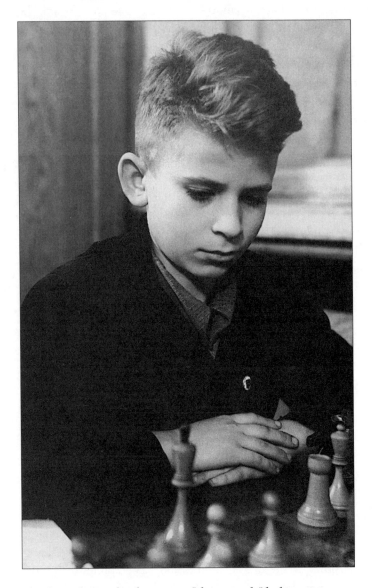

Spassky at eleven, already seen as a "chess miracle" by his trainer, Vladimir Zak. NOVOSTI

Amsterdam Candidates tournament in 1956, making him by that measure one of the top five players in the world—and at the age of only nineteen. It all seemed so simple: a life full of promise, apparently destined for glory. He was now a student. In 1955, he had enrolled at Leningrad University, choosing journalism over mathematics. He says chess competitions prevented him from studying every day—and anyway, he had no talent for math. The young student was already being spoken of as a future world champion. Thanks to his chess, his family jumped the interminable housing queue, moving from one room of fourteen square meters to a "palace"—two rooms of twenty-eight square meters.

Then, just at the age when he was expected to secure his position within the ranks of the world's elite, the highflier's career stalled and went into a spin. The nadir came in an encounter with Mikhail Tal in the 1958 Soviet championship. Spassky needed to beat him to enter the Portoroz Interzonal, lost, and cried for the first time in years. His future opponent for the world championship, Tigran Petrosian, participated in the tournament and watched the game. "When I went up to the board, Spassky raised his eyes. They were the eyes of a cornered animal."

Spassky now discovered how easily the authorities' benign smile could turn to a frown. Later that year, in the student team championship in his home city, he was on first board and was defeated by the talented American William Lombardy, who would be Fischer's chess aide in Iceland. The United States took first place. Criticized for not preparing sufficiently, Spassky was banned from playing abroad for the next two years. He also twice failed to qualify for the Interzonals and so for the Candidates rounds in 1959 and 1962. "My nervous energy was completely destroyed," Spassky recalls.

His game's entering a trough coincided with turmoil in his relationships. In 1960, he parted from Aleksandr Tolush. Mikhail Beilin, who was head of the Sports Committee's Chess Department from 1967 to 1971, remembers, "Tolush was quite depressed after this episode—he didn't have children of his own, and he had spent a lot of time with Boris. He could empathize with bad boys, and he taught Spassky a great deal." Spassky acknowledged his debt to Tolush:

My play became active over the whole board. My imagination, intuition, sacrifices, and tactics improved. I had almost reached my greatest strength, staying cool during a crisis.

Tolush's influence endured. In the 1969 world championship match against Petrosian, long after teacher and pupil split, grandmaster Efim Geller still detected the trainer's fingerprints on Spassky's game. At a critical moment, Geller wrote, "Kasimirovich's cannon roared." But after eight years together, according to Spassky, their relationship slowly wore out: "Tolush complained that I had become an unguided missile."

The coach was exhausted from constantly having to shield his pupil from trouble, with school, the KGB, the USSR Chess Federation. There were also domestic problems.

In 1959, he had married a philology student at his university, Nadezhda Latyntseva (Tolush opposed his choice of bride). A daughter, Tania, was born a year later. Married life cannot have been easy, living with Spassky's mother, brother, and sister in that twenty-eight-square-meter "palace." Shortly after Tania's birth, Boris suggested a divorce, explaining later, "We had become like bishops of opposite colors." Nadezhda refused—and refused to leave the palace. A state of war ensued. Through his trade union chess contacts, Spassky found her a one-room apartment and she finally moved, but the divorce proceedings were still very drawn out, naturally preying on his mind.

During this tough phase, Spassky had a tendency to dwell on lost games, on might-have-beens; a tendency toward melancholy and pessimism. However, by 1962 both his personal life and his chess had rebounded. His divorce had finally gone through, and he had met his future second wife, Larisa Solovieva. They got to know each other on a beach in Vilinagorsk, a small town near Leningrad, discovering that they lived in the same block back in the city. They married in 1966.

Spassky also had a new, more congenial trainer, Igor Bondarevskii. Bondarevskii was descended from the Don Cossacks; his nickname was "Cossack of the Don." War damage to his nervous system prevented him from making the most of his chess gifts, and he competed in his last tournament in 1963. Spassky describes him as sharp, lively, and inquisitive, presenting himself as dignified and modest. He adds that an explosive temperament combined with "ambition and vanity made it impossible [for Bondarevskii] to forgive the sins of others." Nevertheless, Spassky, who revealingly dubbed him "Father," avows that their years together from 1961 to 1969 were "the best of my life." (Bondarevskii remained his trainer until 1972.) "[He] became my friend, clever adviser, excellent coach, good psychologist, and, to a certain extent, my father." Endurance, discipline, the will to fight to the last pawn—these were the qualities the new coach aimed to develop in his pupil.

Under the influence of Bondarevskii, Spassky's results improved steadily, rather than dramatically. At the end of 1961, he won the USSR championship outright, with ten wins, nine draws, and only one defeat. He was runner-up in a tournament in Havana the following year and tied for first place in the USSR championship of 1963, coming second in the playoffs behind grandmaster Leonid Stein. He began to take seriously the prospect of capturing the world title, telling his trainer in 1964, "I will be world champion." He meant he would take the crown from his fellow Soviet, the Armenian Tigran Petrosian.

The Interzonal tournament of 1964 was in Amsterdam, and a first-place tie with Tal, Smyslov, and Larsen saw Spassky into the Candidates, the culminating stage in the world championship cycle. As the result of Fischer's accusing the Soviets of collusion, the Candidates round was held as a series of head-to-head matches. There was also a condition that only three Soviets could qualify for the Candidates, so competition between Soviets at the Interzonal stage was even fiercer than between candidates of different nationalities. To qualify, a Soviet had to finish in third place, while a non-Soviet could qualify by finishing eighth. Spassky thought that unfair.

Tournaments, featuring many players, were the usual form of competition. Spassky had never participated in a lengthy match before—a series of games against a single opponent—and found them physically and mentally draining. Nonetheless, 1965 was his annus mirabilis. He defeated first Paul Keres in an exciting, tightly fought contest, then Efim Geller, then the former world champion Mikhail Tal. So only Tigran Petrosian remained between Spassky and the title. Spassky was not among the Armenian's greatest admirers, characterizing him as the king who "reigned but did not rule"; world champion, but not the strongest in the world. He also felt sorry for himself, a poor student facing the socially and politically well-protected national hero of Armenia.

The 1966 final was held in Moscow, and outside chess circles was virtually ignored in the West. Spassky performed more than creditably, losing by only one point. His and Petrosian's styles were diametrically opposed. Spassky's direct, open, attacking game, often described as "universal," had no systemic weaknesses: He was strong in attack, doughty in defense, exceptional in the middle game, outstanding in the endgame; he was capable of marathon slogs and of stunning miniatures. Petrosian's approach was strategic, slow, and, to those spectators not attuned to its infinite subtlety, soporific. Most chess players have a style, a chess fingerprint—but rarely one as distinctive as Petrosian's. It required an opponent to adapt or die. Asked later why Petrosian had won, Botvinnik said Spassky did not manage "to program himself for Petrosian."

Two months later, in Santa Monica, Spassky won what he describes as the tournament of his life (Fischer finished second). It brought him real money: $5,000. There followed a minor low that some ascribe to the personal contentment brought by his marriage to Larisa and the birth of his son, Vasili, in 1967. (That is not easy to reconcile with his complaint that when he lived alone, too much of his time went into domestic chores, such as ironing his shirts.) Reflecting on 1967, Spassky remembers, "I was a good Soviet citizen. I was traveling, playing, and enjoying life." Back in the Candidates in 1968, he again sailed through against Efim Geller (5.5 to 2.5), Bent Larsen (5.5 to 2.5), and Viktor Korchnoi (6.5 to 3.5), losing only two games of the twenty-six in total. For the win over Larsen, he received the Soviet Badge of Merit. (In 1955, he had been awarded a medal for Valorous Labor, a comparatively run-of-the-mill Soviet decoration, and comments wryly in *Grand Strategy,* "That's all I got.") Once again he faced Tigran Petrosian for the world title. The opening ceremony of the contest took place at the Moscow Television Theatre so that TV audiences could watch. However, once again, Petrosian vs. Spassky failed to ignite the interest of a wider Western audience. Unsurprisingly, the proceedings were conducted in a civilized manner; there were no major rows or controversies.

Most thought that the forty-year-old champion had little chance against the thirty-two-year-old contender. The Armenian's chess had hit a ceiling, though we should remember that he was the only world champion since 1934 to have defended his throne successfully. He was not comfortable with the title or the adulation it brought him from the Armenian community worldwide. In one dazzling game, there was deafening applause in the hall, and a group of Petrosian fans tried to march onto the dais. The British chess official and writer Harry Golombek was there: "Only one aged Armenian succeeded in escaping the attendants and reaching the stage, where he clasped Petrosian by the hand." Petrosian was quoted as saying before his second championship encounter with Spassky, "I never wanted to become world champion. I only wanted to play good chess. For six years now I have not taken a drop of alcohol, nor have I smoked. My doctor told me not to get excited at hockey or soccer matches because I had to have very strong nerves to play chess. But what do I have from life?"

For Spassky, it was the opposite, both in lifestyle and in morale. "On the eve of the Petrosian match," he declared, "I felt magnificent." Still, it was no walk-over. The match swayed to and fro. Spassky divided it into four parts:

```
1. Games 1-9 my sprint and fatigue;
2. Games 10-13 I am a punch bag;
3. Games 14-17 the turning point;
4. Games 18-23 my final offensive.
```

After game seventeen, Spassky was relaxing in his apartment when some heavy blows rattled the front door. "An Armenian guy had discovered my refuge and was trying to storm it. He was shouting: 'Spassky, don't win against our Petrosian!!' " Spassky ignored the threat. "I shouted back, 'Don't you worry, I *will* beat him.' The guy then shut up and disappeared."

He did win, gaining the title by two points, after six victories, four defeats, and thirteen draws. The chess was not always pretty, although some games—the brilliant fifth, for example, in which Spassky advanced his queen pawn all the way to the seventh rank—came to be viewed as classics. Arguably, Tigran Petrosian was the most difficult player to defeat in the history of chess. *Tigr* is Russian for "tiger." Not so much tiger, more snake or cunning fox, commentators thought. He had infinite patience, awaiting exactly the right moment to pounce. Spassky called him "a unique match pugilist. His forte is that he makes it almost impossible to lay a glove on him." Petrosian put it differently: "I try to avoid chance. Those who rely on chance should play cards or roulette."

Moscow 1969: At the microphone, Viktor Ivonin salutes the new world champion, Boris Spassky (fourth from right). VIKTOR IVONIN

Afterward, a fatigued Spassky condemned the protracted qualifying process: "The system has become worse than ever before." Anticipating his defense in 1972, he said, "I want to express beforehand my sincerest sympathy to the challenger who succeeds in breaking through all the trials and obstacles."

5

THE RUSSIAN
FROM LENINGRAD

Our goal is to make the life of the Soviet people still better, still more beautiful, and still happier.

— LEONID BREZHNEV, 1971

In Russia, truth almost always assumes an entirely fantastic character.

— FYODOR DOSTOYEVSKY,
"SOME OBSERVATIONS ON UNTRUTH"

Spassky went to Reykjavik to serve—in the eyes of Soviet society—as an icon as well as a player.

He was a flawed icon, at least in the view of the authorities and many of his peers. He stands out as being a member of the system's awkward squad. How awkward? That is a question that can be answered only within the wider political and cultural context.

When imposing its will, the Party did not operate in a historical vacuum. In *The Soviet Union Since the Fall of Khrushchev*, Archie Brown identifies continuities with the Tsarist era: the tendency to place faith in people, particularly a strong leader, rather than in institutional structures, the dread of chaos, and the high premium placed on loyalty and unity. Added to these are systemic characteristics: the gulf between rulers and ruled and between intelligentsia and the masses, and the perception as normal of such state measures of control as internal passports, secrecy, censorship, surveillance, exile. Fear of anarchy and its correlative, acceptance of order, permeated all classes, providing a widespread distrust of liberalization.

The Great Terror shaped the mentality of Soviet generations to come, creating a society constantly accommodating to the uncertainties of life and to the injustices and arbitrary use of power. Stalin died on 5 March 1953. Khrushchev's revelatory five-and-a-half-hour speech to the Twentieth Party Congress three years later, the beginning of the so-called thaw, was the most momentous political event of Spassky's early life. But the opening of the camp gates did not mean rehabilitation for the thousands of former prisoners. Many Soviet citizens remained convinced that "they must have done something." Suspicion hung in the air like a contagion. And as the historian Catherine Merridale, the author of *Night of Stone,* has it, "Among Stalin's many legacies, the habit of vigilance was the most enduring."

Khrushchev's speech began a debate that could have no closure. A democratic movement had emerged that the regime could crush—but only at a cost it was not prepared to pay. A long, hard, never-resolved battle ensued between dogmatists and liberals, while the Party tried to find some middle ground where it could maintain its power over all aspects of life without returning to the barbarism of the Stalinist era.

Where were the limits of autonomy at any given time? These can be seen only in the reaction of the authorities in the barren volcanic landscape of Soviet cultural life; dissent flared up, was subdued, and flared again. What was expected of chess players was the same as that expected of writers and artists: in the words of the Writers Union, "wholehearted dedication to the ideas of communism and boundless loyalty to the cause of the Party."

On the morning of 14 October 1964, Khrushchev was ousted, attacked by his successors, Andrei Kosygin and Leonid Brezhnev, for "harebrained schemes, half-baked ideas and hasty decisions and actions divorced from reality, boasting and empty rhetoric, attraction to rule by fiat, the refusal to take into account all the achievements of science and practical experience." The twenty-two men who now constituted the Politburo and Secretariat of the Central Committee—the control room of the state—had an average age of sixty-two. Born in 1906, Brezhnev himself had been a communist since 1931. The youngest full Politburo member, Fiodor Kulakov, was born in 1918 and had been a member of the Party since 1940. These were men hardened in the forge of Stalinism, comfortable with the cast-iron language of socialism. The message was that through the efforts of the people, the building of socialism had continued even under Stalin's "distortions." Anyone who was in the public eye, including chess players, was expected to display socialist values.

In *Pravda,* the then Komsomol leader Sergei Pavlov wrote that the regime faced the task of "combating evidence of nihilism, thoughtless and presumptuous rejection of authority, and scornful or ignorant attitudes toward the historical experience of the older generation of Soviet people." He might not have been thinking of chess at that moment, but as chairman of the State Sports Committee, he would play a central part in Spassky's Reykjavik saga.

However, Archie Brown points out that although cultural freedom under Brezhnev was curbed, there was no blanket prohibition on free intellectual activity; instead, the authorities took a pragmatic approach, recognizing the necessity for more openness in natural sciences and, to a limited extent, in the social sciences if the economy was to be modernized. There were also diplomatic considerations, such as the need for better relations with the West as tensions grew with China. But these opposing pressures did not stop Brezhnev from warning that intellectuals who failed to serve the cause of building communism would get what they deserved.

How did the authorities impose their views? In the case of the professional class, it was done primarily through their state organizations. Aleksandr Solzhenitsyn complained bitterly that the leadership of the Writers Union conceived its duty as representing the Party to the writer rather than vice versa. Lev Abramov was in charge of the Chess Department of the Sports Committee for more than eleven years from the mid-1950s: he saw himself as having a two-way role. "I was expressing the opinion of the players to the authorities, and at the same time I was trying to support the general policy of our party and state." He had come to manage chess from a position of high state responsibility and trust. A building engineer by profession, at the end of his professional career he had been chief engineer in construction for the All-Union defense plants. His experience with the Party and government meant that the Sports Committee could generally rely on him to understand what policy should be without being explicitly told.

Officials had an assortment of sticks and carrots with which to keep the elite players in check. The Party's role as gatekeeper to travel was one of its most potent control mechanisms. The Soviet Union's borders were closed to its own people, who had no legal right to travel abroad. There were two classes of Soviet citizen, went a bitter Soviet quip: those who obtained foreign travel passports and those who did not.

To be granted a foreign travel passport, the would-be traveler had to submit an exhaustive personal dossier that included a Party reference on moral and political maturity. Even when all the hoops had been jumped through, a passport could be withheld at the last moment or "lost" in the Foreign Ministry. The would-be traveler was instructed to excuse himself to his hosts on grounds of work, illness, or family commitments. The grandmasters David Bronstein and Edouard Gufeld could testify to lost passports at the last moment making travel to international tournaments impossible. Even Latvian ex–world champion Mikhail Tal was not immune. During the Olympiad in Cuba in 1966, he was involved in an altercation in a nightclub. Hit on the head with a bottle (it is said by an envious boyfriend of the woman with whom he was dancing), he was sent to hospital and was ruled out of chess action for several days. The next Olympiad took place two years later in Lugano. Tal was at the airport with all the other grandmasters when the vice chairman of the Sports Committee approached him and said, "And you, Mikhail Nekhemievich, can return to Riga."

Chess officials of the period all adamantly deny that restrictions were placed on travel as a form of punishment. Their line is that trips had to be limited because of a shortage of funds. Thus, all the cases of restrictions cited to them can be explained by priorities—who was on form, who was already abroad, who had been abroad recently and should give way to another contender equally qualified.

Although Spassky had tasted the authorities' displeasure, his brilliance as a player probably saved him from later restrictions. According to Mikhail Beilin, "Spassky without doubt did things no one else was allowed to do. The higher you reached in chess, master, international master, grandmaster, the more you were allowed to get up to mischief. Others would never have been permitted to go abroad if they acted in the same way as Spassky. He had a very independent character."

As countless Soviet citizens discovered to their cost, independence of character did not amuse the authorities. Spassky could not be free of the Soviet system. Nonetheless, he demanded and enjoyed a rare measure of personal autonomy in belief and expression, an autonomy that he carried into Reykjavik. To comprehend what set him apart, we must return to the war he survived and the city in which he was raised.

"The struggle against Nazism was the greatest test the Soviet people ever endured; perhaps the greatest in the whole history of Russia," writes Catherine Merridale. "The effort of will, the tenacity and stoicism that it demanded were beyond the range of previous experience, more terrible and more prolonged than anything most of the Soviet people, veterans of so many emergencies already, had ever seen."

That was without doubt true of the defense of Leningrad. Nevertheless, there was a substantial element of myth making in the official accounts of the siege, a myth that spoke of the wholly selfless Soviet patriotism of citizens and stressed the heroic role of the Party in sustaining the city and its people. The myth contradicted the reality of panic among the authorities and the continuance of political control by terror, even at the darkest moments during the German attack.

The myth ignored the brutalization of the people. In his *Europe: A History*, Norman Davies comments, "Descriptions of carousing in the Party House, alongside corpses in the street and scientific workers dead at their laboratory benches, only add to the tally of inhumanity."

The myth making that came out of triumph over Germany would affect Boris Spassky in a number of ways. According to the contemporary Soviet journalist and author Vasili Grossman, the hardships of the Great Patriotic War (as World War II was named) had a decisive influence on Russian self-consciousness. With victory at Stalingrad in February 1943, a victory that cost a million lives, Soviet Russians began to differentiate themselves from other nationalities, and the word *Russian* acquired a positive meaning. It is a historical commonplace that Stalin chose to revive Russian patriotism to fuel the Herculean war effort, but he also used the war to proclaim state nationalism. State nationalism was differentiated from the nationalism of modern European countries. It had nothing to do with love of country. The Soviet nationalist had a profound, respectful, and loving attachment to the socialist state that in turn protected and cherished its loyal citizens. State nationalism was to become the sole form of patriotism acceptable to a socialist country. It was state nationalism that Spassky was expected to express in his playing. Soviet chess players must never forget they played in red shirts.

A second source of influence emanating from the mythology of the war was the belief summed up in the phrase *Nashe Luchshe*—"Ours (Means) Better," that the system must necessarily triumph. Its correlative was a constant fear of public belittling, of having the shortcomings of the system exposed. The long-serving Soviet ambassador to Washington, D.C., Anatoli Dobrynin, records wryly in his memoirs that when Brezhnev visited Nixon in 1973, Brezhnev himself instructed the Soviet security service to organize his trip so that "he would in no way appear to the Americans inferior to the president of the United States."

A self-imposed barrier stood in the way of attempts to make a reality of "Ours (Means) Better": the culture of secrecy and isolation that condemned people to live in an astonishing state of ignorance. This was not something that affected only ordinary citizens. Remarkably, in 1959, when Khrushchev was invited to stay with President Eisenhower at the presidential retreat, Camp David, no one around the Soviet leader knew what or where it was. In his memoirs, Khrushchev remembered, "I couldn't for the life of me find out what Camp David was. I began to make inquiries from our Ministry of Foreign Affairs. They said they didn't know, either." Khrushchev worried that the American authorities were slighting him by proposing Camp David, that somehow he was being discriminated against, put into quarantine. Eventually he discovered that it was considered an honor to be entertained in the equivalent of the presidential dacha. "I can laugh about it now, but I'm a bit ashamed. It shows how ignorant we were in some respects."

The chess world was no better informed. A startling lack of knowledge about Fischer's recent history was revealed at a meeting of the chess authorities with Spassky and his team on 13 August 1971 to review the champion's preparation. The report of the outcome by Viktor Baturinskii, the director of the Central Chess Club, records: "A request was made to determine (through Soviet correspondents in the U.S. or by other means) the reasons why Fischer did not take part in any competitions for around a year and a half (1968–1970), where he was during this period and what he was doing, and also to gather information about Fischer's behavior and statements in the future." In the same month, Spassky's "Training Plan" also sought permission to select, purchase, and translate into Russian, foreign theoretical journals so that all relevant data and analysis could be gathered. Censorship and shortage of hard currency entailed seeking official sanction for this basic resource.

Through the 1960s, as Boris Spassky climbed toward the world title, state nationalism became more important in spite of the passing of the war generation. Soviet leaders saw the necessity of trumpeting the very real technological achievements of the Soviet state, in science, in high-tech weapons, in sending a dog into space and then a man. They needed consumer achievements, too, Soviet blue jeans, new apartment buildings. And they needed sporting triumphs. In his study of the Russian mentality, *The Russian Mind,* Ronald Hingley reflects on the Russians' historic capacity and requirement for what he calls "prestige projects." "Gifted in areas as varied as chess, rocketry and athletics,

Russians are often successful when they turn their combined efforts to prestige projects, many of which are functionally effective as well as impressively decorated. One important secondary aim is to capture the imagination of foreign observers in the hope that some may be sufficiently dazzled to overlook the poor living conditions endured by the average citizen."

Soviet citizens saw Spassky's role as defending the outstanding example of "Ours (Means) Better," the USSR's grip on the World Chess Championship. In fighting the American, he became the symbol of the fallen. Before Reykjavik, he received countless letters from Soviet citizens, reminding him of his patriotic duty to turn back the imperialist American who was invading the Soviet chess citadel.

Justifying the Soviet state was what was important to the Party, not the game of chess for its own sake. Of course, says a former president of the Chess Federation of the Russian Federation, journalist Yevgeni Bebchuk: "The party bigwigs felt like that. You should die for the homeland and the Party. As for the games themselves, only chess players were interested. What really matters is that at the board you're a Soviet person." Today he smiles at the memory of the morale-boosting exercises undergone by contestants in student tournaments, with the whole team gathered in the Propaganda and Agitation Department of the Central Committee.

They would sit us down in front of some official who didn't know anything about chess. He would walk about the room. Nikitin, Spassky, and I would be sitting there. He would say, "You realize the honor that you have to defend. Do you understand the honor? Do you understand it properly? Do you understand it or not?" We would just sit there quietly. He would say, "Who is playing today? Ah, Bebchuk, you're a journalist. Do your colleagues realize the honor they have to defend?" "Yes, they understand." "You had better explain it to them. Do they understand it properly or not?"

In fact, there were high-level doubts before the Rekyjavik match as to whether Spassky did recognize his duty as required. Viktor

Baturinskii, the director of the Central Chess Club, was called in for questioning by Aleksandr Yakovlev, the acting head of the Propaganda and Agitation Department of the Central Committee and later Mikhail Gorbachev's right-hand man. "Tell me, does Spassky understand he carries the moral responsibility for the outcome of the match in relation to the entire Soviet people?" Diplomatically, Baturinskii responded, "I hope he does understand." Thirty years after making that statement, he admitted it had been deliberately disingenuous: he was clear that Spassky did not understand.

A former assistant to the chief military prosecutor, Colonel Baturinskii owed both his interest in chess and his legal training to one of the founders of Soviet chess, Nikolai Krylenko, who had encouraged him to take up each in the years after the revolution. Colonel Baturinskii served in the army for thirty-five years. He had been number two in the team prosecuting the key British-American spy, Colonel Oleg Penkovskii. Baturinskii's nickname was "the Black Colonel." After Viktor Korchnoi defected in 1976, he said Baturinskii should be hanged, drawn, and quartered for his role under Stalin.

Blind and hard of hearing, the former senior chess administrator lived out the end of his days at the top of one of the huge, grim, and grimy apartment blocks that encircle Moscow (he died in December 2002). He was still baffled as to how anyone could question why Spassky had a moral duty to demonstrate the primacy of the Soviet system. The answer seemed too obvious to merit discussion: "Of course it was an ideological question."

Given that Spassky owed so much to the Soviet state, how did he fail to appreciate—in the eyes of the authorities, at least—his reciprocal obligations to it? And if he rejected state nationalism, what did he believe in? Two fundamental facts provide a starting point for comprehending Spassky's character and the evolution of his convictions: He was an ethnic Russian, and he was a Leningrader, a denizen of the former imperial capital, Peter the Great's window on the west. In *Notes from Underground*, Dostoyevsky's narrator calls St. Petersburg (as it was and is) "the most abstract and intentional city in the whole round world. (Towns can be either intentional or unintentional.)" In literary terms, it signified a bridge between the low realities of life and the strange, the enigmatic, and the hidden.

In the Western press, Spassky was marked out among Soviet chess players for naming Dostoyevsky as his favorite author. References to the Dostoyevsky-loving player were used to contrast him with the American, who, if he read anything at all beyond chess magazines, read comics. Some Westerners might have assumed that Spassky was taking a risk in his choice of literature. In fact, Spassky's passion for Dostoyevsky was far from defiant; even Stalin is said to have relished *The Devils*. And though some of Dostoyevsky's writings were censored in the 1950s and 1960s, a major new edition of his works was announced in 1971 on the 150th anniversary of the author's birth.

All the same, the qualities of a Dostoyevsky novel, the realism, the psychological depth of the characters, the stress on the dualism of human nature, on nonrational motivation—these made the author the most subversive of prerevolutionary writers. He embraces life lived for the journey, not for its ending—as seen in his *Notes from Underground*. There the hero ruminates that "man is a fickle and disreputable creature and perhaps, like a chess player, is interested in the process of attaining his goal rather than the goal itself. And who knows (nobody can say with certainty), perhaps man's sole purpose in this world consists in this uninterrupted process of attainment, or, in other words, in living, and not specifically in the goal. . . ."

This chimed with Spassky's attitude to chess. Although he was intensely competitive, the process of achieving a result mattered as much to him as the result itself. He also displayed distinct affinities with Dostoyevskian characters. In the novels, there are existentialist choices, constantly faced, choices that will forever mark those who have to make them. A Dostoyevskian character is hard to classify, he or she is incomplete, always with the potential to adapt and evolve. The Dostoyevsky theorist Mikhail Bakhtin writes, "They all acutely sense their own inner unfinalizability, their capacity to outgrow, as it were, from within. . . . Man is not a final and defined quantity upon which firm calculations can be made; man is free, and can therefore violate any regulating norms that might be thrust upon him."

Certainly, Spassky did not conform to the model of Soviet man; his fame and status afforded him the luxury of a self-determination denied others. Although the state lifted him and his family out of poverty, he always rejected any notion that he owed it a debt. Queried on this, he points out that the Russian Tsar Nicholas II also gave allowances to talented children, paid out of his own pocket.

But if, like a latter-day Dostoyevskian character, he contravened the norms of the Soviet state, and in many ways resisted categorization, he also had much in common with Dostoyevsky himself. Dostoyevsky is a profoundly Christian writer, imbued with a belief in the world of the spirit and in life everlasting; these beliefs, he thought, were the keys to moral health. Spassky, raised amid the religious atmosphere of his mother's Russian Orthodox beliefs, was intensely proud of his paternal family's connection with the Orthodox Church. Spassky's favorite among Dostoyevsky's novels is *The Brothers Karamazov*, which carries a heavy dose of theology. The novel also gives a pointer to Spassky's political stance. In the central episode, the trial of one of the three brothers for parricide, the prosecutor claims that in the three are represented Russian Europeanism, national principles, and the ingenuous spontaneity of the Russian temperament. The stress is on Russian. In the period of official Soviet state nationalism, Spassky was a Russian patriot, the inheritor of Russian Orthodox religious culture.

Spassky's university experience would have reinforced his nationalism. It came during a period of convulsions in the arts, what the Leningrad poet Yevgeni Rein called "that half-literary, half-bohemian life that was fermenting in Leningrad." This entailed in part a subversion of Soviet culture. According to Rein, "We started to turn again toward the Western influences, toward contemporary Western culture; we again turned to Russian tradition, saw the nineteenth century, the Age of Silver, in a new light, and again linked up with the ring of tradition."

In *Grand Strategy*, Spassky reflects on his university thesis. Significantly, he had returned to the prerevolutionary period for his choice of subject: *Shakhmatni Listok* 1859–1863, the first Russian chess magazine. He had always had an interest in Russian history, he says. "For this work I had to read journals from the 1860s. I saw the Russian culture of that time. What a beautiful city St. Petersburg was! When I left the National Library, I found myself in the sleepy, dreadful, provincial town of Leningrad. What an abyss when Russia collapsed."

His yearning for the old Russia also explains Spassky's disturbing description of himself as "an honorable anti-Semite." Dostoyevsky was a nationalist Slavophile with a strong streak of anti-Semitism—seen in his crude attacks on what he called "Yidism." Spassky's forthright self-characterization stems from his hostility to the takeover of Russia in 1917 by the international Bolshevik movement, several of whose leaders were Jewish. As so many senior Soviet chess grandmasters and administrators were both Jewish by descent and Communist Party members, we must assume that he was able to separate his professional relationships from his historic antipathy.

Grandmaster Nikolai Krogius remembers Spassky unerringly stressing that he played for Russia and was not glorifying the Soviet Union through his successes. Krogius sniffs, "The authorities tolerated this exposition (possibly, as they say, only for the time being)." "Bourgeois nationalism" was how the authorities would have normally, and critically, described Spassky's brand of patriotism. The KGB considered such an attitude to be a "pernicious and dangerous survival of the past." Nevertheless, as a grandmaster of world caliber, Spassky enjoyed the forbearance of the authorities—a forbearance not accorded to lesser mortals or to those with direct impact on the public, such as poets, novelists, theater directors, and historians. It made the difference between liberty to walk the streets of Leningrad or play abroad on the one hand and the enforced stay in the provinces or the psychiatric ward on the other. How far did Spassky test the tolerance of the system?

As is widely reported, Spassky was not a Communist Party member. But too much is made of that. Some of the characters in this

story—grandmasters Averbakh, Taimanov, and Stein and apparatchiks Baturinskii, Abramov, and Ivonin—were members.
Others—grandmasters Tal, Geller, Krogius, and Smyslov—were
not. The father of the Soviet H-bomb, Andrei Sakharov, declined
powerful "offers" to become a member long before he became
known as a dissident, though he was in receipt of a massive income and other privileges from the state. Spassky insists he was
never under any pressure to join: perhaps he was considered a
lost cause.

The absence of a Party card did not excuse Spassky from political responsibility or from demonstrating the approved political
consciousness. While he saw himself as "politically independent,"
his was a country where the phrase had no meaning. And from
the beginning of his career, in certain non-chess circles he was
being spoken of as someone who should be watched as potentially "politically unreliable."

A thoughtless remark during a championship in Antwerp in
1955, when he was still a teenager, led to an inquiry by the Sports

Genius at work. Spassky (left) and Tal, world champion 1960–1961 (right).
MOSCOW CHESS CLUB MUSEUM

Committee. All innocence, no doubt, Spassky had asked the team commissar, "Did Comrade Lenin suffer from syphilis?" Spassky recollects "the eyes of my apparatchik glittered dangerously." Why risk such a question? "Lenin had been made into an icon, and I was curious about the reality." Only action by the deputy sports minister, Postnikov, prevented the case from being taken up by the Komsomol, which would have threatened Spassky's future.

Officers of the Leningrad KGB were now among those following the career of the chess highflier. Doubtless the organization's plentiful supply of informers kept them in touch with his every word and deed. His independence of spirit was beginning to be observed by some of his colleagues. In 1960, after they had flown to Argentina for the Mar del Plata international tournament, grandmaster David Bronstein told Spassky that they should report in to the embassy. Spassky had better things to do: "David Ionovich, you go, but I won't. I belong to a different generation, to which these rules don't apply."

By the mid-1960s, the non-chess interest in Spassky was such that Bondarevskii urged him to move from Leningrad to the Moscow area. "The KGB is too curious about you," he told Boris. In a studio flat shaken by passing express trains, forty kilometers from the capital, twenty-seven-year-old Spassky lived on his own for the first time.

Being in the international spotlight did nothing to curb his independence. At the 1970 Chess Olympiad in the West German city of Siegen, two years after the Prague Spring and the Soviet invasion of Czechoslovakia, and by now world champion, Spassky took care to shake hands with the entire Czechoslovak team. Even though the Czech authorities must have considered their team members politically reliable enough to travel to the West, Spassky's gesture can still be seen as an intended, if restrained, display of sympathy for that country.

Then, famously and dangerously, in January 1971 he refused to sign a collective letter in support of the black American communist Angela Davis, who had been arrested in the United States. He believed that the world championship should not be used for politics. This refusal was no small matter for the world champion. Leading Soviet representatives of science, sport, music, ballet, and literature had added their names. Botvinnik had signed and had solicited Spassky's signature. The world champion still declined. The chess apparatchik Mikhail Beilin feels generally warm toward Spassky as a person: "He was nice, sympathetic, and most people felt well disposed toward him. I think people liked him for his human qualities but disliked him if they judged him on the upholding of Party values." Yet Beilin disapproves strongly of Spassky's decision. "This letter was signed by different cultural leaders—Spassky was asked to sign on behalf of our chess federation—and it was regarded as a great honor to be asked, a very special honor. So Spassky was being honored by the Central Committee, and he didn't value this honor." To an old communist like Lev Abramov, it was distasteful: "He was a product of the system. The Soviet system provided him with everything he needed for his chess; yet when it came to areas beyond chess, he didn't want to be part of it."

The general reaction was sufficiently negative for the deputy sports minister, Viktor Ivonin, to call a special meeting at the Sports Ministry. Spassky himself was not invited to what bore a strong resemblance to a trial in absentia. The participants included the leader of the Trade Union Sports Committee (of which Spassky was a member), representatives from the State Sports Committee, the Komsomol Central Committee, and the Central Chess Club, as well as the journalist from the news agency Novosti who had drafted the protest letter. As the participants evaluated Spassky's attitude and tried to decide what to do about his refusal, a more general dissatisfaction with him emerged. There was broad agreement that he could not be *forced* to sign. But Botvinnik's influence, Spassky's desire for a new apartment, and unfounded gossip about improper behavior in the presidium of the USSR Chess Federation were all discussed as means of bringing pressure to bear. In the end, it was decided that Ivonin would simply talk to him again, though this proved futile: Spassky's mind was made up. He could not be brought round even by another call, this time from the KGB.

In discussing the preparations for Fischer, Viktor Baturinskii, the director of the Central Chess Club, instanced Spassky's refusal to put his name to the Davis letter as an indication of his immaturity. Mikhail Beilin says that it was in Spassky's nature to delight in outraging others, even at the risk of offending them. This meant saying what nobody else would dare to say. "For example, he was lecturing to a large chess audience in Nizhny Novgorod. He was talking about Estonia as a very nice little country with a very difficult destiny. Such a view didn't appeal to me: there were people who thought it had an extremely happy destiny. His allowing himself to say such a thing is not very agreeable." If as a good Soviet you believed that the USSR's annexation of Estonia was a stroke of good fortune for the country and its people, you might well find Spassky's indirect censure upsetting.

Perhaps there was even a hint of cruelty when Spassky forced unsafe political opinions on a listener. Nikolai Krogius remembers how "in public he often displayed bravado with his paradoxical declarations: 'The communists have destroyed nature,' 'Keres lives in an occupied country [that is, in Estonia],' and so on. Of course, if such statements had been made not by a famous chess player but by an ordinary citizen, then harsh punitive measures would have been taken against that citizen—possibly even a prison sentence."

Obviously, the authorities were fully apprised of Spassky's idiosyncratic outlook. At least when he was at the top, he did not bother to confine his views to his inner circle—though even there he would have known that someone was noting it all for the KGB. Baturinskii complained of "his thoughtlessness" during public appearances, and cited as typical a speech Spassky made to an audience of chess lovers in the city of Shakhty in the Rostov region on 26 September 1971. The speech had been the subject of an outraged letter from the secretary of the Shakhty City Committee of the CPSU, one Comrade Kazantsev:

```
B. Spassky spoke without prompting about his
financial position. He noted that his salary was
300 roubles, which he received in payment for
his post as trainer in the Lokomotiv club,
without carrying out any training duties.
   Comrade Spassky stressed that insufficient
attention is paid to chess players in the Soviet
```

Union, and their labors were poorly compensated.
Explaining the reasons for his nonparticipation
in the USSR championship, he cited the small sum
awarded for the first prize (250 roubles). B.
Spassky noted in his speech that the biggest
prize he had received abroad was the sum of
$5,000, while in his native land it was only
2,000 roubles.

Spassky's salary had been raised from 250 roubles a month to 300 on his becoming world champion. It may not have seemed much to Spassky, but Mikhail Beilin, who signed the necessary document authorizing this increase, recalls the envy Spassky's relative wealth provoked among colleagues: "I remember when the young Spassky received $5,000 in Santa Monica, a lot of people suffered over this as though experiencing a personal loss." To put Spassky's earnings in context, in the late 1960s (after the currency reform) the average monthly wage for a skilled or white-collar worker was 122 roubles.

Spassky did more than just complain about money. At this Shakhty meeting, he startled his listeners by saying, "Basically I am descended from a priest's family. And if I had not made it as a chess player, I would happily have become a priest."

The speech went all the way to the secretaries of the Central Committee, ending up with the acting head of the Central Committee Propaganda and Agitation Department, Aleksandr Yakovlev, who was told that the audience had expressed "bewilderment and indignation" at its contents.

Harsher and potentially more threatening judgments were made of Spassky. Baturinskii accused him of being under the sway of "objectivist views" over the location of the match with Fischer. At a preliminary discussion with the USSR Chess Federation leadership, Spassky had declared: "I consider it inadvisable to hold the match in the USSR, since this would give a certain advantage to one of the participants, and the match should be held on equal terms. . . ."

Broadly, "objectivism" meant expressing views not based on a Marxist-Leninist analysis. The official Soviet reference book, *The*

Great Soviet Encyclopaedia, defined this sin as "A worldview [based on] sociopolitical 'neutrality' and [refraining] from Party-based conclusions. . . . In reality it . . . masks a social and class-based subjectivism . . . objectivism is orientated toward serving, albeit not openly, the dominant conservative or reactionary force of the social 'order of things.'" In other words, Spassky was demonstrating an incorrect political consciousness.

Spassky gave off dangerous political vibrations, but should we call him a dissident? Such he seemed to some contemporary university students. Viktor Korchnoi gives a qualified appraisal: "When I defected, I considered myself a dissident on two legs, while Spassky was a one-legged dissident."

From his post as second in command of the State Sports Committee, and in charge of ten sports including chess, Viktor Ivonin regarded him with a possibly sinister tolerance: "We accepted him as he was, knowing that it was too late to change him. He is a nihilist. We could have helped him in certain ways, to talk and act 'more correctly.' And we tried to do that. But you can't remake a person. So when he said certain things—perhaps in jest—we decided not to react. But he wasn't a dissident."

Yevgeni Bebchuk, the former president of the Chess Federation of the Russian Federation (a republic of the USSR), agrees: "On the other hand, Spassky never accepted the Soviet regime: he wouldn't say that out loud, but he would say it among friends. From the very beginning, he pretended to play the fool, pretended not to know anything. I would often be called to official meetings in my administrative role, and colleagues on the committees would say, 'Well, he's a talented chess player, but he's a little bit strange in the head,' and I would say, 'Well, yes.' He protected himself. It's a kind of survival technique, because in Russian culture they take well to fools; they forgive them a great many things."

Here, Bebchuk is making a peculiarly Russian cultural reference. An established feature of Tsarist Russia, the "Holy Fool," or *yurodivyi* (one of "God's folk"), was a wandering monklike figure, venerated for his or her self-imposed suffering in the cause of humility and intense religiosity. The Holy Fool was credited with mystical powers. But most relevant here, like the king's jester, the Holy Fool also enjoyed a license to poke fun at rulers, expose evils, and tell unpalatable truths. And when some of his contemporaries try to explain Spassky, they express a tolerance of his "eccentricities and unorthodox opinions" in a tone of voice that might be used of such a figure.

Spassky's trainer Nikolai Krogius, the psychologist, says the world champion's politics were the consequence of his complex character—an aspect of which was his hostility to discipline. "He's like an independent artist, a very blithe person, a bohemian type. And as he was the world champion at that time, he thought everyone had to listen to what he said and take his opinion into consideration—though, to be frank, his opinion was not always the last opinion on a subject and not the most considered."

Being opinionated was as much about entertaining as scandalizing. Spassky was certainly that risky type—a joker. Grandmaster Yuri Averbakh has a dramatic analysis of Spassky's approach to life: "Spassky was an actor." In other words, he wanted to be the focus of attention. Averbakh remembers going to Keres's funeral with Spassky, "and everyone was dressed in black, except for Spassky, who came in a red suit. It was very funny because there were a thousand people on the streets and he was the only one who stood out. I wasn't sure whether he simply neglected the usual formalities or whether this was his way of expressing himself. Such exhibitionism was very sad."

Spassky was also highly convivial. Several of his friends and colleagues claim that once he became champion, he shed any former reticence. Then he wanted to be the life and soul of the party and broaden his social life. There was no shortage of invitations. As well as his strongly expressed remarks, he had a fund of amusing stories and was an excellent mimic. Baturinskii and Averbakh were two of his chess victims. Politicians did not escape: Brezhnev was a favorite. He even dared a (passable) Lenin.

Thus, the views of his chess contemporaries offer no single picture of the world champion other than that he was out of the ordinary, of independent character. They remember Spassky the artist, Spassky the buccaneer, Spassky the joker, Spassky the actor, Spassky the nihilist. Spassky the free spirit, *vol'nodumets.* Spassky the frivolous, Spassky the un-Soviet man. Even Spassky the Holy Fool.

However we categorize him, there seems to have been an acceptance by the authorities of Spassky's determination to be his own man and of his distancing himself from the regime. The official answer to their rogue champion was simply to dismiss his views as inconsequential, irritating but not worth taking seriously.

Until, that is, Fischer challenged Soviet ownership of the world title. Then the authorities could no longer escape the tensions between the political role of the world champion and Spassky's obdurate rejection of that role, and between their distaste for his attitudes and admiration for his incontestable greatness as a chess player.

6

LIVING
CHESS

I don't believe in psychology. I believe in good moves.

— BOBBY FISCHER

There is nothing abnormal about a chess player being abnormal. This is normal. — VLADIMIR NABOKOV

How can we begin to understand what goes on inside the minds of world-class players while they are moving pieces on the sixty-four squares of the chess board for hour after hour, game after game, week after week? Months of preparation, mental and physical, precede so grueling a contest as Reykjavik. What resources of skill, intellect, memory, and imagination, of stamina and courage, does a match require?

The British Broadcasting Corporation archives contain a clue in a unique recording of a 1930s interview with Alexander Alekhine. Alekhine is preparing for his title challenge with Max Euwe, the only authentic amateur to become world champion. (Nearly four decades later, as president of FIDE, the sport's governing body, Euwe will preside over the Fischer-Spassky match.) In the precisely enunciated, beautifully modulated diction of the day, the interviewer asks whether Alekhine does not by now know all the combinations in chess. His voice high-pitched and heavily accented, Alekhine replies, "Oh no, believe me, a lifetime is not enough to learn everything about chess."

Like Fischer, Alekhine was a chess fanatic and loner. He lived and breathed chess; he was fiercely competitive, constantly seeking self-improvement, capable of turning violent on the rare occasions that he suffered defeat. His knowledge of the openings was unsurpassed. In Alekhine's time, opening preparation could take elite players up to around move nine or ten, before the game spun off in a novel direction. By the early 1970s, theory had progressed to the extent that often the first fifteen moves would be familiar. Now, in their remarkable memory banks, assisted by computer databases, the chess elite can shuffle through a mental card index consisting of both published games and home-based spadework that may cover them to move twenty-five or beyond. Up to this point they will recognize each position after each move from a game already played, the published analysis of a game already played, or their own private study.

Eventually, however, the sheer immensity of possibilities will land both players in uncharted territory. Indeed, that a board game can generate such intricacy is the real marvel of chess.

Writers trying to convey this complexity have their own pet mathematical picture or comparison to illustrate the scale of the numbers involved. Thus, in *Fields of Force,* his book on Fischer-Spassky, George Steiner states that there are 318,979,584,000 legitimate ways to make the first four moves. It is said that there are more possible variations in a game of chess than there are atoms in the universe (roughly 10^{80}) and seconds that have elapsed since the solar system came into existence (roughly 2×10^{17}). As for chess, it is estimated that there are approximately 25×10^{116} ways for a game to go.

This is the figure for theoretical permutations within the rules of the game. But for any given position, the serious player can immediately rule out of consideration the majority of legal possibilities. Take the opening move. White can advance any of its eight pawns one or two squares and can move each of its knights either to the center or to the side of the board. That is twenty legitimate moves in all. But in fact, almost all serious games begin with a two-move thrust of the king's, queen's, bishop's pawn or the king's knight to the center. So only four of these twenty moves are regularly played.

Even so, one can see how the possible variations soon spiral beyond ordinary comprehension. Assume that in a typical middle-game position there are eight sensible continuations for each player on each move. Over the next five white moves and five black moves, there will be $8 \times 8 \times 8 \times 8 \times 8 \times 8 \times 8 \times 8 \times 8 \times 8$ permutations (8^{10}), or 1,073,741,824; that is more than 1 billion paths down which the game could plausibly twist and turn.

How does a chess player cope with the huge size of the chess cosmos? A layperson might assume that the answer lies in sheer computational ability, and that good chess players are those who can calculate further ahead than mediocre ones. And of course there is some truth in this—though not much. Staring at the board and crunching through the possibilities can get one only so far, for there are simply too many branches on what is a near infinitely sized tree. Today's computers can calculate millions of moves per second. Yet they still struggle against the human insights of the leading grandmasters.

The real explanation of what chess players do is less rational. It is closer to what we might think of as an artist's vision and has to do with a kind of intuition. A chess player examining a position sees not an inanimate set of carved or molded pieces waiting to be moved from square to square, but diagonals and ranks and latent possibilities, what Arthur Koestler described as "a magnetic field of forces charged with energy."

Why do grandmasters recognize that at a certain point in the game, a knight should be positioned on the f5 square rather than c4 or d5? Obviously they might foresee that in certain variations, a knight on f5 defends a crucial square, or threatens a particular combination of moves, or supports a particular maneuver. Or it might be that f5 acts as a temporary staging point for the knight's ultimate destination. However, there can be both more and less to it than that. Grandmasters somehow "feel" that f5 is the right square; it satisfies their conception of the game, fitting into some kind of deep, unarticulated structure. The German grandmaster Michael Bezold spent several months playing chess with Fischer in the 1980s. "He just felt that a certain move was the right move without calculation. And after analyzing, we saw it was the right one." The Cuban-born José Capablanca, world champion from 1921 to 1927, was noted for relying on his intuition but reproached himself for this, as though his innate sense for the game were in some way reprehensible—or less admirable than an approach of pure calculation.

An analogy between chess and mathematics or music may be instructive. All three pursuits regularly produce prodigies—those marvelously gifted and precocious beings so rarely found in the worlds of painting or poetry, drama or literature, ballet or bel canto, or in other forms of art where raw talent needs to build steadily on experience and developed sensitivity. It is barely conceivable that a fourteen-year-old would have a sufficient range of emotions and experience to write *War and Peace* or paint *Guernica*. But he or she could play Elgar's violin concerto, propose a mathematical proof, or become U.S. chess champion. Genius in chess is a magical fusion of logic and art—an innate recognition of pattern, an instinct for space, a talent for order and harmony, all mixed with creativity to fashion surprising and hitherto new formations. Max Euwe said of Alekhine, "He is a poet who creates a work of art out of something that would hardly inspire another man to send home a picture postcard."

Comparing the beauty of chess and music, Harold Schonberg, the senior music critic of *The New York Times*, wrote, "If chess were as popular as music, if as many people responded to its subtleties and nuances, the masterpieces of Steinitz, Capablanca, Alekhine, Botvinnik, and Fischer would not be held far below the masterpieces of Bach, Mozart, Beethoven, and Brahms."

The creative imaginations that go into a great chess game and a great piece of music are closely allied. Spassky has been called the Mozart of chess; like Mozart's music, his chess was a brilliantly fluid combination of form and fantasy. He himself took pride in being labeled the "Pushkin of chess," explaining in a Yugoslav magazine that it was "because of my elegant and har-

José Raúl Capablanca y Graupera, world champion 1921–1927, giving a simultaneous display. NEW IN CHESS MAGAZINE

monic style, I suppose." Musicians are often good chess players and vice versa, while mathematicians often excel at both chess and music. Mathematicians see in certain equations the artistic beauty that chess players see in certain combinations. Max Euwe trained as a mathematician. A law in vector theory is named after the early-twentieth-century German world champion Emanuel Lasker. Mark Taimanov is a virtuoso concert pianist.

The splendor of Fischer's chess lay in its cleanliness, its simplicity; if his moves were notes, they were struck not to impress an audience, not to delight himself by their wit or ingenuity, not to achieve beauty (though they had their beauty). They arose out of the logic of the board and Fischer's profound yet unfathomable sense of harmony.

There is a passage in Stefan Zweig's novella *The Royal Game,* that celebrates the uniqueness of chess, while also drawing parallels with music and mathematics.

Every child can learn its basic rules. Every bungler can try it. And yet it requires within those unchanging small squares the production of a special species of master, not comparable to any other kind, men who have a singular gift for chess, geniuses of a particular kind, in whom vision, patience and technique function in just as precise divisions as they do in mathematicians, poets and musicians.

One artist who proclaimed the aesthetic qualities of chess was a moving force in the Dada movement, Marcel Duchamp. Duchamp achieved notoriety in 1917 through showing a urinal as an exhibition piece under the title *Fountain*. It symbolized his contempt for bourgeois art and was a pioneering exhibit in the revelation of everyday artefacts as objects d'art. But at this time chess was already on its way to taking over Duchamp's life, eventually ruining his marriage. On his honeymoon, he analyzed chess problems until, it is said, one night, in a rage, his wife glued the pieces to the board. Later he abandoned art altogether for chess—competing for France in the chess Olympiads. He had a unique perspective of both the artistic and the chess worlds. "From my close contact with artists and chess players I have come to the conclusion that while all artists are not chess players, all chess players are artists."

Of course, creativity is a necessary but not a sufficient condition for high achievement at the game. Just as professional musicians have to practice continuously, so chess professionals need constant study. They must be abreast of the latest opening innovations. They must plow through the games of their peers. They are always topping up their mental store of patterns, improving their judgment and deepening their feel for various types of position. They also need constant competition in order to remain battle sharp.

Along with artistic vision, memory is a vital ingredient in the chess player's makeup. And all world-class chess players have shown an astounding ability to recollect games. Fischer's total recall struck even fellow professionals with awe.

However, a chess player's memory is of a particular kind. During World War II, a Dutch chess master and psychologist, Adrian de Groot, made a breakthrough in our understanding of the chess mind. De Groot conducted a series of experiments in which he showed a variety of chess positions to a variety of players, from the expert to the beginner. They were exposed to these positions for just a few seconds, after which they were given a chess set and asked to reconstruct them. Their ability to do so correlated closely with the strength of their chess. Max Euwe, who took part in these tests, never failed to place each piece correctly.

De Groot showed his subjects typical chess positions such as one might come across during a typical game. Later, psychologists widened his experiment by conducting similar tests with randomly placed pieces. The results were intriguing. When the pieces were positioned arbitrarily, the expert performed no better in reproducing the board than the beginner. What the expert could do was recognize regular patterns of pieces. Thus, after the castling maneuver on the king's side of the board—when the king moves to the knight square and the rook leaps over it—white will routinely have several pieces on certain squares (for instance, the king on the g1 square, a rook on f1, and pawns on the f2, g2, and h2 squares). A chess player needs almost no time to absorb such a familiar cluster of pieces. Such clusters can be regarded as akin to phonemes in language; they are the game's basic building blocks. The top chess masters can instantly make out thousands of such clusters.

Just as some people have an affinity for language, some will also have a natural aptitude for pattern recognition and retention, which is then enlarged by study—perhaps physically expanding the relevant area of the brain itself, as tests have shown happens to London taxi drivers who have to memorize all London streets to gain a license.

This capacity to recall positions has led to staggering public feats, one from grandmaster Miguel Najdorf. Najdorf was born in Poland in 1910 but was in Buenos Aires for the chess Olympiad when German tanks crossed the border into Poland in 1939. He stayed in Argentina, and during the war he took up a challenge to play forty boards "blindfold." The term *blindfold* is chess player's argot; in practice, Najdorf sat with his back to his opponents as their moves were read out to him. This required keeping in his head the positions of 1,280 pieces (initially) on 2,560 squares. He had undertaken the challenge after losing all contact with his family, hoping they would read of his exploits in the press. He won the vast majority of games, but there is no evidence that this news reached home.

✦✦✦

Given the skills required of the chess player, and the repeated mental strain from playing game after game after game, it is small wonder that, in George Steiner's words, "this focus produces pathological symptoms and nervous stress and unreality."

The image of the near insane chess champion must be approached with caution. For the vast majority of grandmasters, mastery of chess is combined with a normal social and emotional life. Spassky had a life outside chess recognizable to chess players and non–chess players alike, a family, hobbies and passions, feuds and friendships. Yet the number of great players whose behavior away from the board has been eccentric, bordering on the outlandish, cannot be ignored. Some champions have clearly lived on—and a few have crossed—the fine line between genius and insanity.

Before Fischer, the United States had produced only one player with an unquestionable claim to being the world's best, Paul Morphy, who came from a wealthy New Orleans family a century earlier. Morphy was Fischer's favorite player of all time; he characterized him as "perhaps the most accurate chess player who ever lived." As a young man, Morphy demolished the foremost players in the United States before traveling to Europe in 1858 in search of stronger opposition. There, too, he trounced everybody in sight. Like Fischer, who came to identify with him closely, Morphy's exploits over the board captured the nation's headlines and imagination. His name was used to market various products, such as cigars and hats. Although he did little apart from chess, Morphy loathed any suggestion that he was a professional, deeming it more respectable to live off an inheritance from his parents. He also despised the chess "scene." Still only in his twenties he descended into a state of paranoia and depression and became a recluse. Occasionally he was seen wandering the streets of New Orleans, muttering to himself in French. At the age of forty-seven, he was found dead in a bathtub, surrounded by women's shoes.

The first official world champion, the Prague-born Wilhelm Steinitz, who did scratch a living from chess, became convinced at the end of his life that he could beat God, even if the Lord were granted a pawn and a move head start. Akiba Rubinstein, a Pole, one of the preeminent players in the early twentieth century, was certain that other players were out to poison him; he lived in an asylum from which he journeyed to the chessboard. In the same decade, the Mexican master Carlos Torre removed all his clothes while traveling on a public bus in New York. His breakdown may have been triggered by a relationship with a young woman that had gone sour. From that moment on, he never recovered sanity. Was chess partially responsible? International master Bill Hartston, a psychologist, says, "Chess is not something that drives people mad; chess is something that keeps mad people sane." Clearly, it failed to do this for Morphy and several others. What about Fischer? His later life appears to supply the answer.

The chess mentality offers rich pastures in which psychoanalysts may safely graze. Freudians in particular have delighted in speculating on what subconscious drives govern the average chess player. Ernest Jones, pupil and biographer of Freud, wrote a paper in 1930 entitled "The Problem of Paul Morphy." He focused on the relative impotence of the central piece, the king, leading him to the startling deduction that chess is "adapted to gratify at the same time both the homosexual and antagonistic aspects of the father-son contest." Grandmaster Reuben Fine, himself a psychoanalyst and author of a book about the Fischer-Spassky match, was also taken by the role of the king and the sexual connotations of the game of chess. Ignoring female players, he maintained that the king aroused castration anxiety among men, since it "stands for the boy's penis in the phallic stage, the self-image of the man, and the father cut down to boy's size." Fine concluded, "Chess is a contest between two men in which there is considerable ego involvement. In some ways it certainly touches upon the conflicts surrounding aggression, homosexuality, masturbation, and narcissism."

Fine used his psychoanalytic tools to analyze Fischer. He saw particular import in Fischer's statement that he would like to "live the rest of my life in a house built exactly like a rook." According to Fine, the libidinal undertones expressed in this desire are impossible to ignore. The preference offered "a typical double symbolic meaning: first of all it is the strong penis for which he apparently finds so little use in real life; second, it is a castle in which he can live in grandiose fantasy, like the kings of old, shutting out the real world."

The Freudian view remains ultimately unfalsifiable and so not, in the view of many philosophers, scientific: certainly in this extravagant form, it is difficult to take seriously. What a survey of great players tells us is that all human life is there: drunks and womanizers, the happily married and the lonely, the businesslike and the otherworldly, the religious and the atheistic, the democratic and the totalitarian, the honorable and the treacherous. But alongside their brilliance, at their competitive acme they share one other quality—an uncommon steeliness of character.

In no high-level sport does a player need to be tougher psychologically than in chess. In most sports, nerves dissolve in the flow of the action; in chess there is a deadly surfeit of time for brooding. Most professional games last several hours. A match against the same opponent can go on for several weeks. A whole hour can pass waiting for an opponent to make a move, while the inevitable question nags insistently: Has a weakness been found?

If panic, doubt, or defeatism creeps in, the affected player may begin to see less clearly, begin to adopt too cautious an approach or, in desperation, too cavalier a style. The conviction may grow that an opponent is seeing further and deeper. Inspiration becomes impossible. The British journalist and chess fan Dominic Lawson puts it vividly:

In all sports confidence is important. In chess, a game which, unlike all those others, is entirely in the mind, with no trained limbs to take over when the brain is in crisis, a collapse of confidence is terminal. Above all, across the board the opponent can sense this mental bleeding, as clearly as a boxer can see blood oozing from his adversary's head.

As in all walks of life, in chess there are various mechanisms for handling the stress. It is possible that Fischer coped in part by channeling it into rage. Certainly some players (notoriously, for example, Mikhail Botvinnik) have a talent for loathing an opponent, a loathing that improves their performance at the board, sharpens their sense of competition, and channels their aggression. Korchnoi is in that class, too, capable of whipping up antipathy for a single game.

Though very competitive by nature, Spassky belonged to a far rarer breed. Like Smyslov and Tal, he wanted to befriend his opponents, to create an atmosphere conducive to weaving creative magic. For him chess was more artistry than slow-motion Sumo wrestling. And like Taimanov, as an artist he needed the stimulus of spectators.

Of course, Spassky had learned to control his emotions and to stifle any expression of feeling, though in earlier days he was often ill after a tournament, afflicted by tonsillitis and a high temperature. But later on, the German grandmaster and psychologist

The unrepentant Bolshevik. In 1961 Botvinnik (on left) takes his revenge on Tal and wins his third world title. NEW IN CHESS MAGAZINE

Helmut Pfleger measured the stress levels (blood pressure and so on) of a number of grandmasters in a major tournament in Munich. He discovered that Spassky was the calmest. Spassky's serenity was an asset: any champion would have had his nerve tested by the manner in which Fischer stormed his way to the final.

7

BULLDOZER TO REYKJAVIK

As far as world championship events are concerned, Fischer is in some danger of becoming the Yeti of the chess world. Indeed, to organizers of such events, he must seem as elusive and as fearsome as the abominable snowman.

—HARRY GOLOMBEK, THE LONDON *TIMES*

OCTOBER 1970

In the world championship cycle, the Zonal, the Interzonal, and the Candidates, the United States, like the USSR, was considered a zone in its own right, Zone 5. The U.S. Championship doubled as the U.S. Zonal, with the rules stating that the top three placed players would qualify. However, for several years Fischer had boycotted the tournament. His grievance was that it was too short: with only eleven rounds, a player who suffered a loss of form for one or two days could be put out of the running. The organizers said they could not afford a longer tournament. In 1969, Fischer was absent again; the three players to qualify for the Interzonal were William Addison, Samuel Reshevsky, and Pal Benko.

Fischer had not played competitive chess for eighteen months, and many thought he would never return. Then, to general surprise and delight, he agreed to participate in the Soviet Union vs. the Rest of the World in 1970 in Belgrade. To even greater amazement, when the Danish grandmaster Bent Larsen demanded that he play on Board One for the Rest against the leading Soviet, pointing out quite reasonably that he had achieved the best tournament results over the previous two years, Fischer yielded the point and agreed to step down to Board Two. It meant that he played Petrosian rather than Spassky.

Despite his voluntary concession, Fischer was fuming. Knowing how he could take his anger out on tournament organizers, the press monitored his every movement. Soviet grandmaster Mark Taimanov says reports on Belgrade Radio were akin to battlefield dispatches: "Fischer has left the room," "Fischer has ordered dinner in the restaurant." However, the American's humor soon improved; though handicapped by a lack of practice, he beat Petrosian in the first two rounds and drew with him in the last two. Meanwhile, Spassky and Larsen shared the honors with a win apiece. (Spassky's win became famous—achieved in seventeen moves; it was one of the quickest in grandmaster history.) The Soviet Union edged to victory overall by a single point.

Representing their countries, Fischer and Spassky were to meet at the chess Olympiad at Siegen in West Germany in 1970. Naturally, there was great pressure on both men. Spassky was spotted puffing away tensely on cigarette after cigarette before they faced each other. Hundreds gathered in the hall to watch the game; Fischer had ensured that the table was kept several yards away from the spectators.

Those who could make out the position were not to be disappointed: it was a truly fabulous game. Fischer, with the black pieces—a minor disadvantage—quickly gained equality with one of his favorite openings, the Grünfeld Defense, and, as is common in the Grünfeld, sniped away at white's center. The American then planted a knight on a secure square, c4, on which it was both safe from attack and, within its surrounding area, a dominating presence. Yet Fischer seemed to underestimate Spassky's attack, involving rook, knight, and queen, on the other side of the board. The winning combination was delightfully elegant, an unexpected rook sacrifice, winning Fischer's queen. The chess correspondent of the London *Times*, Harry Golombek, praised Spassky for having played "in true world champion style."

When Spassky emerged victorious after five hours and thirty-nine moves, the Soviet ambassador to West Germany, Semion Tsarapkin, kissed him with joy. Spassky was lucky: according to then West German chancellor Willy Brandt, Tsarapkin was nicknamed "Pincers." "The ambassador's powerful jaws sometimes snapped with a force suggestive of the intention to pulverize his words." Tsarapkin was given the chessboard on which the match had been played, signed by all the grandmasters there save one—Fischer.

In an interview later, Spassky said of this win that he had succeeded in working himself up "into that special state of élan without which any tour de force is impossible. Fischer himself may have unwittingly contributed to my high spirits. It has always been a pleasure to play against him." Spassky told the interviewer that he regarded Fischer as the most likely challenger for his crown and that he held him in high esteem as a man who loved chess passionately and for whom the game was everything. In a display of empathy, he described Fischer as "very lonely. That is one of his tragedies."

So Fischer was back, and a series of impressive tournament results followed; he was apparently growing stronger with each game. As he once again approached his best form, to the neutral chess observer it began to seem a catastrophe that the self-destructive American had disqualified himself from the world championship cycle. But help was at hand from Fischer's guardian angel, Ed Edmondson.

Colonel Edmondson had a bearing that could only be American: square jawed, upright, solid. He had entered the byzantine world of chess administration in the twilight of his military career in the U.S. Air Force, where he edited its *Navigator* magazine. The United States Chess Federation was in chaos when he took over in 1967 as the first ever executive director. Run from a shabby office in Greenwich Village in New York, the USCF had few members and no money. He turned it around, seeking donations, building up the membership base, and moving to new headquarters.

For years, the ever cheerful director of the U.S. Chess

Federation acted as Fischer's unpaid agent, standing between Fischer and the potential consequences of his extreme conduct. Now the colonel and Pal Benko hatched a plan. Rules had been bent for Fischer before; they could be bent for him again. If FIDE agreed, and the other players in the U.S. Zonal agreed, Benko would give up his Interzonal place to Fischer. Some reports suggest this was Edmondson's idea; Benko says it was at his initiative, since only Fischer had a realistic chance of the title. The prospect that one of the three American Interzonal contenders might make way for Fischer had been the talk of the chess world as early as the Siegen Olympiad. In any case, Edmondson persuaded FIDE to accept the deal. As for Benko, he received a modest payoff from the U.S. Chess Federation of $2,000. Fischer's place in the world championship had been bought for him—and bought cheaply, given the potential rewards.

Fischer's rapture was modified: as usual, there was a last minute hiccup when he expressed his dissatisfaction with the money on offer. His threat not to take up his Interzonal spot after all provoked this anguished plea from Colonel Edmondson:

More than anything else, I want to help you to become World Champion. I can only do so if there is a high degree of cooperation and faith between us. I strongly urge you to play in the Interzonal and in the Candidates Matches, trusting me as you progress to fight every step of the way for the best possible playing and financial conditions on your behalf.

I believe you appreciate this fact and ask that we again confirm agreement on the following.

Honorariums

A.	Interzonal	$4,000
B.	Candidates Match, Quarter-Final	$3,000
C.	Candidates Match, Semi-Final	$3,000
D.	Final Candidates Match	$4,000
E.	World Championship Match	$5,000
	Total guaranteed honorariums	$19,000

The honorariums, Edmondson pointed out, were in addition to the prize money. Then there would be expenses. "I will also guarantee that your 'pocket money' will be twice that given to other contestants in each event." In addition, he promised that Fischer would be put up in the most luxurious hotels and that the conditions at every stage in the world championship cycle would meet Fischer's high standards. The plea worked, and Fischer was off to the walled city of Palma de Majorca in the Balearic Islands—and the Interzonal.

So Fischer began a miraculous year in the history of chess. As the scale of the miracle became apparent, a burgeoning wave of press and public interest emerged that would swell all the way to Reykjavik.

The November/December 1970 Interzonal took place in the concert center in Palma, the Sala Mozart, overlooking the bay, the cathedral, and the old fort. There were twenty-four competitors; many were already famous names in the world of chess, including Efim Geller, Vasili Smyslov, Mark Taimanov, Lev Polugaievskii (USSR), Lajos Portisch (Hungary), Bent Larsen (Denmark), Wolfgang Uhlmann (East Germany), Svetozar Gligoric (Yugoslavia), Vlastimil Hort (Czechoslovakia), Henrique Mecking (Brazil), and Robert Hübner (West Germany). But it was Fischer who drew the spectators. Crowded onto the dark yellow carpet, they strained to glimpse his board.

The top six would advance to the knockout stage, where they would be joined by former world champion Tigran Petrosian and Viktor Korchnoi, the latter having qualified as the losing finalist in the Candidates match against Spassky in 1968. Fischer began well but hit a bad patch, losing to Bent Larsen. In the second half, he abruptly stepped up a couple of gears and, in a stupendous run, eventually won the last seven games, taking first place by the huge margin of 3.5 points. Grandmaster Uhlmann, who also qualified for the Candidates, said, "It's simply unbelievable with what superiority he played in the Interzonal. There is a vitality in his games, and the other grandmasters seem to develop an inferiority complex."

While the Soviets relaxed and played bridge between rounds, Fischer barely emerged from his room at the plush Hotel Demar. The list of conditions he had placed on his attendance at the tournament was as long as ever and included glare-free fluorescent lighting and a schedule that took account of his religious practices, meaning the strict observance of his Sabbath. To fit in with that, Larsen had to rise early for his rendezvous with the American. "Many of us have decided that this will be the last time that Fischer gets such special treatment. What he wants, he gets. But no more!"

Eight players were now left to compete in the Candidates round for the right to face Spassky: Taimanov, Korchnoi, Geller, Petrosian, Larsen, Uhlmann, the brilliant, highly strung Hübner—and Fischer. He was drawn in the quarter-finals with Taimanov, the match to be played at the University of British Columbia in Vancouver.

Until this match, Mark Taimanov had lived an enviable double life, conducting his chess in tandem with a career as a highly respected classical pianist. He performed duets with his wife, Liubov Bruk; their work together has earned them a place in the record collection *Great Pianists of the Twentieth Century*. Their pianist son, Igor, would join them on the concert platform. Taimanov made occasional forays into journalism and led an otherwise normal existence. To the Soviets he appeared, in many ways, to be a model citizen.

Then forty-four years old, and so a relative veteran, Taimanov had come across Fischer several times in tournaments over the years. Like many others, he was astonished by Fischer's single-minded devotion: "I swear that I never saw him without a chess set." Despite Fischer's evident promise from a young age, Taimanov had been one of the few to be skeptical that he would achieve the breakthrough to the superleague. For all the American's maturity at the chessboard, Taimanov thought the adolescent Fischer suffered from a weakness. He was "too deeply convinced that he is a genius. Self-confidence that borders on a loss of impartiality in assessing one's potentialities is a poor ally in a difficult contest."

If overconfidence was a failing, it was not one Fischer ever attempted to rectify. He saw himself as the firm favorite in the Taimanov match. He was not alone; the noncommunist press was of the same mind. Only Taimanov insisted he could win, dismissing Fischer as a mere computer. Even the Soviet Communist Party daily *Pravda* must have been pessimistic, failing to print this self-assured forecast.

Taimanov prepared hard, helped by former world champion Mikhail Botvinnik, who handed over his enormous Fischer file in its entirety. This had been compiled a year earlier, in 1970, as negotiations dragged on for a Botvinnik vs. Fischer match supposed to take place in the Dutch town of Leiden. The plans had been aborted after Fischer insisted the victor would have to win six games, draws not to count. For the organizers, this had major financial implications since it meant that, in theory, the match could go on forever. It was not a risk they were willing to take.

Botvinnik's analysis of Fischer's play was full of fascinating, detailed insights. Through a painstaking deconstruction of all of Fischer's published games, he claimed to discern certain themes and patterns that Fischer consciously or unconsciously adopted. The Russian drew a number of conclusions—for example, that Fischer had a penchant for long moves with his queen, and that in the endgame he preferred a knight to a bishop. Also in the endgame, observed Botvinnik, his king was often dispatched on deep forays across the board. Taimanov was grateful but felt that ultimately "it didn't help me—in the Russian saying, this straw was not for the right horse."

In addition to the file, Taimanov was backed by the thorough organization of the Soviet chess machine. He was supplied with three grandmasters: Aleksandr Kotov led the team, supported by the highly thought of, but young and relatively inexperienced, Yuri Balashov, and by Yevgeni Vasiukov, an old sparring partner. It was not Taimanov's ideal squad. "I wanted Tal. He was a friend of mine, and in case of defeat I would rather have had Misha with me." But Botvinnik thought he was too bohemian and that his fondness for drink might render him incapable of the long hours of sober analysis required of a second. Puritan sports apparatchiks in the Central Committee also disapproved of Tal's three divorces.

By contrast, in terms of the actual chess, Fischer was without assistance. He had hoped to bring grandmaster Larry Evans along as his second, but Evans refused because of Fischer's twin demands that he abstain from journalism and leave his wife at home. Colonel Ed Edmondson, however, was there to help with the arrangements and with resolving any disputes.

The game started several days late, this time because of an objection by Fischer's opponent. To Taimanov's annoyance, the organizers had attempted to preempt a Fischer tantrum about the spectators by setting the board in a cramped room at the back of the campus library. Taimanov, used to playing the piano in front of a large and appreciative concert audience, said it was too stuffy. After some haggling, they compromised on the student cinema, which seated 200. Victory would go to the player who racked up five-and-a-half points; there would be a maximum of ten games.

Fischer won an epic first game in eighty-nine moves. He won the second and the third games. Taimanov blundered badly in the second. After a postponement, taken on Taimanov's request on health grounds (he was diagnosed with high blood pressure), Fischer won the fourth game, then the fifth, again after a shocking Taimanov howler. And then Fischer won the sixth. It is difficult to portray to non–chess players the magnitude of such a shutout. A typical result between well-matched players might be, say, six wins to four, with nine draws. Fischer had just beaten a world-class grandmaster six games to none, with no draws. The British chess player P. H. Clarke wrote that "this performance by Fischer may be the best, in statistical terms anyway, ever recorded in a single competition."

Taimanov's defeat turned his hitherto settled life inside out. This pillar of the Soviet chess establishment suffered the wrath of a system that felt betrayed and disgraced—even scared—by the scale of his rout. In his account of this episode, *I Was Fischer's Victim,* Taimanov writes about his "civic execution." "If on the eve of the match I was officially and popularly reputed to be 'an exemplary citizen' . . . I suddenly fell into the flames of ruthlessly destructive criticism by the authorities at all levels."

His "civic execution" began on 5 June 1970, on his return from

Vancouver when he was passing through Soviet customs at Moscow's Sheremet'evo Airport. He had done this dozens of times before, always without incident. Now he found himself thoroughly searched, on the orders of the senior customs official on shift, named in the report of the incident as Comrade Dmitriev. Taimanov's suitcase had been delayed, but in his hand baggage the officials discovered a copy of *The First Circle* by Aleksandr Solzhenitsyn. They also found a large sum in dollars, Taimanov's prize plus unused subsistence money. Taimanov then told Comrade Dmitriev that in his suitcase was a letter containing 1,100 Dutch guilders that he had failed to declare on entry. Taimanov had been asked by Max Euwe to take this letter to grandmaster Salo Flohr—the money was payment for articles Flohr had published in Dutch periodicals. "Since I was asked by the president of FIDE, a person who enjoys respect in our country," Taimanov would explain, "I did not consider it appropriate to refuse him." To a suspicious mind, it looks as if the customs officers knew in advance what they would hit upon.

Taimanov was in effect put on trial by the Sports Committee—hauled before them for these two customs offenses, bringing in both undeclared currency and a book that the minister Sergei Pavlov told him was too repulsive even to pick up. "By the expression on their faces," Taimanov wrote, "I might have robbed the Bank of Canada and smuggled millions of dollars into the country."

Taimanov's importing of a foreign edition of Solzhenitsyn's novel was potentially a serious offense. In 1969, the author had been expelled from the Writers Union for "conduct anti-social in nature and fundamentally at variance with the principles and tasks formulated in the charter of the Writers Union," and could not be published in the Soviet Union—his last work was published there in 1966. He had opposed the publication of his work abroad but his books were still accused of "being used by Western reactionary circles for anti-Soviet aims."

In his letter of explanation, Taimanov protested, unconvincingly, that the Solzhenitsyn book was essential reading because foreign journalists were always interrogating him about the USSR's most famous author. He had not read any of Solzhenitsyn's books before, and "I thought that it would be expedient to familiarize myself with at least one of them. Of course I intended to dispose of the book afterward . . . but I forgot to do so." He went on, "I consider this mistake to be a serious misdemeanor on my part, which can only be explained by a state of shock caused by what I had been through."

Of course, he knew—everybody knew—that the real charge was what Pavlov, in his secret report to the Central Committee on 21 June, called "the unprecedented defeat of a Soviet grandmaster." In the minds of the officials, a Soviet grandmaster's losing six to nil to the representative of U.S. imperialism was equivalent to an act of intentional ideological sabotage. Taimanov puts his treatment down to the fact that "I was the first. And they thought something lay behind it, something political."

Today, the broadcast journalist and chess specialist Naum Dymarskii insists that Taimanov's "offense" was possession of the forbidden book. "But if Taimanov had won, the customs would have ignored it." Indeed, Taimanov tells how at Sheremet'evo the customs official had asked, "Why did you lose? If you had beaten Fischer, I would have carried all the volumes of Solzhenitsyn's books myself to your taxi." Taimanov managed to retain a sense of humor through the ordeal, laughing at a joke "by my friend the cellist Mstislav Rostropovich that Solzhenitsyn had been arrested for carrying one of my chess books."

He was not the only scapegoat. Aleksandr Kotov, the head of Taimanov's delegation, was also attacked for showing a marked failure of leadership. Kotov admitted that Taimanov had played like a machine that had completely broken down. He, Kotov, was then accused of being disrespectful to Comrade Dmitriev, the customs official. He denied this: "We talked in the politest manner." In his "explanatory letter" to Pavlov and the Council of Ministers Committee for Physical Training and Sport, Kotov wrote that he had actually thanked Dmitriev for teaching them a lesson well learned. The panic is palpable; so is the humiliation.

At the time, the repercussions for Taimanov were sobering—he thought that they were meant as a caution for the world champion. He was thrown out of the USSR team and forbidden to travel for two years. He was banned from writing articles, was deprived of his monthly stipend, even stripped of his title, honored USSR Master of Sport. (The title was eventually rewarded in the last days of the Soviet Union.) As if this were not retribution enough, the authorities prohibited him from performing on the concert platform. From being an elite member of Soviet society, with a comparatively comfortable lifestyle, Taimanov was now a discredited figure facing financial ruin. His marriage was also affected. He wrote later that his "unpredictable fate" had "shattered the family unity."

Few of Taimanov's friends and colleagues were brave enough publicly to come to his defense, though many privately sympathized with his plight. There was, however, one exception—Boris Spassky. In the postmortem, the world champion put a rhetorical question: "When we've all lost to Fischer, will all of us be dragged on the carpet?" Spassky also showed his irreverent side. Baturinskii wanted to know if a physician should have been sent to help Taimanov. "Yes," interjected Spassky, "a sexologist." "I see, Boris, that you are in a jovial mood," was Baturinskii's irritated response. Taimanov remains grateful to Spassky that the world champion also backed him publicly. "Everybody criticized me, and Spassky was one of the few who openly defended me to the press by saying, 'Whatever the result, as a match it was very interesting.' How they dared to print it I don't know."

Fischer's next match was against Bent Larsen. Fischer was again the favorite, but Spassky predicted a tight struggle. "Larsen is a little stronger in spirit." The Dane had been the only other Western player to pose a challenge to Soviet hegemony in the previous decade. He had also beaten Fischer twice. After bids were taken to host the contest, the players settled on the U.S. city of Denver as the venue.

Larsen believes that accepting this was his fatal mistake. Accustomed to the gentle summer breezes of northern Europe, he found himself sweltering in a Colorado heat wave. "I couldn't play. I just couldn't play. And I couldn't sleep. They had the hottest summer since 1936. It was so hot that people who worked in offices were allowed to stay at home."

The first game got under way on 6 July in the playing hall of a women's college, Temple Buell. Fischer won. He won the second game and then the third and the fourth. After the fourth, Larsen complained of feeling ill and exhausted, and the doctors ordered a break. Fischer then wrapped up proceedings with two more wins in a row.

Recall that Fischer had swept majestically through the last seven games in the Interzonal. With the victory against Taimanov by six games to zero and now Larsen by the same score, he had achieved nineteen consecutive wins against outstanding opposition, a feat in chess that had never been equaled. One hypothetical parallel would be a tennis player taking the Wimbledon title without dropping a single game throughout the tournament.

Although chess was still confined to the back pages, public interest in Fischer was now gathering momentum. President Nixon sent Fischer a letter:

I wanted to add my personal congratulations to the many you have already received. Your string of nineteen consecutive victories in world-class competition is unprecedented, and you have every reason to take great satisfaction in your superb achievement. As you prepare to meet the winner of the Petrosian-Korchnoi matches, you may be certain that your fellow citizens will be cheering you on. Good luck!

The winner of the Petrosian-Korchnoi duel was the forty-two-year-old former world champion Tigran Petrosian. The result of his match with Fischer would determine the challenger to Boris Spassky. The Fischer juggernaut seemed unstoppable.

Petrosian and Fischer had met eighteen times previously, with three victories apiece and twelve draws. Petrosian was known as the maestro of the draw. He had a unique technique, which, despite being highly effective, had not endeared him to the millions of chess fans around the world. He shunned complexity, taking preemptive defensive measures whenever possible. He would lull his opponents into a false sense of security, often inveigling them into overreaching. Then he would grind them relentlessly down with deadly strategic precision, pressing home the tiniest positional advantage (an apparently inconsequential move of the queen's rook's pawn might baffle spectators; eight moves later it would invariably turn out to be on the perfect square).

Athens, Belgrade, and Buenos Aires all bid for the match. Petrosian wanted to play in Greece, Fischer in Argentina for two reasons—they were offering the most money, and they had the best steak. Lots were drawn to settle it, with Buenos Aires triumphant.

Fischer fever may not yet have circled the globe, but its arrival in Argentina was unquestionable. Buenos Aires was a chess city—host to over sixty clubs. The organizers had offered $7,500 for the winner, $4,500 for the loser. The match would take place in one of the most prominent theaters, the San Martín, at the center of the capital's cultural life. It was situated on the equivalent of Broadway, the Avenida Corrientes. Chess was now "entertainment."

Tickets went on sale at nine A.M. (the games began at five P.M.), by which time several thousand people were already lining up. The regular audience was one and a half thousand, a very high number for a game not previously regarded as much of a spectator sport.

Everywhere he went, Fischer was mobbed by adoring, starstruck crowds, from teenage girls to old-age pensioners. They had a very different conception of personal space from the solitary American: they tried to shake his hand, grab him by the arm, or pat him on the back. He would wrench himself away in horror. He got into the habit of slinking out through back doors, walking against walls, hoping to outpace his fans with his huge strides. Buenos Aires foreshadowed the Reykjavik media circus; the local and international press sought out off-board details such as Fischer's favorite snack (a grilled kidney sandwich).

The opening ceremony was on 29 September. Fischer was tardy, as usual. His opponent was asked, "Do you think that Fischer's lateness is a battle of nerves?" Petrosian thought not: "It is a question of upbringing."

In a letter Fischer wrote afterward—it is unclear whether it was ever sent—he admits that he was nervous before the Petrosian match kicked off but claims that he was reassured by how scared the Armenian looked. And, avers Fischer, Petrosian had good reason to be fearful. When world champion, he had been the instrument through which the Soviets lied about Fischer's character and ability at chess. So Petrosian's moment of truth had arrived. This accusation was most unfair. The Armenian had been editor of the Moscow chess magazine *64,* which had been critical of Fischer, but he had always been respectful of the American's ability.

Apparently, even Petrosian's expression was too much for Fischer to live with. The two players had been booked into the same skyscraper hotel, Fischer on the thirteenth floor, Petrosian on the tenth. Fischer soon asked to be moved. He explained to the chief arbiter, the German grandmaster Lothar Schmid, that when he met Petrosian in the elevator, the former world champion's face was so sad, he could not bear seeing him.

Fischer had laid down a host of conditions about the lighting, the table, the chairs, the clock—none of which unduly disturbed his hosts. Also at Fischer's request, the first three rows of seats in the theater were kept empty. Rona Petrosian, small and plump, who each match day would prepare a flask of coffee for her husband, had a reserved place in row four.

Although the organizers had done everything they could to satisfy Fischer, this did not stop someone throwing a stink bomb at the back of the hall (the stench did not reach the platform), nor did it prevent the finely calibrated lighting from breaking down. And it did not stop Fischer from complaining to the arbiter about the way Petrosian walked out of view after his moves.

The relative serenity owed much to the presence of both Colonel Edmondson at Fischer's side and Petrosian's team leader, Viktor Baturinskii. Additionally, both players knew and trusted the chief arbiter. Lothar Schmid had been plucked from playing in a tournament in Berlin as the only arbiter acceptable to the two sides. He was among the few foreigners ever to be at the receiving end of a grin from Baturinskii, in public an iron-faced archetypical Stalinist. Schmid knew that Russians kissed each other on meeting, so on first seeing Baturinskii, he threw his arms around him; the Soviet former colonel was startled into smiling.

Game one began on 30 September. Halfway through, when

Fischer found himself unexpectedly on the defensive, the lights blew. The clocks were stopped and Petrosian left the stage; Fischer, meanwhile, carried on—sitting there and staring at the board. His Soviet opponent complained to the arbiter that Fischer was benefiting from free calculation time—contemplating his next move in the gloom while his clock was not running. Fischer allowed Schmid to restart the clock, while he remained thinking in the darkness.

Fischer won that first game, his twentieth consecutive grandmaster victory. But any expectations that he would dispatch Petrosian in the fashion in which he had destroyed Taimanov and Larsen were to be dashed in game two. Fischer, suffering from a bad cold, played poorly. When he offered his resignation, the audience began loudly to chant Petrosian's name. Did Fischer at last have a real fight on his hands?

With one win apiece, there followed a series of three draws. Fischer's fans were in a state of high anxiety. For the American—who sought to win every game—a draw was a semidefeat. For Petrosian, who sought in every game not to lose, the same result was a partial triumph. What Fischer needed was to restore his psychological advantage with a second victory.

Once it came, in game six, Petrosian collapsed. He took a few days off, complaining of exhaustion, and was diagnosed with low blood circulation. Fischer identified this as the moment of his opponent's psychic disintegration. He said, "I felt Petrosian's ego crumbling after the sixth game." Petrosian's comments support that: "After the sixth game Fischer really did become a genius; I, on the other hand, either had a breakdown or was tired, or something else happened, but the last three games were no longer chess." Indeed, when the Armenian returned, Fischer quickly wrapped up the proceedings. President Nixon wrote to Fischer, "Your victory at Buenos Aires brings you one step closer to that world title you so richly deserve, and I want you to know that together with thousands of chess players across America, I will be rooting for you when you meet Boris Spassky next year."

Although there were no major rows, Petrosian complained later, "A player feels at a disadvantage when he knows that he is playing in the city and the hall where his opponent wants to play,

Flattened: (from top) Mark Taimanov, Bent Larsen, and Tigran Petrosian. NEW IN CHESS MAGAZINE

that the lighting is such as his opponent ordered, that while one of the players will receive a superpurse, the other will not. It is not that without a superpurse it is hard to play chess, but that you unwittingly begin to feel a certain discrimination, a sense of injury, almost of humiliation." He added that tortuous match negotiations left Fischer's opponents softened up, much as troops under attack in the trenches were softened up by a preliminary bombardment. This formed the basis of a warning to Spassky.

In Moscow, Petrosian was credited with having accomplished what Taimanov had not: at 6.5 to 2.5, this was defeat with dignity. But a non-Soviet player was now the challenger for the world crown for the first time in a quarter of a century. Spassky was asked about his prospects of retaining the title but gave nothing away: "The one thing I can say is that I think the match will be a very interesting one." All the evidence suggests that, privately, Spassky was convinced that he could and would win.

8

TROUBLE IN
PARADISE

*What I really like is when I'm in a festive mood and my
friends are in a wonderful mood, too. . . .*

— BORIS SPASSKY, ON LEAVING FOR REYKJAVIK

On 19 June 1972, the chairman of the USSR Council of
Ministers Committee for Physical Training and Sport—in
short, USSR sports minister Sergei Pavlov—held a farewell
reception for Boris Spassky and his team on their departure
for Reykjavik. His deputy, Viktor Ivonin, joined them, together
with Viktor Baturinskii. Spassky and Pavlov made short speeches.

This was no joyful sendoff, as for smiling troops departing to
war with flags waving and families cheering. The atmosphere
seemed strained, an air of battles being refought, entrenched positions justified. Spassky told them that his group had gelled and
thanked the Sports Committee for its organization. He felt well
prepared and well rested. He had lost some weight and even felt
younger. He singled out grandmaster Isaac Boleslavskii for his
usefulness and mentioned that he had played a sparring game
with Anatoli Karpov. Then he justified his decision not to have a
head of delegation, a doctor, a cook, or a translator in Reykjavik:

"Such people would have had to be compatible with the team." He also rebutted rumors within the chess community that he had not worked hard enough. The match, he prophesied, would be a celebration of chess.

In reply, Pavlov dwelled on the historic nature of the event that was about to take place. In spite of all the difficulties in the negotiations, the Soviet conditions for the match had been satisfied. Those in the room would have understood that the chairman's allusion to "difficulties" was not referring only to the Americans or FIDE, but also to the world champion. Then Pavlov uttered two warnings to the team. Firmness was essential. If someone behaved toward them in a "boorish way," they must be boorish back. Pavlov tried to make this sound like a little joke. But it was clear to the audience that he meant what he said and that the remarks contained an implicit reproach. The word *boor* had already been used in a personal attack on Fischer in the Soviet chess magazine *64*—an attack ordered by Pavlov. The chairman went on to caution the team not to be caught up in the Fischer mystique—the notion that the U.S. grandmaster was bestowed with some kind of transcendent, irresistible power. Then he wished Spassky victory, the assembled party raised their glasses, and the reception was over.

What exactly was Pavlov hinting at? What "difficulties" had Spassky and his team created? Little was known about the Soviet chess machine in the West, except that it was phenomenally successful; but the image was of ruthless efficiency, of a culture and political system that permitted no dissent or internal squabbling. The reality, at least in the buildup to Reykjavik, was the reverse.

⸪

Boris Spassky and the chess authorities had been bracing themselves for a duel with Fischer since the spring of 1971, before the American had even taken on Taimanov in the first of the Candidates matches.

Normally, grandmaster arrangements would be managed through the USSR Chess Federation, but because of his position as world champion, Spassky jumped a stage of the administrative hierarchy, discussing his plans directly with the State Sports

Committee leadership. A significant first meeting took place on 1 March 1971, when Spassky and his trainer, grandmaster Igor Bondarevskii, met the deputy sports minister, Viktor Ivonin, to discuss the champion's program for the year ahead. This meant a schedule that would cover both his personal training and the array of commitments incumbent upon him as world champion, the training he would carry out for the trade union chess club, his participation in matches, international tournaments, public chess duties, even rest and recreation. The world champion was ex officio the leader of Soviet chess.

Viktor Ivonin is a central figure in our story. His daily record of the meetings and talks he held offers a unique contemporaneous source for the Soviet side of the championship. Sports Minister Pavlov had taken personal charge of the USSR preparations for the Munich Olympics, so Deputy Minister Ivonin became the senior governmental point of reference for Fischer's challenge.

Short, shrewd, jolly, and still full of energy in his seventies,

The deputy sports minister Viktor Ivonin. Trying to get through to Spassky?
VIKTOR IVONIN

Ivonin is evidently a survivor. His career opened on the floor of a Leningrad electric power station, where at fourteen he started as a metal worker during the siege. There he became a Party activist, beginning the ascent that has taken him through all political upheaval to the spacious office he now occupies as the executive director of Russian Lotteries. He progressed steadily through the ranks of the Komsomol, went briefly to the Sports Committee, and then, in 1962, moved to the CPSU Central Committee, working in the sports section (he was a sports enthusiast). In 1968, when Pavlov became chairman of the State Sports Committee, he asked Ivonin to become his deputy: they had known each other well in the Komsomol and the Central Committee. Ivonin thought highly of Pavlov, but he hesitated for a short while because Pavlov was notoriously difficult to work with. They ended up being colleagues for fourteen years.

Politically, there was more to the story. Pavlov was on his way down. A tough Stalinist who had gained entry to the highest echelons of the Party as head of the Komsomol, he was a professional propagandist and orator, skilled at brutal assaults on those he and the authorities regarded as "enemies of the state." He was known for his violent temper—though, says Ivonin, "the whip was not his principal weapon." In the mid-1960s, he backed the hard-line Aleksandr Shelepin, who mounted an unsuccessful challenge to Brezhnev's leadership. Shelepin was ejected from the Party Secretariat, dispatched to the outer darkness of the trade union movement. Pavlov fell with his mentor, and when, in 1968, he accepted an offer he could not refuse to become head of the State Sports Committee, it was a substantial loss of rank, influence, and authority. As first secretary of the Komsomol, he was a full member of the Central Committee; as chairman of the Sports Committee, he was reduced to being a nonvoting ("candidate") member. However, he made the best of it, coming to be seen as a fine statesman of sport.

When Spassky and Bondarevskii arrived at Ivonin's office, the central question was the probable identity of the challenger for the title. Spassky and Bondarevskii said Fischer would certainly be a contender, and they predicted he would reach the final. Forecasting his challenger was vital. Chess players cannot train effectively in a vacuum; the training has to be tailored to the opponent they expect to confront.

Although the world championship cycle still had a long way to run, from this moment, Spassky's preparation would be focused on the American. Ivonin held a further series of meetings to appraise Fischer's chess qualities. The tone was one of respect, almost awe. His technique was exemplary. He looked after his physical fitness. The enigma of his personality was discussed with curiosity and apprehension. There was longstanding resentment at Fischer's earlier claims that Soviet players were dishonest and sold victories to one another for money. But was Fischer a genius, or mad, or both? The question was raised with Sergei Pavlov at the Sports Committee in March.

Old habits die hard. Not long after this committee meeting, an article entitled "The Subject Is Fischer" appeared in the magazine *64*. This served up 1,400 words of acidic anti-Fischer vituperation. A non–chess journalist, Anatoli Golobev, wrote the piece under Pavlov's instructions. This extract gives the flavor: "A difficult childhood predetermined his place in the chess world as well as his ignorance in most spheres of social life, unthinkable for a contemporary cultured person"—presumably a broad hint that Fischer was *nekulturnyi*, rude and uncouth. "By the way, much of his 'extravagant behavior' stems from this—from his mixture of ignorance and childlike spite."

It may have been their minister's style, but several other members of the committee regarded this heavy-handed mauling as a hugely embarrassing mistake. When all was said and done, they knew Fischer as an exceptional player. The grandmasters also despised the item as the political journalism of a chess nonentity. Mikhail Beilin was head of the Sports Committee's Chess Department from 1967 to 1971. He recalls, "Many in the chess world were sympathetic to Fischer: when you look at his games, you're not interested if he attended school or not."

The committee members resolved that henceforth only serious and objective articles on Fischer as a chess player should appear in Soviet chess magazines—personal criticism was to be outlawed. It was a decree they stuck to in the face of a number of provocative Fischer outbursts—such as at the time of the Larsen match, when he bragged that he would destroy any Russian he faced. Pavlov had to be restrained from demanding a tough rejoinder in the Soviet press.

Nevertheless, even articles praising Fischer's chess tended to remind Soviet readers of his less laudable characteristics. He caused genuine umbrage in the Soviet official breast. No doubt bound up with this hostility was the Soviet sense of inferiority. In an internal report, the Director of the Central Chess Club, Viktor Baturinskii, complained angrily and inaccurately: "Fischer is provided with considerable moral and material support, and for these purposes the U.S. Chess Federation has received around $200,000 from various organizations." He went on, "Appearances by Fischer are organized in the press, on the radio and on television, during which he gives assurances that he will become world champion in 1972 and makes insulting remarks about Soviet chess players."

The pattern of approbation followed by condemnation was repeated in an article by international master Vasili Panov. Comparing Fischer and Spassky, the author noted: "Both are masters of the art of fine maneuvering and of combinational attack, both have the ability to squeeze out the smallest positional advantages, and both have perfect endgame technique . . . the creativity of Spassky and Fischer represents the culmination of all the achievements of the second half of the twentieth century." But in the same article, he homed in on another aspect of Fischer's character, quoting the American: " 'Chess provides me with happiness and money. . . . I follow what happens to my capital closely. I want to have a magnificent villa and an expensive car of my own. . . .' " Panov seemed horrified. "American patrons of the arts, now paying generously for Fischer's appearances, do not know much about chess. But they understand success! For them there are only winners and losers. And only success pays!"

Evaluating Fischer as both a man and a player became a high priority. In June, after Taimanov's defeat, a bruised Taimanov and his now abject team manager, Aleksandr Kotov, gave an assessment of Fischer to the Sports Committee. What was remarkable about Fischer, they said, was his "demonic influence over his opponent when he sits at the table." The long-held view of Soviet grandmasters that Fischer was a tournament player, not a match player, was inaccurate. Kotov and Taimanov blamed themselves for underestimating Fischer. They were struck by his habit of continuing to study chess even over dinner.

It was not all gloom. They thought their experience showed that Fischer was slow to get into a match; in the first three games he was sweating. A potential Achilles heel for the American was his narrow opening repertoire. Finally, said Taimanov, there was only one player who could beat him: Boris Spassky.

Together with a note from several other Soviet grandmasters, this review of Fischer was passed on to Spassky, though Fischer's matches against Larsen and Petrosian were still to be played. At the beginning of June, Spassky's team was assembled. It consisted of three grandmasters: his longtime coach, "Father" Igor Bondarevskii; Nikolai Krogius, a psychologist; and Efim Geller. Krogius had been part of Spassky's training team, with Bondarevskii, since the autumn of 1967 and was to continue working with him until 1974.

Each had a specific task. Bondarevskii's job was to study in minute detail 500 of Fischer's games in an attempt to identify deficiencies and weaknesses. Krogius had developed a technique for appraising players' psychology and was now applying it to Fischer. He aimed to find the critical positions in his games and assess Fischer's thought processes, studying also his reaction to defeat. He would carry out the same process on Spassky and compare the two. Geller would concentrate on the openings.

Later, Krogius complained that Spassky had ignored the results of his toil, just as Geller grumbled that Spassky had not followed his openings advice. Ivonin recorded in his diary that Spassky had paid little attention to the notes on Fischer commissioned from other leading Soviet grandmasters such as Tal, Smyslov, and Petrosian, nor had he taken the opportunity to discuss Fischer with them in person. The champion had his reasons, some less respectful than others. "We don't need general advice from old men," he opined to Ivonin. And he was determined that these "old men" should not discover any of the new weapons he was developing for use against Fischer. "The most important thing is we won't be able to tell them *anything;* we're scared information may leak."

It was and remains quite normal for grandmasters to fear that their ingeniously worked-through ideas might seep out to the wider world, but Mikhail Beilin describes this as a Spassky obsession and claims that the champion had been suspicious of others since childhood: "He would keep quiet; it was his nature, and he wouldn't trust or believe anyone." The world champion also believed that some grandmasters, Petrosian for one, actively disliked him. He had grounds to be wary. Because foreign travel and the other rewards for success were so dependent on the favor of the authorities, Moscow chess was a wasps' nest of rivalry, intrigues, and plots.

So for Spassky the formation of a tight, loyal team was vital. To Bondarevskii, Geller, and Krogius, an Estonian player was added. Ivo Nei had captured the USSR Junior Chess Championship in 1948. He was only an international master, a lack of foreign tournament play having cost him the chance of the grandmaster title. Baffled by the choice, some put it down to Nei's being a close friend of his fellow Estonian Paul Keres, whom Spassky was said to have idolized. Certainly Spassky was an admirer of Keres. But talent with a tennis racket was the primary reason for Nei's selection. A former Estonian tennis champion, his major role was to keep Spassky physically fit. He was likable and ebullient, and according to Nei, he and Spassky enjoyed a freedom of conversation the champion did not share with the others. Looking back, Spassky says he trusted Nei, and it is probable that he felt more at ease with the unpretentious non-Muscovite than with the other denizens of the Central Chess Club.

However, the Sports Committee felt Nei to be an extremely poor choice. After all, he had little to offer in terms of chess analysis; he was not in the same class as the others, and if Spassky required a physical trainer, then a real expert should have been found. The KGB also objected to the non–Party member Estonian; during the match, doubts about him would take a more menacing turn.

By August 1971, as Petrosian prepared to meet Fischer in the last of the Candidates matches, Spassky discussed the details of his preparation with the Sports Committee. Baturinskii had already informed Ivonin that the world champion had not worked much in the previous year. Ivonin told Spassky he should be playing more in the Soviet Union, where the competitors were stronger and fought more fiercely.

Since becoming world champion, Spassky had played ninety-two games, eighty-eight of them abroad. Ivonin suspected that Spassky did not want tough competition. He appeared to be suffering from post–world championship loss-of-form syndrome.

In July 1971, in a small tournament in the Swedish city of Göteborg, Spassky had managed eight points out of eleven (five wins, six draws). In the Alekhine Memorial tournament in Moscow in November/December 1971, he was placed only joint sixth, below the new prodigy, Anatoli Karpov, and ex-champions Smyslov and Petrosian. He had agreed a series of unimpressive short draws. But he was not the only champion to have avoided tough competition. In a later article in the chess magazine *64,* Vasili Panov commented: "Not one of our world champions, with the exception of Botvinnik, played even once in the Championship of the USSR—the strongest contemporary tournament—while they held the title. That is why they lost their feel for hard-fought battles. Even in the competitions in which the world champions were magnanimous enough to appear, they didn't throw themselves fully into it, didn't crave first place, and often—oh, how often!—instead of passionately searching for paths to victory were satisfied with modest 'grandmaster' draws and now and then conceded first place to a braver and more ambitious competitor."

If he were minded to make excuses, Spassky could point to personal preoccupations—private troubles that the Sports Committee tried to help him resolve. He was unsettled by the obligations that fell to him as the leader of Soviet chess. He had to ensure that Bondarevskii and Krogius had permits to live in Moscow and that Bondarevskii gained a much needed pay increase. He wanted to change his Moscow flat in Prospekt Mira; he described the Stalin-era apartment as noisy and claustrophobic, with nowhere to put his books or work. He wanted more money. He had to pay alimony to his first wife and provide for his mother. His second wife, Larisa, had come to Moscow with their child, and they too had to be taken care of—a suitable kinder-garten found for the little boy, Vasili. With all these expenses, 300 roubles a month was not enough, he told Ivonin.

As a senior politician, a deputy minister, Ivonin also received 300 roubles a month. He initially told Spassky that the Sports Committee did not have sufficient money for chess as well as for other sports in the Soviet Union. Privately he thought that com-pared to other people, Spassky had a privileged enough life al-ready; the real problem was that Spassky knew how sports stars lived abroad. However, Spassky's demands could not be ignored, and when they met again in late November, Ivonin capitulated. Spassky was awarded an increase to 500 roubles a month—the same as a Soviet minister and the first Soviet sportsman to be re-munerated at this level. The Council of Ministers—the govern-ment—had to approve the increase as an "exceptional personal salary."

On 16 November, Viktor Baturinskii, director of the Central Chess Club, wrote a report to the Sports Committee on Spassky's training, expressing the authorities' disquiet at the champion's at-titude to the defense of his title. Clearly exasperated, he ex-plained Spassky's unsuitability to carry the Soviet flag and gave a merciless review of the world champion's general readiness for the mission ahead:

```
As a result of his difficult childhood and gaps
in his upbringing, he allows himself to make
immature statements, infringes sporting
procedures, and does not display the necessary
level of industriousness. Certain individuals in
our country and abroad try to aggravate these
weaknesses, nurturing his delusions of grandeur,
emphasizing his "exclusive role" as world
champion in all sorts of ways and encouraging B.
Spassky's already unhealthy mercenary spirit.
    Two points cause particular anxiety:

    a) He spends a great deal of time on improving
his living conditions (exchanging his flat,
```

buying a dacha, repairing his automobile), and
this may in future influence his training, which
demands the full devotion of his energy and
time . . .

b) Thoughtlessness during public appearances;
his attention has been drawn to this several
times.

The very next day, the Sports Committee lost control of Spassky's preparation.

Within the structure of government, the Sports Committee was answerable to the Council of Ministers. But the Soviet Union had two (unequal) sources of governing authority. Operating alongside the government, at this time led by Andrei Kosygin, was the real center of power, the Communist Party. At the top of the Party was the Central Committee. It had a cabinet, the Politburo, the pinnacle of the power structure. The Central Committee and its secretaries were at the heart of the political system, and the general secretary, Leonid Brezhnev, was the true leader of the country. (This caused puzzled head scratching in diplomatic circles: how could Brezhnev pay state visits abroad when he had no official governmental position?) Any issue with major ideological implications went to the Central Committee for discussion and decision. If the response was positive, the government ministry would act; if not, not.

Without informing the Sports Committee (in other words, the deputy minister, Viktor Ivonin, and the bureaucrats who would have to make all the practical arrangements and find the money for them), Spassky initiated a meeting with a senior functionary in the Central Committee and handed over his outline "Training Plan." The unnamed functionary conveyed it to Piotr Demichev, the Central Committee secretary whose beat covered chess. Chess fell under "ideology," and Demichev had been the secretary responsible for ideology since 1961—he was also a candidate, or nonvoting member, of the Politburo. Spassky himself says that he never met Demichev.

Why did Spassky take this radical step and give his schedule to the Central Committee, the control room of the Party? He says it was because of his growing friction with Baturinskii; he wanted to bypass him—and with him, presumably, the other Sports Committee apparatchiks.

Although this was a world championship, the Central Committee would not normally have intervened; usually such matters would have been left to the Sports Committee. Asked if he resented Spassky's gambit, Ivonin simply says that such a move by a top sportsman with Party connections was not unknown ("a world champion is a world champion"), but that in this case Spassky had no need to go to Demichev. The Sports Committee, says Ivonin, was already implementing his wishes. Ivonin assumed that Spassky just wanted the Central Committee to put its authority behind his personal demands, including finding a new apartment.

In any case, two days later, the chairman of the Sports Committee, Sergei Pavlov, a man utterly familiar with Soviet ways of power, had his first sight of the world champion's program to retain the title. As he read the cover letter, with at least surprise, and probably anger, he realized that Spassky now outgunned the chess bureaucrats. The initiative concerning Spassky was out of the ordinary, and the champion had generated it. This in itself would have irritated Pavlov, but perhaps his response would also have been tinged with personal bitterness and envy. He had been a Party boss. He had helped Brezhnev dispose of Khrushchev. Now here was a Central Committee secretary going over his head to meddle in his bailiwick.

```
To Comrade S. P. Pavlov

I ask you to examine closely the questions posed
here and to report back to me.
P. Demichev
```

Attached was Spassky's plan, now circulated to them via the second most powerful body in the country:

Preparations for the match: Spassky-Fischer
(in summary)

The main goal is victory. Our collective is responsible for the result. It consists of: grandmasters B. V. Spassky, I. Z. Bondarevskii, E. P. Geller, N. V. Krogius, I. P. Nei.

1. Everything connected with the match preparations must be secret. All those taking part in the preparations must sign a document stating that they will not reveal an official secret.

2. All members of the working community are at the disposal of B. V. Spassky until the end of the match.

3. A permanent base is needed for work and rest outside Moscow. A dacha for seven people.

4. Finances. Estimate of expenses for the entire preparation period.

5. A head of preparations is needed who will deal with organizational issues.

6. Supply of food and medical care.

7. Arrival for the match two weeks before the start. Aim — acclimatization and organization of a working routine.

8. Talks about the location and dates for the match are to be carried out directly by B. V. Spassky in consultation with the entire collective and other competent individuals.

```
Personal requests of B. V. Spassky:
Exchange of flat (has been going on for two
years)

The general plan of preparation consists of
1. Physical
2. Chess
3. Psychological

1. Physical. Aim: maximum professional capacity
for work

2. Chess. Objective analysis of the strong and
weak sides of Spassky and Fischer. Theoretical
preparation.

3. Psychological — steadiness in the struggle.

B. Spassky
Moscow 17.11.71
```

Many of these points had already been raised with the Sports Committee, though two of Spassky's demands—that everyone involved in his training should be sworn to secrecy and that the location of the match should be for him to decide—were new. The last worried the committee: they wanted Spassky to concentrate on chess and leave the rest to them.

Demichev's one line was enough. His request to be kept informed raised the stakes for the Sports Committee. In Soviet culture, it stated "the Party views this match as ideologically important." In other words, "Watch out!" Or, as Spassky expresses it in English, he had succeeded "in jumping through Pavlov's head."

After receiving it, the Sports Committee was, or at least saw itself as being, unusually complaisant toward Spassky, even when it became plain that he lacked faith in them. For example, the committee wanted to send a doctor, a translator, and its choice of journalist to Reykjavik. Spassky insisted that they send a grandmaster, Isaac Boleslavskii, rather than a professional chess writer. And he rejected a doctor and a translator, telling Ivonin, "We don't need a translator, we can do everything ourselves. It's a matter of trust." Decoded—and of course Ivonin understood the code—that meant Spassky thought the translator would be a KGB officer, there to observe him. The committee would have had to approve these staff and arrange their passports. Ivonin's note of the conversation gives Spassky's remark three exclamation marks.

The balance of power had shifted to the chess champion. "Heads down" became the rule in the Sports Committee. "Why risk intervention?" muses Beilin. "Pavlov was no idiot. This was now Demichev's and Spassky's responsibility. Okay, so you guys take responsibility."

Today, Spassky remembers that he was not given the team he wanted and denied the interpreter and cook of his choice—Karpov in 1978 had a squad of forty, he complains. He is also disdainful about his lineup: "Krogius was not much of a psychologist. . . . In Reykjavik, 1972, he was useless. Nei was a tennis partner, not much of a chess player. Geller was the only one who helped me." But the truth is that the committee did its best to convince Spassky that a head of delegation and the other assistants were necessary. The limited chess team in Iceland was the team Spassky himself had assembled.

On 4 January 1972, in a secret memo to Demichev covering every aspect of Spassky's training, including his diet, Pavlov tried to reassure the Central Committee that everything was in hand.

> Scientific workers and specialists from the
> Academy of Medical Sciences and the All-Union
> Scientific Research Institute for Physical
> Training have been brought in to provide
> thorough medical care, organize the appropriate
> nourishment, and devise recommendations for
> quickly reestablishing the ability to work after
> major mental, nervous, and psychological labors.

```
The issue of providing high-calorie foods is
being decided jointly with the RSFSR Ministry of
Trade.
```

In the ensuing months, with the world champion's family finally settled into a newly built, plush four-room apartment in Vesnin Street in the elite diplomatic quarter, Spassky and his team moved from handpicked dacha to handpicked dacha—Krasnaia Pakhra thirty-five kilometers from Moscow (where he was billeted during his championship match with Petrosian), Arkhys in the North Caucasus, Sochi on the Black Sea, and finally Ozera near Moscow. In Ozera they lived in a sanatorium where defeated German field marshal Friedrich von Paulus had been held after the war. The Sports Committee kept an eye on the facilities and living conditions—and tried, as discretely as it could, to establish how hard Spassky was working.

Unhappily, the training paradise now created contained a number of serpents.

By the time he arrived in Reykjavik, Spassky was feeling the strain caused by the breakdown of two key relationships during his training period, one with the director of the Central Chess Club, Viktor Baturinskii, the other with the champion's personal coach, Igor Bondarevskii. There was also a quarrel with Mikhail Botvinnik, opening a rift sufficiently wide for Botvinnik to refuse to sign a petition to save the struggling magazine *Moscow Chess* from closure simply because Spassky's signature was also on it.

The consequences of the breach with Baturinskii, in particular, were to be serious. Spassky put at arm's length the man who had direct responsibility for chess and chess players, who led the negotiations with the Americans and with FIDE over the location of the match, and who might have been a highly effective team leader in Iceland.

The immediate cause of this dispute appears trivial. Spassky wanted to lend his car to a friend. To do this, he needed a duly notarized letter of authority (as is still the case in Russia today).

Colonel Viktor Baturinskii, former military prosecutor and director of the Central Chess Club. Preparing his moves? OLGA BATURINSKAIA

In late November 1971, Spassky drafted such a letter and asked Baturinskii to affix the Central Chess Club seal and countersign it. Baturinskii refused. He was not qualified to sign, he told Spassky. (Actually, he thought there was something suspect about the document and believed Spassky would do better to take it to a lawyer.) The champion took this as a personal slight and made it plain that as far as he was concerned, Baturinskii was no longer to be trusted. From this point on, Baturinskii was effectively excluded from close contact with the preparations.

Even in his final years, as a blind, hard of hearing, apartment-bound pensioner, Baturinskii's memory of Spassky's attitude revived an indignant anger. As a Soviet, he desperately wanted Spassky to triumph. Equally, as a Stalinist by upbringing, he had little time for the free-spirited Spassky, who felt that when the world champion spoke, the chess world should follow.

In terms of personality and politics, there was an inevitability about his break with the champion. Some surmise that Spassky created the car issue to confront Baturinskii and distance him from the match.

Spassky informed the authorities that he objected to Baturinskii representing him at FIDE in negotiations over the match conditions. Ivonin tried dissuading Spassky. Strictly speaking, he said, Baturinskii had been correct not to sign the letter of authorization. But Spassky's mind had been made up. In any case, at that point, Baturinskii drew the line. "I told Ivonin that I refused to go. He said that my passport and all the documents were ready. I said that's not important—if someone who ought to trust me doesn't trust me, I just won't go."

The row undoubtedly upset Spassky and drained his energy. In practical terms, the negotiations for the match were left in the hands of Geller, who understood chess, and Aleksandra Ivushkina, the deputy head of the Sports Committee's International Department, whose work covered relations with international sports federations. She spoke excellent English, had wide experience in working with other federations, and knew the Sports Committee's position. In terms of legal acumen, though, it was hardly the sharpest team.

Spassky's breakup with Baturinskii affected the conduct of the match. The other breakup—with Bondarevskii, his longtime coach—affected his preparation. Bondarevskii and Spassky had begun to work together in 1961, as the future champion's career and personal life ran aground. Intriguingly, he was later to part from Bondarevskii as his second marriage was also foundering. Spassky's winning the title had changed both relationships. Bondarevskii had not been trainer to the world champion. Suddenly he was. Similarly, Larisa had not married a world champion. She complained that when Boris took the title, he began to dominate all aspects of life— he even gave her advice on how to cook soup.

For several years, there had been hints of trouble to come. According to Spassky's autobiographical section of *Grand Strategy*, during the 1969 title match with Petrosian, the Bondarevskii-

Spassky relationship had broken down over the living arrangements Bondarevskii had made (too far out of town, Spassky thought). However, they eventually made up. Spassky respected Bondarevskii and acknowledged that he had to accept him as he was. Looking back at the dawn of his relationship with his third and last trainer, Spassky remembered, "He knew how to stimulate me and make me work. That was his secret."

That was his perspective in 2002. Thirty years earlier, things looked rather different. On the morning of 2 February 1972, Bondarevskii told Ivonin that he and Spassky could no longer work together and they had come to an amicable agreement to part. There was no real communication between them, said Bondarevskii, so they accomplished little. Since he became champion, Spassky had practically ceased to listen to his recommendations. Nor was Bondarevskii satisfied with Spassky's work rate. Before he saw Ivonin, he visited Baturinskii. Baturinskii remembered the conversation thus: " 'Viktor Davidovich, I'm stepping down from this job'—How can you refuse to work only three or four months before the beginning of the match? You are his chief trainer—you're putting him in a very difficult situation. 'It's impossible to work with him, impossible. I am standing down. He doesn't follow my instructions: he gets on with all sorts of other things. With so little time before the match he can't *concentrate*.' "

Nikolai Krogius draws a distinction between the old Spassky and the new, between the aspiring world champion and the title holder. "Previously (for example, during the preparations for his 1969 match against Petrosian), Boris might initially disagree with a proposal, but later, having thought about it, he would often (usually on the following day) admit that it was sound. Bondarevskii and I would joke that Spassky must be persuaded in two stages: first a refusal, then a yes. But now, having said no, Boris stubbornly maintained his position—frequently without foundation."

Some believe that Bondarevskii abandoned the team because he feared his trainee was heading for defeat and was apprehensive of being associated with failure.

The same reason may explain the simultaneous resignation of V. I. Postnikov, then president of the USSR Chess Federation and a friend of Bondarevskii's. Postnikov was succeeded by his deputy,

Yuri Averbakh—no one else, according to Averbakh, was willing to take on the risk. Averbakh says that from this moment on, he grew pessimistic about Boris's prospects. Only Bondarevskii's force of personality could induce Spassky to keep slogging away—to work up the necessary mental sweat. Yes, Spassky labored, "but in a light style, let's say."

But plenty of people are inclined to side with Spassky in the dispute. According to Yevgeni Bebchuk, the former president of the Chess Federation of the Russian Federation, the coach was a very difficult person. "He was an ingenious coach, a prince among coaches, but his rudeness was quite impossible. When he became Spassky's coach several years earlier, Spassky had needed his skills as a trainer, irrespective of his character. But when Spassky was at the height of his profession and Bondarevskii swore at him—he had always sworn at him—Spassky would no longer put up with it."

Vera Tikhomirova also knew Bondarevskii from their hometown, Rostov on Don. An expansive, formidable woman, she had survived Stalin's famine and terror to become the Russian Federation's women's chess champion, though at this point she taught chess for the Federation's sports committee. Vera retains a maternal love for Spassky. In return, he loves her as would a son. Her verdict on Bondarevskii: "He was said to be strong-willed. But he wasn't. He definitely didn't like taking responsibility."

The day of Bondarevskii's departure, Spassky, Geller, and Krogius arrived in Ivonin's office to give their side of the story. Bondarevskii did not believe in their success; he was not completely committed. Spassky would no longer put up with being treated like a child, spoken to in harsh language. What is more, Bondarevskii had not kept up with theoretical advances in openings: now that Geller was in the team, Bondarevskii was of no real value. Spassky added that he, Spassky, had been the first to declare they had to part.

To sweeten the pill, the group gave Ivonin a reassuring summary of their labor to date. Thanks to the Sports Committee, their personal problems, the dacha, flats, salaries, and living permits, had been resolved. The group was conducting its studies in a businesslike fashion, the creative work was going well, and the preparation plan had been successfully fulfilled. In groundwork they were probably ahead of Fischer. Ivonin noted: "They said Spassky would have a significant edge against Fischer in the opening because Fischer would not have time to rework his very limited repertoire."

Whatever the basis for Bondarevskii's departure, the original group had been working and living closely together; the loss of a member was inevitably unsettling. If there had been a driving force in the group, it was Bondarevskii. With Spassky as the new leader, the team simply performed what he wanted of them. An independent leader could have forced Spassky to do what he needed but did not care to do. Geller filled Bondarevskii's place, but he was not at all suited to it. Unwilling to confront Spassky himself, he would quietly take Nei to one side. Could Nei cajole the champion to work?

"Obstinate, with a dimpled chin and a slow waddle, Geller looked more like a former boxer or elderly boatswain who had come on shore than the world-class grandmaster he was," is the portrait drawn by Genna Sosonko in *Russian Silhouettes*. Spassky praised him as "a very complete player. . . . His diligence was extraordinary. He developed his talent by sitting on his backside, and his backside developed in turn thanks to his talent." He belonged to a very elite club of those having a plus record against Fischer; over the course of his career, he had beaten the American five times.

Geller came from the most cosmopolitan city in the Soviet Union, the southern port of Odessa, and outwardly had the familiarity and warmth of the Jewish neighborhood where he grew up. However, Spassky once said the good nature was on the surface; underneath, Geller was envious and hostile. He was also wholly Soviet in outlook, deeply suspicious of the West and what he saw as its corrupt and devious ways. In his book *Soviet Chess,* Andrew Soltis quotes Geller as saying that success in chess awaited only those players of deep morality and high intellect who were "free from the flaws and evils rotting through the capitalist system." Bondarevskii's departure put this problematic character at the champion's right hand in training and at the match.

With all these distractions, how effective and concentrated was Spassky's preparation?

There are many gossipy tales of slackness; some might well come under the heading of *vranyo*—the Russian weakness for exaggerated, often preposterous untruth. Given Spassky's insistence on complete secrecy, only a select few were granted any real insight into his training. One engaging story that seems short of genuine eyewitnesses recounts how Bondarevskii made his exit after Spassky was given a weekend off and came back a fortnight later. Another tells how visitors saw Spassky whiling away the time with whiskey and copies of *Playboy* magazine.

Still, that Spassky had a considerably more relaxed schedule than his opponent is unquestionable. Yuri Averbakh recalls that his first action when he took over as acting president of the USSR Chess Federation after Postnikov's sudden resignation was to visit the camp for himself: "Spassky was sitting there with Geller and Krogius. . . . On the table were cards and dominoes, and when lunchtime came Spassky pulled out a bottle of whiskey. Everything became apparent to me immediately."

Boris Spassky insists that he worked and worked hard. Ivo Nei agrees but adds, not enough. Spassky maintained then and maintains now that he operates best with a clear mind, that physical fitness was crucial. Hence the tennis, skiing, and swimming. It is also true that the champion, in Mikhail Beilin's warm assessment, "loved life, loved to relax, to talk and spend time with friends, to repose. He wasn't like Korchnoi, for instance, grinding away for eight hours." A typical day would begin with Spassky regaling his team over breakfast with the Greek myths he had read the night before and would later include his ration of sport, leisurely meals—and five hours for chess.

"The main deficiency in our schedule was Spassky's flippant attitude," says Krogius. "He believed that he understood Fischer well, and that he, Spassky, would 'find the key' to Bobby's chess during the match. He was encouraged to hold this view by those leading Soviet chess players who had written accounts of Fischer's and Spassky's styles of play. Keres, Smyslov, Petrosian, Tal, and also Botvinnik (who expressed his views orally) unanimously dismissed the possibility of any fundamental changes in the American's game, especially in the opening. Only Korchnoi identified fresh features in Fischer's chess evolution. But since Korchnoi's opinion was directed at Spassky in personal and harsh terms, Boris did not pay it much attention."

In May, when another grandmaster, Isaac Boleslavskii, came to assist, the work rate was stepped up. Spassky's play, it was reported back to Ivonin, was becoming more imaginative as well as more accurate. This coincided with the date being fixed for the match—no doubt concentrating the title holder's mind. On a visit, Baturinskii noted the improvement: "Each day, six to seven hours are dedicated to chess analysis, and three hours to physical training (tennis and swimming in the pool)."

Whatever the regime, Vera Tikhomirova was struck by the good health radiated by the champion and his team. "I remember when they visited me in my office for a photograph, they looked so healthy and so 'plume-y'—bright eyed and bushy tailed—that I asked myself, 'Did they really work or just enjoy themselves?' "

Spassky's troubled relationships, the negotiations over the match, the aggravation over his apartment, his incapacity for hard grind—these combined to ensure that he arrived in Reykjavik in less than a settled state and underprepared. But his conviction that there would be a feast of chess in Reykjavik and that he would win at the table in a historic victory was undiminished. "He really wanted to go down in history," says Mikhail Beilin. "He always denies it: I've asked him that ten times, and he always says, 'What do you mean?' But I'm confident he really wanted to go down in history." And he did—his name forever being associated with the staging of an extraordinary event in a small island state in the North Atlantic.

9

BIG CONTEST,
LITTLE ISLAND

Islands are places apart where Europe is absent.

—W. H. AUDEN AND LOUIS MACNEICE,
LETTERS FROM ICELAND

Fischer had already made his views on Iceland devastatingly clear. For the U.S. forces, it qualified as a "hardship posting," he claimed, and GIs had to be paid a special extra allowance to compensate them for serving there.

This was untrue. It was also unfair. Upon arrival in 874 C.E., the Norwegian Ingolfur Arnarson, the first settler in what is now the nation's capital, must have gasped at the spectacular scenery: in the distance a towering snow-capped volcano, in the foreground white steam blowing off the shore. He named this area Reykjavik, meaning "Smoky Bay." The land runs alongside a sea inlet, bordered on three sides by water. There is a whiff of sulfur in the air.

This bleak, windy, isolated island has a magnificent, if austere, beauty. It is a country of glaciers and geysers, of marsh and wild, hardy grass. In winter, night lasts all day; in summer, day lasts all night. Appropriately for the match, this volcanic country sits across a great subterranean divide, the Mid-Atlantic Ridge.

In 1972, Iceland was inhabited by only 210,775 people and had barely fifty miles of paved road outside the capital (nowadays, the most common vehicle is a four-wheel drive). Nearly half the population lived in Reykjavik.

In support of Fischer's prejudice, the city's modern urban planners certainly had a great deal to answer for. Despite its stunning landscape, Reykjavik has been transformed into an aesthetic shambles. Part of the explanation is too rapid expansion. At the end of World War II, the city was barely more than a fishing village. In the subsequent quarter of a century, it grew dramatically but in an ad hoc fashion, with housing developments dotted haphazardly around the grandly desolate landscape. The shops and office buildings were often in gray concrete, while the houses were white with brightly colored roofs. In 1972, there were few modern hotels, and communication with the outside world was poor. Then as now, there were almost no imposing buildings to dignify the capital's center.

At first sight, Iceland did not seem a plausible candidate to host a match that was arousing worldwide interest. Could this remote island cope logistically? The country had no history of putting on events of this scale; indeed, it had never bothered to compete in such international auctions.

How did the World Chess Championship arrive in Reyjkavik?

Fischer had played all three of his Candidates matches in the Americas, at Vancouver, Denver, and Buenos Aires. He proposed to Max Euwe, via Ed Edmondson, that the final be held in the United States—even though playing on American soil would have given him a clear advantage. He flatly refused to consider the USSR as an option. Among other things, he feared for his safety there. Spassky, for his part, had security concerns about the United States. But nor did he want the match to be held in the USSR: he suspected some of his colleagues would support Fischer, and that would unsettle him.

If not the United States or the USSR, then where? At the start of the process, FIDE had announced that any city in the world could bid to host the championship, their sealed envelopes to be received by 1 January 1972. Several would tender sums that, for a chess match, were unprecedented.

When Spassky beat Tigran Petrosian in Moscow in 1969, the prize was $1,400. This time, from the outset, the award was to be of a different magnitude. Belgrade, the capital of chess-mad Yugoslavia, offered a hundred times more, an astounding $152,000. A second Yugoslav city, Sarajevo, sealed a bid of $120,000. Buenos Aires proposed $100,000, as did a third Yugoslav city, Bled. There were bids from the Netherlands, Rio de Janeiro, Montreal, Zagreb (the fourth Yugoslav city), Zurich, Athens, Dortmund, Paris, Bogotá, and Chicago (this last being disqualified for late arrival). Reykjavik pledged $125,000, the equivalent of fifty cents for every man, woman, and child in Iceland, the entire amount to be underwritten by the government, although the organizers hoped to more than recoup the outlay through the sale of TV rights.

Gudmundur Thorarinsson, president of the Icelandic Chess Federation (ICF), coordinated the bid. Gudmundur had been elected to the ICF post (in his absence) two years earlier: the nomination had come from his brother, Johann, a much better player, one of the best in Iceland. Johann also first suggested the Icelanders tender for the match. Thorarinsson says he only reluctantly agreed to spearhead the effort: after all, he had a full-time job as a consultant civil engineer. But he also nursed political ambitions, and the campaign was one way to be noticed. It helped that he belonged to the center-left Progressive Party, then in the coalition government, and was on good terms with Prime Minister Olafur Johannesson.

Both Spassky and Fischer were asked to list their preferences. At this stage, Spassky's two chief desires were to play on neutral ground and not to split the match between two cities. He was also anxious about the weather. Holland was his preference. The Icelanders could point out that Reykjavik had a climate similar to Spassky's home city, Leningrad.

The climate, in contrast, never seemed to trouble Fischer much. "Money, money, money," was what he cared about, or so he said. His preference was always likely to be the highest bidder, Belgrade, where he had been widely admired since competing in the Interzonal in Yugoslavia as a fifteen-year-old. This admiration for Fischer was an obvious drawback for Spassky.

How, then, to decide? For the Soviets, the necessity of thrashing out a deal, of seeking the middle ground, was the beginning of a painful awakening. They had held a monopoly of the championship since the war. Details of any squabbling remained behind closed doors. Behind those doors they had been able to determine the site, the conditions, the prize. Now the authorities had to learn the art of compromise and to do so in doubly difficult circumstances, dealing with the Americans and dealing with Spassky.

Disarray and vacillation reigned. The possibility of playing half in the United States and half in Leningrad was canvassed. When this idea was abandoned, the list of preferences became Amsterdam, Iceland, Bled—or, if not in Europe, then Argentina. Later the order read Reykjavik, Dortmund, Paris, and Amsterdam. There was a further shuffling before the final list was produced. Interestingly, the money on offer seems to have been irrelevant to the Soviets' decision-making process.

Small wonder, then, that in this confused atmosphere the first major row between the Soviets and FIDE occurred through what might have been a simple misunderstanding over the deadline for submitting lists of preferences. This had initially been set for 31 January 1972, but the Soviets believed Euwe had then brought it forward to 27 January: he maintained that the new date had merely been a FIDE request to speed the process along. The Soviets handed in their list on 27 January. The Americans handed in theirs four days later, when, to Moscow's great annoyance and consternation, Euwe accepted it as arriving in time.

The price Euwe paid for his management of the location issue was that the Soviets would never again fully trust him to be impartial. Internal Soviet documents impugn his integrity, accusing him of being "indulgent" toward Fischer. The Soviets were further incensed when, during a trip to the United States, Euwe publicly predicted that Fischer would be victorious. In Euwe's defense, it should perhaps be said that rather than being on Fischer's side, he was on the side of the match taking place—but for the

Soviets, in the light of Fischer's behavior, this amounted to much the same thing.

Fischer and Spassky eventually submitted four locations each. The Americans chose Belgrade, Sarajevo, Buenos Aires, and Montreal; the Soviets chose Reykjavik, Amsterdam, Dortmund, and Paris. Thus the Soviets' favorite city was capitalist, the Americans' communist (though Yugoslavia was not within the Soviet sphere of influence). To put it another way, for both contestants, climate and cash superseded politics.

Negotiations stretched out over the next two months. On 7 February, Edmondson arrived in Moscow to hammer out a deal. He was both liked and respected there, knowing how to get on with his hosts (for instance, confiding in them his reservations on Fischer's personality and behavior). Because there was little between the financial inducements offered by Belgrade and Reykjavik (especially given an explicit commitment from Iceland to pay the players 30 percent of the TV revenue), and because Spassky was adamant that he would find a Yugoslav summer insufferable, Edmondson signed an agreement for the match to be staged in Iceland.

Euwe's sigh of relief had barely been exhaled before he received the news that Fischer, holed up in New York, was refusing to acknowledge the Moscow pact. He repeated that he wanted to compete in Belgrade or on American soil.

Desperately, the FIDE president sought a way out. On 14 February, he offered a compromise: to stage the first half of the match in Belgrade, the second in Reykjavik. It was a middle way that suited neither city. In Belgrade, there was resentment that Iceland would host the climax of the match. In Reykjavik, the concern was that one player might secure such a commanding lead in Yugoslavia that by the time the championship moved to Iceland, it would be as good as over. Fischer accepted the compromise. In Moscow, anger and frustration had erupted again. Ivonin described the atmosphere there as a madhouse. In his diary, he noted, "Protest to the very end."

However, in his talks with the Soviets, Euwe had a major advantage: The world champion was impatient for the match to go ahead. At some point between 2 and 5 March, Spassky decided to let the two-city verdict stand, insisting that all the arrangements must be laid out in a comprehensive contract. The Soviets couched their face-saving retreat in altruistic terms. They would reconsider their attitude, they wrote in a letter to FIDE dated 5 March, for the sake of the millions of chess fans around the world and in view of their friendly relations with the Yugoslav chess authorities.

To finalize the details, representatives of the United States, USSR, Icelandic, and Yugoslav Chess Federations were summoned to a meeting in Amsterdam in late March. Euwe must have been confident that the imbroglio had been resolved, for he was off on a goodwill tour of chess federations in the Far East; the deputy president of FIDE, N. Rabell Mendez, a Puerto Rican, stood in for him. Euwe was surprised and hurt by Soviet criticism of his absence.

In spite of Fischer's rejection of his last undertaking, Ed Edmondson acted as Fischer's delegate. Negotiations lasted a few days. By 20 March, every aspect of the conduct of the match had been hammered out; the final session lasted until three in the morning. The rules were designed to cover all the minutiae, from the drawing of lots to determine who would begin with the white pieces to the question of exactly how late a player had to be (one hour) before the game was forfeited. The process was long and tiresome, but the atmosphere was relatively amicable. It appeared to be all wrapped up.

With Fischer, things could never be that simple. Two days later, the occupant of room G6 in upstate New York's Grossinger's resort hotel fired off a telegram.

Littered with spelling and typing errors, it was addressed to the head of the Yugoslav Chess Federation and to his Icelandic counterpart, Gudmundur Thorarinsson. In ninety words, Fischer repudiated Edmondson's agreement and threatened not to appear unless the financial arrangements were changed so that all the income from the match, less expenses, went to the players.

To his credit, the Icelandic official sent back a courageously curt, handwritten reply: "Re your cable 22 Marz [sic]: any changes of the financial agreement in Amsterdam are out of the question. G. Thorarinsson." From Grossinger's there came a one-line response. Fischer refused to play at all in Iceland. The conditions were "unexceptable [sic]."

For the Yugoslavs, the match was becoming too much of a gamble. They now refused to host it unless they received a deposit of $35,000 from the United States and USSR Chess Federations as surety against the match not going ahead. The Soviets unwillingly agreed, even though they thought Spassky was allowing himself to be humiliated. The Americans—for whom this constituted a far greater risk—did not agree.

Perhaps Fischer understood that for Euwe an ultimatum was, in the American writer Ambrose Bierce's phrase, the last warning before making concessions. Nevertheless, FIDE sent Fischer an ultimatum: He must confirm by 4 April that he was prepared to play under the Amsterdam conditions. Back from the U.S. Chess Federation came the soothing—if confusing—response that "Mr. Fischer is prepared to play at the agreed times and venues. Paul Marshall will finalize negotiations in friendly fashion on our federation's behalf."

Working for Fischer now was a Manhattan-based show business attorney, Paul Marshall. Marshall had first met Fischer in 1971 through a client, the British entertainer David Frost, and over the next few months would be active on the challenger's behalf at critical turns in the story. As a highly successful lawyer, he was used to getting his own way, though the combination of Fischer, FIDE, and the Soviets was a challenge for which no amount of time in Hollywood could have prepared him.

In the absence of an American financial guarantee, the Yugoslavs dropped out, leaving FIDE's two-city arrangement in tatters. Once again, Gudmundur Thorarinsson seized the opportunity—offering to host the entire match if the opening could be delayed until 1 July. Acting unilaterally, Euwe agreed: If Fischer failed to show up in Iceland, later in the year Spassky would play for the title in Moscow with Tigran Petrosian, the losing finalist in the Candidates match.

⁂

Although Euwe was now advocating Spassky's preferred location, the Soviets were nonetheless seething at what they perceived to be the FIDE president's bias. Fischer had effectively ignored the 4 April ultimatum, yet Euwe had continued to seek a solution,

President of the Icelandic Chess Federation Gudmundur Thorarinsson. He believed it was not the match of the century. It was the match of all time.
ICELANDIC CHESS FEDERATION

one acceptable to Fischer. A secret document—with serial number 14279, dated 29 April 1972, drawn up for the Central Committee of the Communist Party—alleged that Max Euwe was "under the thumb of the American grandmaster." "The pretender sets a precedent and is followed by the president," was the bitter summary by the Soviet news agency TASS.

On 8 May, Euwe received a telegram that finally appeared to resolve matters: "Bobby Fischer agrees to play in Iceland according to the program sent to him—but under protest." The signatures on the telegram were those of Edmondson and Marshall. According to Euwe, the text was drafted by these two and read to Fischer over the telephone. Only when he agreed to it in their hearing was the telegram sent.

Fischer himself had signed nothing. However, Edmondson sought to reassure Euwe that the absence of Fischer's signature had nothing to do with his intention to play. But what did the phrase *under protest* imply?

10

BOBBY
IS MISSING

People indulge Fischer's caprices. The very mention of his name on the radio or in the newspaper fills me with a feeling of disgust and indignation. If I were B. Spassky, I would consider it beneath my dignity to play against such a type.

—VERA MAKAROVA, SOVIET PENSIONER—

IN A LETTER TO TASS

Fischer trained for the most important match of his life almost completely in isolation.

What chess support he received came from two sources. Ken "Top Hat" Smith was a chess master and world-class poker player who always wore a flamboyant black silk top hat during card games. Slightly too small for its owner, the hat had been acquired in an auction and was alleged to have been discovered in Ford's Theatre in Washington, D.C., on the night that Abraham Lincoln had been assassinated there. Whenever he won the pot, Smith would slam this hat on the table and shout, "What a player!" He always drew a crowd. Such a valued customer was he that the Hilton hotel in Las Vegas would send a private jet to pick him up from his home in Dallas. "No-limit Texas hold-'em" was his game, and he was good at it, winning tens of thousands of dollars.

From Dallas, Smith ran *Chess Digest* magazine and, later, a chess publishing business. For two years, he had been supplying

Fischer with chess literature from around the world: books and magazines on openings, the middle game, endings, analysis of all kinds, the moves from games played in topflight tournaments. To feed Fischer's unquenchable thirst, Smith would fly in with suitcases crammed full of material. Player and supplier were never intimate, and if Smith wanted to get in touch with Fischer, he would have to do so through one of Fischer's other contacts, using a complicated coding system. (After Fischer went to Iceland, Smith traveled to Reykjavik with yet more literature.)

Fischer's other aide was Bob Wade, a kindly, accommodating, New Zealand–born international master, a resident of south London and owner of a vast chess library. He had a more specific task: at Ed Edmondson's request, he had sent Fischer copies of all the games he could find that had been played first by Taimanov, then by Larsen, and then, at the Candidates final stage, by Petrosian. Now Edmondson gave him the same brief for the world championship.

With infinite pains, Wade researched and compiled all of Spassky's published games; some were well-known, others were located in obscure journals. The folder ended up at over a thousand games and over a thousand pages. He dispatched it to Fischer via Edmondson, who had it bound in red velvet. Fortunately, it reached its destination, for the work had been done by hand and there was no other copy.

By this stage, Fischer was in seclusion at Grossinger's, in the Catskills in upstate New York. In the so-called borscht belt, Grossinger's was an institution, popular with the Jewish middle class: a former farm, it had been converted into a huge hotel complex complete with tennis courts and bridle paths. Many famous people had stayed there, including Eleanor Roosevelt. It was also a favorite retreat for sportsmen, such as baseball legend Jackie Robinson and the undefeated world heavyweight boxing champion, Rocky Marciano, who had Grossinger's emblazoned upon his robe.

For over thirty years, Wade has kept the letter that came back from Grossinger's on receipt of his meticulously prepared material. There was not a word of thanks. Instead, he was greeted by a torrent of abuse for failing to abide by Fischer's preferred method of displaying the moves. Wade had written them across the page rather than down the page. "Can't you follow even the simplest instructions?" He was rebuked for having "cut corners." There was nothing for it but for Wade painstakingly to copy out each move again, working almost from scratch. "The tone reminded me," says Wade, who was a chess coach for many years, "of how a teacher might speak to his schoolchildren." Wade was paid £600, £200 of which was considered "a bonus" for his conscientious labors.

For Fischer, this dossier was to be his constant companion until July 1972. At Grossinger's, he would take his meals in the dining room accompanied only by the dossier. If he ventured out, he would take it down to a local restaurant. He tended to eat Chinese or Italian dishes. (The waitresses were never pleased to see him because he took up two tables.) For the rest of the time, he was in his hotel room, absorbing the contents of the red file, trying to discern patterns and identify weaknesses. As always, he would rise late and then work deep into the night. Journalists who knocked on the door of his quarters—a white villa—were told to "go away." One or two chess colleagues went to visit him. Larry Evans says, "We would play over Spassky's games—usually in the wee hours of the morning. We would have rock radio blasting." But essentially Fischer worked alone. Evans explained to *The New York Times*. "I probably have more influence on him than anybody else, and that's exactly zero."

Fischer stayed at Grossinger's until 5 June and then went to California for tennis; he wanted to improve his fitness. He also attended a service of the Worldwide Church of God. His flight to Reykjavik had been scheduled for Sunday, 25 June, in good time for the official opening on Saturday, 1 July and the first game the next day.

He flew back to New York on Tuesday, 27 June, and moved into the Yale Club as a guest of his New York lawyer, Andrew Davis. It was four days before the official opening of the match.

⦿⦿⦿

The Soviet party had arrived in Reykjavik on 21 June to settle in and acclimatize. In Iceland at that time of year, there was practically no darkness, only "white nights." Spassky was thoroughly comfortable with this; it was the season of merrymaking in his home city, Leningrad. The Soviets took up residence in the best hotel in Reykjavik, the Saga, with Spassky occupying room 730—the presidential suite at the secure end of a corridor. With its wide views, Empire-style furniture, and gold-plated taps in the bathroom, his accommodation no doubt made a pleasing change from Moscow. The champion played tennis with Ivo Nei up to eleven o'clock at night, while Geller and Krogius prepared for the chess battle ahead.

A comparison of the two players' teams is instructive. Spassky had arrived with Geller, Krogius, and Nei—chess players all, two grandmasters and an international master. Lined up on Fischer's side were thirty-nine-year-old attorney Andrew Davis, educated at Yale and Oxford, and Fred Cramer, a past president of the United States Chess Federation, who had taken over from Edmondson as the challenger's emissary. Fischer also summoned Paul Marshall to his side. A journalist for *Life* magazine, Brad Darrach, attached himself to the Fischer squad and later wrote an exuberant, blow-by-blow account of the whole experience.

Fischer had not yet chosen a second; grandmaster William Lombardy took the position at the last moment. Lombardy was strikingly different from the rest of Fischer's team. He was a chess player of high class: in 1958, he took the World Junior Chess Championship with a perfect eleven victories, no draws, no losses—a truly remarkable accomplishment—and he went on to become U.S. champion twice. Unlike Fischer, he had beaten Spassky. This victory, in twenty-nine moves, came when he led the United States to first place in the 1960 World Student Team Championship in Leningrad. But chess was only a part of his vocation: he was a Roman Catholic priest, possibly the greatest chess-playing cleric since Ruy Lopez in sixteenth-century Spain, originator of the eponymous opening that was Fischer's favorite.

Rotund, with small eyes peeping out of a podgy face framed by sharply razored muttonchop whiskers and a vestigial mustache, Lombardy tended to divide opinion in Reykjavik. Some thought him approachable, affable, gregarious, and humorous. Others found him insufferably stiff and pompous. Some reported that he was loyal and dependable. Others, such as the writer George

Steiner, regarded him as scheming and "sinister." Certainly, one of the sights of the match was Father Lombardy holding a press conference in clerical garb.

Both Davis and Marshall were accustomed to Fischer's unpredictability, and each had already resigned once over his repudiation of agreements they had negotiated for him. Yet, in common with so many other acquaintances of Fischer's, they were prepared to forgive what in other clients or friends would have been unforgivable. Marshall was "amazed" when Davis telephoned suddenly, seeking his help on Fischer's behalf as though there had been no breach. However, he took his client back on, traveling and acting for him without billing his time or expenses—a New York lawyer taking pro bono to extremes. He reflected on his client in terms appropriate for Charles Dickens's Tiny Tim: "Bobby never made any money in his life. Everyone who dealt with him when he was fourteen, fifteen, used him. If there was any money to be made, they took it. They'd call him up and say, 'Come on out here, we'll pay your bills and we'll give you a couple of bucks on the side.' And when it was over, they'd stick him with a huge hotel bill. Here's a fifteen-year-old kid with an enormous bill, no money, all alone, crying."

Of course, by 1972 Fischer was no longer a child, and by rights there should have been no further negotiation on money. The financial arrangements appeared to have been settled. The winner would receive $78,125, the loser $46,875, and the two contestants would each take 30 percent of TV and film rights. But Fischer's approach was always to agree to nothing, sign nothing, confirm nothing. With only days to go before the scheduled start, he now argued that the pot should include 30 percent of the gate receipts—estimated to total $250,000. The Icelanders balked: the venue, the exhibition hall, could seat some 2,500, and they were depending on this revenue to cover their costs.

Although Fischer was in New York on 27 June, and so already twenty-four hours late for his timetabled appearance in Reykjavik, his imminent arrival was still expected. And if he did not arrive? The Icelandic Chess Federation press spokesman,

Freysteinn Johannsson, had no press statement ready for such a contingency.

On 28 June, Fischer was booked onto another flight from John F. Kennedy Airport. All the arrangements were in place, including a supply of fresh oranges that he insisted should be squeezed in front of him for fear the Soviets had tampered with his juice. Although the challenger's financial demands had not been conceded, his lawyers were cautiously optimistic that he would be on the plane. Marshall, who was overwhelmed with work at his practice, was quoted in the press:

> I received a call from Andy [Davis] from the limousine taking the two to the airport. It had just passed over the 59th Street Bridge when I spoke to Andy, and I said to him, "Congratulations." He said, "Don't congratulate me yet—it's a little early." We both laughed and signed off. I was a happy man. . . . I wouldn't have to see Bobby for two and a half months, I thought. I went home and my wife congratulated me. I kissed my kids for the first time in weeks. I slept well, went to the office, had a good morning and went out for lunch. I picked up a paper and saw—oh, no, he hadn't gone yet. I grabbed a quick drink.

Davis himself had boarded the plane. But amid the airport passageways, in scenes worthy of a Marx Brothers film (starring Greta Garbo), Fischer stopped to buy an alarm clock, caught sight of the hordes of cameramen waiting to record his historic departure—and bolted.

He took refuge in the Tudor-style family house of a childhood companion, Anthony Saidy, in Douglaston, in the New York borough of Queens—2 Cedar Lane. A medical doctor from a Lebanese family, Saidy had once won the U.S. Open Chess Championship. Fischer felt at home with the Saidy family, relishing the Lebanese cuisine prepared by Anthony's mother.

Davis later blamed the media for thwarting his client's desire to be veiled from the public gaze. Others suspected darker motives for his turning the flight to the championship into a flight from the championship. Some theorized that the cause was not the paparazzi, but a stalemate over Fischer's latest financial stipu-

June 30. Fischer at John F. Kennedy Airport. Then he ran down the corridors, looking for a way out. ASSOCIATED PRESS

lations. In Davis's briefcase were demands for a better TV deal, the loser's share of the money in Fischer's hand at the outset, and 30 percent of the gate. *The New York Times* found that hard to believe: the amounts were trivial compared with the fortune he could make on becoming champion.

A second hypothesis held that Fischer was deliberately conducting a war of nerves against his opponent. With the challenger still absent, the press claimed the champion was "on the edge already." A *Washington Post* reporter visited Fischer in Douglaston and put this to him. "I don't believe in psychology. I believe in good moves," the challenger rejoined.

To add to the Icelanders' woes, Fred Cramer had arrived on 27 June and offered a foretaste of his part in the drama. He had presented a list of expected requirements about lighting and other arrangements, then thrown in an unexpected demand—a new arbiter, a non–chess player. The experienced and respected German grandmaster Lothar Schmid was apparently unacceptable as chief arbiter. This was curious if only because, when a teenager, Fischer had stayed with Schmid in his family home in Bamberg. Passing off the underage chess genius as his nephew, Schmid had taken him to a casino in Bad Homburg, a suburb of Frankfurt am Main, where he observed that Fischer was not a risk taker. The quietly spoken, patently decent Schmid had also refereed Fischer's last match in the Candidates round, against Petrosian. The manner in which he carried off that task had marked him out for the final. Chess was not Schmid's only interest. His family-owned firm, Karl-May-Verlag, published the writer of westerns, Karl May—after Goethe, Germany's best-selling author.

While Fischer hunkered down in the Saidys' house, the impasse between Icelandic officials and his lawyers pushed the U.S. presidential nominations down the front page. With Fischer's attorneys haggling over the financial terms, it did not escape the reporters that Dr. Saidy's father, Fred, was coauthor of *Finian's Rainbow*, the musical about the filching of a pot of gold. Contributing to Dr. Saidy's stress was the fact that his father was seriously ill and needed hospitalization. Fischer told Anthony not to worry: Fred's illness would not disturb him.

On the day of the official opening, Saturday, 1 July, *The New York Times* covered the story on its front page: "Bobby Fischer's erratic posture toward the World Chess Championship has touched off a wave of debate and discussion in New York and Moscow as well as Reykjavik, Iceland." TASS, the Soviet state press agency, wrote that a "disgusting spirit of gain" motivated Fischer. Ed Edmondson said, "He's putting on some kind of act—for what I don't know." He, Edmondson, thought that the odds were two to one that Fischer would not play. When the match was delayed, a reporter noted: "Everyone hated Bobby. He put himself in the hot seat, and every man in the room would have gladly pulled the switch. But nobody could afford to let the son of a bitch burn. So what did they do? They stopped the world. Now if we all fall down on our knees, Bobby might be willing to get on."

Icelanders accused Fischer of extortion. In Reykjavik, rumors circulated as in wartime. Among the most popular were that Fischer was in hiding after his arrival in the country a week earlier on a United States Air Force jet or alternately after being smuggled ashore in a rubber dinghy from a U.S. Navy submarine.

Already chilled by the prospect of the whole project's collapsing, the organizers now faced a problem for which no preplanning could have prepared them. In the absence of the challenger, should they go ahead with the opening ceremony of the match? Absurd though it might be, there seemed no other plausible answer than yes. To proceed as though the match would, at some stage, commence was the surest way to ensure that it did actually commence. That, at least, was the theory.

⸭⸭⸭

So, almost as though everything were in order, the dignitaries gather at Reykjavik's National Theatre for the scheduled event. The seat next to Spassky's is empty. As befits the magnitude of the occasion for their country, Iceland's president, Kristjan Eldjarn, and the mayor of Reykjavik, Geir Hallgrimsson, are both present, together with the city councillors. So too are the prime minister, Olafur Johannesson, and the finance minister, Halldor E. Sigurdsson, who has guaranteed the cost of the project up to five million Icelandic kronur. The heads of the Soviet and U.S. embassies are in their places. Max Euwe, the president of FIDE, has flown in from Holland. Chief arbiter, Lothar Schmid, has arrived from Germany. They are aware that this event may be a charade. The public bonhomie conceals anxiety and a smoldering sense of grievance.

However, the most embarrassed and fraught figure of all is the man responsible for the match's being held in Iceland, Gudmundur Thorarinsson. This should be his moment. He is down to make the opening speech, winning plaudits from the Icelandic establishment to launch his political career. Instead, he is seized by panic, sweating and fearful of being late. He has been in the Loftleidir hotel since ten o'clock, listening, he says, to "demands and demands and new demands." At 4:50 P.M., with little progress made, Andrew Davis stands up and says, "Forget it.

Fischer won't come and there'll be no match." There are ten minutes to go before the opening, and Thorarinsson finds himself racing to the National Theatre. Knowing that Fischer has no intention of leaving New York, he will have to appear on stage in front of his country's president. Worst of all, he is still dressed in his working clothes.

The drive to the National Theatre is spent in frenzied internal debate: Should he tell the audience it is over or simply open the match with his fingers crossed? He arrives at 5:15 P.M., fifteen minutes late, and begins the longest walk of his life, to the rostrum:

> A high official at the Foreign Ministry came running to me when I came through the door, and he said, "What kind of a man are you? This is the height of rudeness. Everybody is waiting and you come dressed like this." He took me by the arm and he said they're waiting and the rostrum is there. So, I went alone, fifteen meters or so to the rostrum. I looked at the balcony, where the president of Iceland sat. He was an elderly, experienced man. I think he guessed what kind of a dilemma I was in. We looked at each other, and about a meter from the rostum I made a decision. I will open the match. Then I won't close any doors. I can always tell them later that it's over. But if I say now it's over, it's really over. Somehow I got through a speech, one I hadn't prepared. And I opened the match.

The president of Iceland makes no speech. The government's welcome is given by the minister of culture magnus, Torfi Olafsson. The mayor then talks pointedly of an ongoing chess game. "It is obvious that human beings do not for long wish to be pawns on a chessboard, even if they are in the hands of geniuses." Euwe's speech is half explanatory, half apologetic, expressing the hold Fischer has over the officials. "Mr. Fischer is not an easy man. But we should remember that he has lifted the level of world chess for all players." At the cocktail party after the ceremony, Thorarinsson comes in for criticism from his Icelandic colleagues. " 'Keeping the government waiting is something one doesn't do. If you're going to organize this world championship, you'll have to change your habits.' I couldn't let on; it would have been all over the world press. I just said, 'I'm sorry, I shall try to do better. It won't happen again.' "

In fact, government ministers have more to worry about than Thorarinsson's working clothes. Iceland's economy is wholly dependent on fish, and they are preparing to announce the extension of the country's fishing limits from twelve to fifty miles, confirming a threat that had been made a year earlier. The new rules will come into force on 1 September 1972. With Great Britain's fishing industry already suffering from an earlier extension, London's rejection of the move is inevitable, meaning that this tiny nation, whose entire air force (one helicopter) had recently been incapacitated, is heading for a showdown with one of the mightiest military forces in the world. (In the event, with American backing and a devastating weapon, a wire cutter that traps and cuts trawl ropes, causing thousands of pounds' worth of

Left to right: Soviet ambassador Sergei Astavin, Boris Spassky, U.S. chargé d'affaires Theodore Tremblay. A vin d'honneur *for being there.*
ASSOCIATED PRESS

damage through lost catches and, worse still, lost nets, Iceland will secure its extension.)

Fischer's aide Fred Cramer dismisses Fischer's absence from the ceremony, describing it as "a musical concert with speeches in Icelandic which he wouldn't have understood." Meanwhile, one man seems to have guessed what is going on. Spassky chats amicably with Yugoslav grandmaster Svetozar Gligoric, telling him that he is looking forward to a two-month vacation, and then will return to Moscow to play Petrosian.

As Thorarinsson pondered his next move, Fischer was still in Douglaston, immured in Sabbath observance. His demands were still on the table, and there seemed no question of his boarding a plane. Out of sight of the world's press, he was refusing to respond to letters, take calls, or answer the door.

With the match in a quagmire, there now came two attempts at its rescue: the first from the heart of Nixon's White House, the other a true deus ex machina from one of the richest men in Britain, whose decision to intervene came as he was in a car driving through London.

The Icelandic government might have played a part in securing the first intervention. Although it had no direct role in the match, national prestige was at stake, and the prime minister, Olafur Johannesson, was deeply concerned at the possibility of failure. He and Thorarinsson were in the same political party, the Progressive Party, a center-left farmers movement. And Gudmundur Thorarinsson decided he had to ask him for assistance.

He, Thorarinsson, had been searching nonstop for a way ahead. Could he persuade Spassky and Fischer to talk to each other directly? The champion was refusing to call his challenger but readily agreed to take Fischer's call if the American rang. Fischer, however, seemed unlikely to respond to a request to phone Spassky. Spassky then summoned the Icelander to a meeting at his hotel.

He said, "Gudmundur, this is a very serious situation. This can only be solved at a higher level." I looked at him and said, "Well, yes, maybe that is the way. We'll solve it at a higher level." And after we shook hands I went to see the prime minister. I said, "We're in serious trouble, and I think you should come into the picture. You have to phone the White House and ask them to use their influence on Fischer." "Oh, no, no, no, no," he said. "You're a young man, and things don't happen that way." Then he thought about it and said, "If you're quite determined, I'll do what I can." And he phoned the American embassy.

But the Russian and the Icelander were at cross-purposes. Thorarinsson was so focused on bringing the American to the match, it did not enter his mind that Spassky might need help himself. The prime minister then called in the U.S. chargé d'affaires Theodore Tremblay. Would the American government lend a hand?

Tremblay was intensely irritated with Fischer. At the opening ceremony, his wife had been sitting next to the empty chair, on the other side of which sat Spassky. But he was inclined to help. Uppermost in his mind, in a fragile phase in U.S.-Icelandic relations, was the U.S. base at Keflavik. The Icelandic coalition government—the only NATO country with communist ministers—was considering its future. Closure could have strategic consequences for the Western alliance. Iceland's geographic position, midway between the United States and the Soviet Union, made this desolate island an invaluable ally. The Soviets were pressing on with a new blue water naval strategy, and Iceland served as a critical forward observation post, monitoring Soviet ship and submarine movements.

As well as protection, Keflavik had brought employment and wealth. Yet many Icelanders felt resentment rather than gratitude: the base led to anxiety that Icelandic culture was threatened by the alien presence of so many foreigners. The ambiguity toward America was nothing new. At the end of the nineteenth century, a visitor depicted the American whaler "dashing ashore in his civilian dress, and flinging his dollars everywhere, drinking, roistering, catching the ponies, and scampering off, frightening the Icelander out of his wits." And in his 1948 novel, *The Atom Station*, the Nobel Prize–winning Icelandic author Halldor Laxness catches this dissonance in the image of two small boys playing chess while the radio blares out American music. The heroine reflects: "I contemplated once more the civilized peace of the chess game amongst the din from the American radio station."

Over and above the geopolitical considerations, Tremblay was also fond of the Icelandic people. "I hated to see this thing blow up in their face because of Fischer's ignorant attitude." He recalls the prime minister telling him how much Iceland had laid out for the match and asking, "Is there any way we can get him here?"

Back at the U.S. embassy, Tremblay sent a telegram addressed to the secretary of state, William Rogers, and copied to the National Security Council and the CIA. It recited that the chargé had been summoned by Olafur Johannesson to express concern at Fischer's nonappearance: the United States government was not accountable for the imbroglio, but Fischer's actions, he said, were an insult to Iceland, and cancellation would cost seven million kronur. "Everyone knows that Fischer erratic [*sic*] and not susceptible to control by USG but actions were bound to hurt US image." The prime minister had asked Tremblay to relay this concern to the White House. "While he realizes it might not do any good, he would appreciate an immediate attempt to persuade Fischer to live up to his agreement."

Given that these events unfolded over a weekend, it remains unclear whether Tremblay's telegram produced any result. We can simply observe a chain of events: Johannesson's request preceded Tremblay's action, which was followed by a call to Douglaston made by the national security adviser, Dr. Henry Kissinger.

In an interview with the authors, Dr. Kissinger rejected any idea that this call was made in an official capacity. "It was not a big political thing. I did not have a big staff paper to say you've got to do this. It somehow came to my attention." Kissinger makes no claims for his own chess expertise. "I am a rank amateur." He refused to play the Soviet ambassador Anatoli Dobrynin, a keen player, in case it gave his adversary an insight into the way his mind worked. The opening words of Kissinger's conversation with Fischer have entered chess lore: "This is the worst player in the world calling the best player in the world." He recalls, "There was a difficulty in the operation, an upset. I just wanted

Fischer to know that his government wished him well. I wished him well."

Thorarinsson learned from the "American attorneys" about Fischer's reaction.

> They were in the room with Fischer when Kissinger phoned. Kissinger had said to Fischer, "America wants you to go over there and beat the Russians." And Fischer changed, becoming like a young soldier going to war. When they asked him later, why did you change your mind, he said something like "I have decided that the interests of my nation are greater than my own."

No doubt the attorneys felt suitably humbled at so selfless a display of patriotism by their client—and puzzled by his continued failure to leave his Douglaston foxhole for the battlefront.

After his call, next move Fischer. THE WHITE HOUSE

Meanwhile, in Reykjavik, the American team was pushing Thorarinsson for financial concessions in ways he had never experienced and thought utterly unreasonable. He felt that if he yielded to one of their demands, he would simply open the door to many more. "So we very stubbornly said, 'This is our offer. We will live up to it, but this is all we can do and we're not changing it.'" Almost admiringly, he recollects their tactics. "They would always say, 'This is nonsense. We're against it. We are telling you this as a friend: To save the match, you have to do this and this. Otherwise there will be no match.' There was no hostility. They were just giving me advice! They came with papers and they said, 'There's no problem, you just sign here.'" The Icelander was in culture shock:

> These lawyers were different kinds of people from what we knew in Iceland. It seemed to me that money was the driving force and that everything that was legal was allowed. We didn't see it like that. In Iceland it's more about ethics than the law. And when they said the word *money*, the sound of their speech changed, and the look on the face changed. Money! Money! Money!

Money, however, mattered to the Icelanders, too. They were at a disadvantage. If there were no match, they would lose their whole investment, and for a tiny country, this represented a large sum. Thorarinsson has not forgotten how Andrew Davis rubbed this in: "He said, 'You're losing everything. You just have to give us the gate money and this and that, and we shall make sure Bobby is here.'" The Icelander was under attack from all directions. The journalist Brad Darrach accused him of wanting to hand the match to the Soviets. The local press charged him with damaging Iceland's international reputation. One editorial griped, "Why can't he negotiate? He seems impotent."

Thorarinsson was not the only one on the receiving end. Tremblay informed the State Department by telegram that his mission was dealing with a "large number of financial and facultative requests from Fischer's reps. . . ." He wanted to put on record demands he had not granted. For example, Davis had asked the U.S. government to guarantee Fischer a sum of $50,000 on the grounds that his bid for a percentage of the ticket proceeds had been turned down. Davis's argument took some lawyerly chutzpah: the U.S. government should help out, he argued, because of the risk that his client would be responsible for a breach in U.S.-Icelandic relations. Tremblay wrote, "This was rejected as exaggerated. Icelanders regard Bobby Fischer as a unique individual, and while his antics may not aid the US cause, it is highly unlikely that public or official blame will accrue for the delay or possible cancellation." Cramer had also requested on Fischer's behalf diplomatic number plates—and was told this was unnecessary. At two A.M. on Sunday, 2 July, Darrach woke Tremblay to insist that four marine guards were required around the clock to ensure Fischer's security.

All of this was infuriating the Icelandic government. The prime minister had particularly taken umbrage at Davis's claim that Iceland would look to the U.S. government for reparations if the match fell through. Johannesson had also resented a demand by Fischer's representatives that the United States guarantee Fischer's security. According to Tremblay, "the prime minister re- marked acidly that the government of Iceland is quite capable of providing the requisite security."

Tremblay was far more anxious about the impact of Fischer's be- havior than he let on to his superiors back in Washington. The Soviets, he thought, were winning the propaganda battle. "Sure they were. Boris was his charming self. The guy's a real charmer. He's handsome and sophisticated and well educated: he's got everything going for him. And here's this other guy refusing to turn up."

Probably sensing trouble, Davis changed tack and asked for a postponement. The excuse? His client was suffering from fatigue. Davis and Cramer promised doctors' certificates that failed to ma- terialize. The mood in Reykjavik was somber, the organizers living on their nerves, the city still alive with speculation. The corre- spondent of *The New York Times,* Harold Schonberg, wrote: "There is something sad about the stage which has been so care- fully prepared and conceivably may never be used."

Max Euwe, president of FIDE, held back from contacting Fischer directly. For six months, the match had been one long headache; now he was quoted as saying, "Fischer does not speak to me unless, perhaps, it is to order me to get him a taxi. I do not want to meet him." All the same, without seeing any medical evidence, he allowed Fischer two extra days to arrive, on the grounds that the challenger was ill.

While all this was going on, the world champion was marginalized. The Soviet team in Reykjavik was informed that the drawing of lots was to be postponed from 2 July to midday on 4 July. Geller phoned Moscow to pass on the news. On behalf of the USSR Chess Federation, Baturinskii sent a furious cable to Schmid. He accused Fischer of "busying himself with blackmail" with the connivance of the FIDE leadership. His failure to appear for the opening, the drawing of lots, and the first game on 2 July was a violation of FIDE rules unprecedented in its history. Fischer deserved disqualification, said Baturinskii. For his part, Euwe had taken "the more than unattractive role of Fischer's defender." On his own initiative, he had postponed the match following a "nonexistent request" on the grounds of Fischer's "imaginary illness."

Citing chapter and verse from the Amsterdam agreement, Baturinskii declared that if, beginning at noon on 4 July, measures were not taken to follow FIDE rules and the agreement, the USSR Chess Federation would consider the contest "wrecked" by FIDE and Fischer. The threat was plain: they would declare the match null and void.

When Geller challenged Euwe over the postponement, the FIDE president used Spassky as his excuse: "I wanted to save the match because Spassky wants to play so much." Geller recounted this to Ivonin, who dismissed it as an outrageous argument. What they could not have known is that the world champion had indeed tacitly given Thorarinsson and Euwe the go-ahead to try to salvage the competition.

In the early afternoon of Sunday, 2 July, Spassky had a long conversation with Euwe, who then proposed an evening meal with himself and an American millionaire chess fan, Isaac Turover. Geller and Krogius believed Spassky could return with honor to Moscow, and, sensing the champion's vacillation, urged him to miss the supper where he might be prevailed upon to give ground. Spassky ignored them: the next day, it was reported he had consented to the delay.

But then came a second call attempting to save the match, just as it looked as if Fischer was going too far.

.•.•.

Driving to work in London early on Monday morning, 3 July, Jim Slater was upset by a radio report on the challenger's nonappearance in Reykjavik.

Slater was a businessman whose company, Slater Walker Securities, had been formed in 1964 when he was in his mid-thirties. His partner, Peter Walker, had left the business to become a Conservative member of Parliament and a government minister under Edward Heath and (later) Margaret Thatcher. At the time of the Fischer-Spassky match, the company reportedly had a controlling interest in 250 companies around the world. Supremely confident, decisive, ruthless in business, Slater had by then amassed a fortune of, in his own words, "£6 million and rising." A gambler by nature, he allowed himself one big luxury: to play bridge for thousands of pounds with stronger opponents.

Slater was a chess fan and supporter of the game, subsidizing the annual Hastings tournament. In the years following Fischer-Spassky, he would, alongside the former British champion and journalist Leonard Barden (who provided the vision and organization), transform the state of British chess by channeling funds into junior competition.

Now he decided that he could easily afford the money to send Fischer to Reykjavik—or expose the American as a coward. He would double the prize, putting an additional £50,000 ($125,000) into the pot. Arriving at his office that Monday morning, he passed on his offer through Leonard Barden, who then spoke to Paul Marshall, giving the U.S. attorney some background details about this championship angel. Marshall then talked to Fischer. Slater says he also telephoned his friend David Frost, who in turn rang his friend Henry Kissinger. Kissinger then contacted Fischer. What motivated Slater? "As well as providing me with a fascinating spectacle for the next few weeks, I

Millionaire businessman James Slater. He put up the money to save the match. JAMES SLATER

could give chess players throughout the world enormous plea-sure."

Slater's offer made headlines in London's *Evening Standard.* His house was soon swarming with reporters. When he returned from work, he enlightened his astonished wife: "I had a good idea on the way to the office." The good idea was couched in challeng-ing terms: "If he isn't afraid of Spassky, then I have removed the element of money."

It is not altogether clear how the British offer finally persuaded Fischer. Paul Marshall certainly had a hand, initially pushing it as the answer to all Fischer's financial demands. "But he wouldn't ac-cept it. His experiences with people promising things had taught him not to believe them, particularly with money. And he wanted proof. And he said no." Marshall tried to change his mind. Phoning Barden, the attorney took his place in the gallery of

callers that saved the match. "I said if I were them, I would re-
phrase the offer. Slater should say he didn't think his money was
at risk, because Fischer was just making excuses. He should say
that deep down Fischer was frightened. I said Bobby might be
piqued by that challenge—and he was. I knew Bobby was very,
very competitive and combative and would not like to be thought
of as a chicken." Slater denies this version of events. He maintains
it was always his idea to express his offer as a taunt. He never
spoke to Fischer and never received a word of gratitude from him.
"Fischer is known to be rude, graceless, possibly insane. I didn't
do it to be thanked. I did it because it would be good for chess." In
the meantime, there were reports that Mrs. Marshall, a professional photographer, informed the press where Fischer was staying, in an attempt to smoke him out of his bunker.

Kissinger's intervention, the extra money, the wording of the offer, the media camped outside the house in Cedar Lane, perhaps
also information from Reykjavik that disqualification would follow
if Fischer failed to arrive by midday on 4 July—one or a combination of these tipped the balance.

On 3 July, Fischer drove through the pre–Independence Day
evening traffic to JFK Airport. At Kennedy, he transferred to an
Icelandic Airlines station wagon and was smuggled on board a
plane, flight 202A. The flight, scheduled for 7:30 P.M., took off at
10:04 P.M. All the other passengers had been kept waiting, and a
few had been bumped off the flight. In Moscow, the Foreign
Ministry rang Viktor Ivonin to report that the American challenger was on his way.

Marshall told the press that the problem had never been the
money. It was the principle. His client felt Iceland was not treating this match or his countrymen with the dignity that it, and
they, deserved. His private view was that before Slater's offer,
Fischer "had already in effect defaulted. He was pretty well determined not to go."

Marshall chaperoned Fischer on the journey to Iceland, accompanied by his wife, Bette. Fischer had initially prohibited
Marshall from bringing her along, claiming she would distract her
husband. Marshall circumvented this injunction by booking a
seat for her at the other end of the plane. "And a quarter of the

way through the flight, I figured Bobby was above jumping, so I asked my wife to come back and he welcomed her very pleasantly, as though the previous conversation hadn't happened."

The Icelandic grandmaster Fridrik Olafsson had the role of Fischer's official greeter, meeting him at his seat, escorting him to the receiving line, performing introductions, and driving with him to Reykjavik. As a precaution, all journalists and photographers had initially been corraled into the airport building—but a public relations officer at Icelandic Airlines was tempted by the fruit of worldwide publicity and fell. He cut the reporters loose.

Olafsson's plan crumbled as Fischer arrived at the top of the gangway in the early hours of 4 July.

All went well until Bobby came out on the ramp and saw the crowd of journalists and photographers waiting for him below. Seeing this, Bobby dashed down, hardly noticing the dignitaries that had lined up there for him, pushed aside the journalists and photographers, who were in his way, and jumped into the nearest car of the convoy. While this was going on, I had been left standing in the doorway, staring in amazement at the commotion and looking at Bobby dashing down the steps.

Olafsson was a phlegmatic, dignified man who reserved all his aggression for the chessboard. (One of the world's leading grandmasters, he had little real competition at home. He was, says Thorarinsson, "a genius who came out of nowhere.")

Gradually things calmed down; the members of Bobby's party got out of the plane and went to their cars. Soon the convoy was on its way to Reykjavik with a police escort at a speed of 150 kilometers an hour—the protocol for a visit by a head of state.

There was a sting in the tail for the organizers of the match, says Olafsson. "This was Fischer's first impression of Iceland—and it was that the organizers didn't keep their word."

Thorarinsson was now a man relieved, even if Fischer had ig-

Olafsson (right) standing. ASSOCIATED PRESS

nored him in the chaos of the reception at Keflavik airport. He sought out Spassky, to thank him for his advice to refer upward to a more senior rank. But when they met, Spassky, for once, was angry. He charged Thorarinsson with having broken a promise. Suddenly the truth dawned on the Icelander. "I realized that I had misunderstood the whole thing. The Soviet government felt that Spassky was being humiliated and they had called him back. Spassky had wanted me to involve the higher authorities in Moscow, not Washington." Now that Fischer was in Reykjavik, Thorarinsson had a new battle on his hands: to keep Spassky there, too.

11

WHO'S
SORRY NOW?

*This atmosphere of unreality is likely to prevail through-
out the match. . . .* —THEODORE TREMBLAY, CABLE

From the airport, Fischer was taken straight to the house, placed at his disposal in a quiet road in a half-built suburb called Wodaland. The jackpot prize in a forthcoming state lottery, it had not been lived in. (The winner would later complain that it was not strictly new, as promised in the lottery promotion.) When Fischer showed up, there were still bricks and mounds of earth on the street. From here, it was a two-mile hike to the center of town. Fischer soon abandoned it in favor of the other accommodation reserved for him—a three-room suite at the hotel Loftleidir. While this was one of Iceland's best hotels, it was functional rather than luxurious, looking like an airport terminal, low-rise, set off from a big thoroughfare, with a façade of precast rectangular windows and paneling.

Fischer granted the BBC an interview, conducted by a well-known science correspondent, James Burke, and produced by Bob Toner, who has good reason to remember the occasion: "We started recording and Fischer looked very bored and for two reels we got nothing, twenty minutes of nothing, just one-line answers. I thought my career was disappearing down the tubes. But then, in between reels, he asked Burke what kind of events he normally covered. Burke said he had reported on the *Apollo* launches, and you could see Fischer's interest light up. And he said, 'You mean you go to Houston, you go to launch pads?' 'Yes,' said Burke, 'I know Neil Armstrong very well.' After that Fischer couldn't stop talking."

Soon after Fischer's arrival, Paul Marshall held a news conference, adopting an emollient tone. Fischer was sorry to be late and he applauded Spassky for waiting for him. Andrew Davis, Fischer's other lawyer, was far less loquacious, drawing on his pipe while looking balefully through his bifocals. However, Soviet composure, both in Moscow and in Reykjavik, could no longer be preserved, and the Soviet delegation responded with a news conference of its own. Euwe had not followed FIDE rules. Fischer should have been punished for various violations.

Yet again, Thorarinsson was off to seek prime ministerial intervention. This time, Johannesson summoned Sergei Astavin, the Soviet ambassador. He praised Spassky's forbearance and asked Astavin to do what he could to ensure the match took place.

Theodore Tremblay wired Washington that "the Russians had become increasingly difficult . . . to the extent that the match again seemed threatened." Tremblay, like Spassky, thought a direct approach should be made to Moscow and suggested as much to the prime minister. He has a different account of the prime minister's meeting with the Soviet ambassador. According to Tremblay, Johannesson said the Russians "should quit being so silly."

In Moscow, the major concern was still over Spassky's state of mind, and they wanted a week's postponement. It was felt that the world champion had been distracted by having to deal with Fischer's antics and would be too wound up to play properly. It was also felt that Fischer had arrived in good form—though how they could possibly have known that is unclear (after all, unlike Spassky, who had had time to settle in, Fischer was probably jet-lagged).

Then the temperature rose further. Up to this point, dissatisfaction with FIDE and Fischer had been voiced in Moscow by chess players, journalists, and, most significant, the Sports Committee. But now intervention came from a more elevated political level, the Central Committee of the Communist Party. Aleksandr Yakovlev, then acting head of the Propaganda and Agitation Department, fumed over the "humiliation" of the world champion. He blamed Viktor Ivonin for in effect helping the Americans by not summoning Spassky back. Spassky should leave, he pronounced.

Whoever did not actively support the Soviet system was against it. Even a senior figure like Ivonin was not immune. He recorded: "Yakovlev accused me personally several times of not creating a situation where Spassky could come home. He said that in a way, given my position, I was helping the Americans." The functionary went on and on in the same vein. An experienced Party politician, Ivonin responded by consulting a psychiatrist about how Spassky could be persuaded to return even if he was determined to stay. Having received some guidance, he told Yakovlev that he was indeed ready to fly to Reykjavik. "It's very easy to give advice but not so easy to take responsibility," remembers Ivonin. "And when I told Yakovlev that I would go, he said, 'No, no, don't. We'll talk about it later.' And he rang me a bit later with the news that [Party secretary Piotr] Demichev had said, 'No need to fly. Spassky must not be the first to leave.' After that, Yakovlev's energy subsided."

The situation was not helped by the far from straightforward communication between Reykjavik and Moscow. The champion's team used Soviet journalists' telephones to speak to Sports Committee officials, including the minister, Sergei Pavlov. The TASS correspondent Aleksandr Yermakov overheard Moscow being counseled that Spassky was in a strange frame of mind; care must be taken in dealings with him.

There are numerous accounts of Pavlov telephoning Spassky and pressuring him to return to the USSR. Some have him ordering the world champion back and meeting a brave refusal. Such a command seems unlikely. Spassky was world champion and in charge of his own defense, and he still believed he would win.

Furthermore, Ivonin has no record of his recall being discussed in the Sports Committee. Yermakov recollects the phone call but says that Spassky phoned Pavlov, not the other way around. He remembers Spassky talking in a quiet and conversational tone, and not for long. Pavlov, he says, was trying to help the world champion deal with the situation, advising him to consider declaring the match void, but finally agreeing that he should stay. On 7 July, Pavlov told Ivonin that his place was by Spassky's side. Ivonin left for Reykjavik four days later.

A problem for the far-off Moscow bureaucracy was that events were moving fast. Fischer had already plunged the proceedings into a new controversy, locking himself away from officials and sending his second, Lombardy, to act for him at the drawing of lots to determine who would open with the advantage of the white pieces. This was too much even for Spassky. First the empty chair, now a replacement at this crucial ceremony. He read a short prepared statement in Russian and left the room; suddenly the future of the match was again in doubt. His statement protested against the postponement of the match and accused Fischer of violating the rules and insulting the Soviet people. A just punishment was required. This could only mean forfeiting the first game.

Spassky's reaction triggered a plethora of meetings in hotels around Reykjavik, at all hours of day and night. Spassky wanted an apology as well as an appropriate sanction imposed on Fischer. Even after a three-hour meeting between Fischer's and Spassky's representatives, the matter remained unresolved.

Victor Jackovich, later a U.S. ambassador, was the only American diplomat in Iceland who could speak Russian. He was brought in as an interpreter:

> None of us in the embassy was familiar with the rules or with FIDE. This could be a fiasco, we thought, if the Russians walk out and claim a forfeiture of the entire match. And maybe that's where we're headed. The Soviets were tough customers, and understandably unhappy about the circumstances. We were having to interpret what Fischer was trying to do, and what he was trying to do was anyone's guess. Afterward, discussing the episode with

colleagues, we said, Well, maybe the Russians missed a beat there; maybe it would have been expedient for them to have walked out.

Paul Marshall's view was that the Soviets' emotional involvement in the match gave him a bargaining edge:

[It] allowed for an odd combination of tactics; fun, joyful tactics, because they were so damned serious about it all. It was like a bad movie with a load of snarling Russians. It wasn't that hard to negotiate if one took a position that they didn't like. You could make fun of them, and knowing that the fun would be publicized really helped a lot.

The organizers were not having much fun. They had to deal with the Soviet claim that Fischer forfeit the first game. All knew the latter was out of the question for Fischer. "The situation is critical," Euwe declared. "I don't know if the match will be played at all."

Schmid concedes that the Russians were within their rights to demand the first game, but when he and Euwe met Spassky, "I tried to make a joke of it and said, 'How about a pawn head start in game one instead of a point?'" This raised a rare Soviet smile. Schmid reminded them that in other competitions the Russians had arrived a day late because of travel hitches—even once for a tournament in Reykjavik—and they had been allowed a postponement. This, he maintained, set a precedent.

A grueling second meeting between Thorarinsson, Euwe, and Spassky's seconds was held late in the evening at the Saga. This time Thorarinsson took the role of white knight:

Dr. Euwe fought with them for a long time. I tried to be neutral and didn't say much. When it came to three or four in the morning, both Schmid and Euwe were becoming very, very tired. Suddenly Dr. Euwe gave in. He said, "I see there is no other way. I declare the first game lost." And they all stood up. For me it was clear it was all over, there would now be no match. I banged my hand on the table and said, "This is impossible, and it's my fault.

Because according to the laws of chess, you can't lose a game by forfeit unless the clock has been started. We are the organizers, and we failed to start the clock." It was a drowning man grasping at something. And the Russians all sat down.

This moment of inspired casuistry immediately terminated the forfeit debate but was not enough to rescue the match; there were still the required expressions of contrition. On 5 July, the Soviet delegation issued a statement, read by Geller at a press conference. Hastily translated, it complained that "an unprecedented in the history of chess situation [sic]" had arisen when the world champion was made to wait. This was also the infringement of FIDE rules. The absence of the challenger at the opening and his three-day delay were insulting. This breach had been "taken under the protection" of Euwe. There followed a proposition with which few could quarrel: "All that have [sic] happened were enough to B. Spasski [sic] to discontinue the negotiations and leave for home. The only thing that is keeping him hitherto from taking this step is his understanding of the match meaning [sic] for the world of chess and for hospitable Iceland."

Decoded, the statement added an extra condition for the survival of the match. As well as Fischer's apology, the Soviets now required Euwe's condemnation of Fischer's behavior and an admission by the president that he had violated FIDE rules by postponing the match.

Earlier, Fischer's team had gone a short way down the apology route, offering a terse handout written by Marshall: "We are sorry that the world championship was delayed. . . . If Grandmaster Spassky or the Soviet people were inconvenienced or discomforted, I am indeed unhappy, for I had not the slightest intention of this occurring." Geller rejected it at the press conference as entirely inadequate—it had been mimeographed and was unsigned.

Euwe was in the audience, which had now gone quiet. In what Lothar Schmid called "a great gesture by a great man, saving the match," he immediately rose to do his part in meeting the Soviet conditions. The USSR embassy interpreter, Valeri Chamanin, jotted down Euwe's words on his own copy of Geller's statement. The president admitted breaking FIDE rules "for special reasons," for which he apologized; he condemned Fischer's behavior, and he accepted that Spassky could not be expected to play within the next four days.

The press conference spontaneously erupted in applause, although they also greeted with ridicule Euwe's assertion that Fischer did not *intend* to cause trouble. *The Washington Post* commented that everybody thought Fischer and his companions were the villains. A *Los Angeles Times* article filed from Iceland was headlined BOBBY FISCHER AS THE UGLY AMERICAN. However, the Soviets too came in for criticism. The British papers reported an attack by Ed Edmondson. If the Soviets claimed victory because of Fischer's failure to appear, they would be "showing themselves in their true colours as grasping, greedy, deceitful nonsportsmen." Edmondson added, "I do not intend this to be a personal attack on Spassky because we all know that he is being guided—I should say misguided—by the Russian Ministry of Sport."

Immediately after Geller's press conference, Fred Cramer called one of his own. Concessions were out of the question. If

Dr. Max Euwe, president of FIDE. Apologies all around. ASSOCIATED PRESS

any apologizing was to be done, Cramer said, Dr. Euwe should apologize to the Americans. He had broken the rules in favor of the Russians. As for Fischer, he "felt he hadn't violated the rules."

Meanwhile, Tremblay had met Lombardy and Marshall for what the chargé called a strategy session "aimed at getting the contestants to the chessboard and reversing the propaganda trend that had been heavily pro-Spassky." *The Washington Post* depicted Fischer's entourage as part of the problem: Lombardy and the lawyers were professionally closemouthed, Cramer the opposite. The *Post* remarked: "All in all, the Americans add up to a great team—for Spassky."

The outcome of the meeting was a new letter of apology by Fischer to Spassky. Fischer, in one of those sudden, unexpected, and inexplicable U-turns that had dotted his career, now decided on an act of abnegation. He scrawled a note in which he proposed giving up every cent of the prize money and competing simply for the love of chess. Horrified, Marshall and Darrach worked on the text through the night, finally persuading Fischer to delete any reference to relinquishing the prize. Marshall was quoted as having described his task as "feeling like a cop trying to talk a jump case off a ledge."

The letter was delivered to Spassky's hotel room in the early morning while he slept. Fischer offered "sincere apologies" to Spassky and apologies to Euwe and millions of chess fans for his "disrespectful behavior in not attending the opening ceremony." He also confessed that he had been carried away by his petty dispute over money. However, the hand of the lawyer is plain. After the opening paragraph of soft soap, the next paragraph carefully argues the case against a forfeit of the first game, casting doubt on the Soviets' motive in demanding it, especially when they had apparently accepted a postponement. Anyway, the apology goes on, surely Spassky would not want an unfair advantage? Then, following best public relations practice, it concluded with an appeal to Spassky's honor: "I know you to be a sportsman and a gentleman, and I am looking forward to some exciting chess games with you." In the circumstances, it was a psychological masterstroke. How could the champion not be disarmed? The U.S. embassy released the letter to the press before the Soviets had a chance to react.

It worked. Opinion swung toward the American challenger for the first time. The match was back on.

On 7 July, lots were drawn. Again Fischer was late, leaving the Russian to sweat it out once more. When the American arrived at the playing hall, according to Darrach "bursting out of the cab in a glitter-green slubbed silk suit with wide pointy shoulders," he at first failed to notice Spassky. The world champion "stood staring at the broad green back, his smile crumpled and his tan two shades lighter. Big and vital and overdressed, Fischer looked every inch the arrogant superstar. In a sweater that had lost its casual flair, Spassky looked like a guy who had asked for an autograph and been told to buzz off." The Moscow evening paper *Vecherniaia Moskva* recorded the draw:

> Spassky did what even a chess beginner would do: he squeezed a pawn in each hand, made several loops around the stage with them, then approached his rival and stretched his hands in front of him. Fischer pointed at the hand containing the black pawn.

Spassky would start with the white pieces.

There is now an interval in the drama, a breathing space for the harried actors. The first game has been rescheduled at the Soviets' request (or ultimatum) for 11 July. Spassky relaxes over a salmon fishing expedition. Gudmundur Thorarinsson rests. Paul Marshall returns to his less troublesome clients in New York. Lothar Schmid has to fly back to Germany briefly to tend to his son, who has fallen off a bicycle while pedaling downhill and is suffering from a head injury. Fischer can slip into his routine of sleeping by day and bowling and eating U.S. steaks by night at the Keflavik military base.

12

RAGE

RULES

Ajax, heavy with rage. —SOPHOCLES

When the curtain goes up again, Fischer is in the playing hall. But a new character is on stage and in frustrated turmoil: Chester Fox, an ambitious, young, would-be film-maker with bushy sideburns, tightly curled red hair, and dressed to impress in a wide-lapeled trench coat. He speaks some Russian. When he smokes in times of trouble (from this point, almost continuously), he forgets to puff and the cigarette burns until it melts the filter between his fingers. Fox is agitated. "Tell me, do I look like a rapist?" he asks a journalist. "Am I in here to rape somebody? All I want to do is make a deal." Fox's lawyer, Richard Stein, does his best to curb his client's outbursts.

Although of limited experience, Fox had been granted exclusive rights to film and to photography inside the sports hall by the Icelandic Chess Federation. The deal was for Fischer and Spassky to receive 30 percent each of the revenue, with the other 40 percent being split evenly between the ICF and Fox. Fox was recommended by Paul Marshall, who claims that he could not find another filmmaker interested in the job. Aspects of the deal bewildered Thorarinsson. The Icelander was surprised that a one-man business was apparently the sole contender for the contract.

> We got no money up front. It became clear later that they had a special agreement with Chester Fox behind our backs, and probably Fox paid the Americans something to secure the agreement without our knowledge.

For Fox it was potentially a big break. With the unprecedented international interest, with TV stations hungry for pictures, having the monopoly must have seemed like having the key to the bank.

When the drawing of lots had taken place, Fischer had raised no complaints about the arrangements in the hall. The British chess master Harry Golombek, a vice president of FIDE who stood in for Euwe, complimented the Icelanders on "the best playing conditions in the history of chess": closed-circuit television throughout, 15,000 square feet of red carpet, 1,000 green chairs at ground level, 6,000 feet of curtaining to keep out the daylight.

Nervous officials waited in the hall night after night for a Fischer visit, but he kept deferring an inspection. When he eventually showed up, some forty hours before the first game, only the thirty-two pieces and a familiar swivel chair, especially flown in from New York, met his approval. The hand-carved lead-weighted chess set was made by an English company, John Jacques & Son. As for the leather-bound chair, it was designed by Charles Eames, originally for use in the lobby of the Time-Life Building in New York, and had been found at a shop on 600 Madison Avenue. The Michigan manufacturer of the chair Herman Miller had given the Icelandic organizers a $50 discount as "a token of our friendship and respect" for the Icelandic people. The official price was $524.

No matter what they had heard about the challenger, the naturally courteous Icelandic officials must have been disconcerted by what followed. The table, the chessboard, the lighting, the proximity of the seating to the stage, and the cloth-swathed towers in which the cameras were hidden—all were declared unsatisfactory. The $1,200 custom-built mahogany table should have its legs shortened, the sumptuous chessboard changed, the front rows of seats removed, the camera towers pushed right back to a point where filming would be nigh impracticable, the lighting brighter—no, less bright; no, brighter than that. Above the board was a four-meter-by-four-meter fluorescent fixture containing many bulbs. The Swedish-trained lighting engineer Dadi Agustsson was patient and sympathetic.

> I liked Fischer. He learned very quickly. If I gave him one explanation about the lighting, I would not have to explain it again. Of course he was difficult, but he was not unfair. He just wanted the lighting a certain way, and it was quite clear what he wanted. He wanted it to be such that he didn't notice it—not too hot, he didn't want shadow, he didn't want glare. Spassky wasn't interested. I'll always remember what Spassky told me. He said he used to study chess in his mother's kitchen with a tiny table lamp. After that he never thought about lighting. "Leave it to Fischer," he said.

It was nearly three A.M. before Fischer got around to looking at the chessboard. "There are just too many spots in the stone. It needs to be clear." At the request of Thorarinsson, Gunnar Magnusson had designed the table and board. The table was a rich mahogany with a matte varnish. There were two lower ledges for water. The chessboard itself was green-and-white marble. One of the nation's best masons, Thorsteinn Bjornsson, had worked the stone. The factory had never made a chess set before—they specialized, among other things, in tombstones. Icelandic officials now yanked Bjornsson out of bed at six and told him he had thirty-six hours to make another board. "What do you mean, another board," he shouted. "We made three already. What's wrong? Is he crazy?" Later, Bjornsson had his men cut the two-and-a-quarter-inch squares, binding them together with crushed marble and transparent glue.

As for the camera positions, once Fischer had gone, the

Icelandic officials and Cramer thought that they could find a compromise behind his back—a little shift away of the towers and one row of seats removed. Cramer checked his notes to see if there was anything else his boy might object to. "I've been through it all," he said. "As far as I can see, the only thing left is the air."

Six minutes after the scheduled start of the first game, Fischer appeared to the applause of the audience. At last, the championship was under way, and with a game that left grandmasters openmouthed.

Spassky played the opening and middle game with great caution and the first two hours were devoid of thrills. The queens came off at move eleven, a pair of knights at move sixteen, a pair of bishops at move eighteen, a pair of rooks at move nineteen, the two other rooks at move twenty-three, and the two other knights at move twenty-eight. That left six pawns and a bishop each. Most players would agree to a draw immediately upon reaching such a lifeless, evenly balanced position. There was no scent of victory for either side. There seemed to be no possibility of stirring up the position. Fischer had plenty of time to make his moves and was ahead of Spassky on the clock.

Then, on move twenty-nine, Fischer did the unthinkable. Picking up the remaining black bishop in the long fingers of his right hand, balancing it with his thumb, index, and middle fingers, he stretched out his arm and in one movement plucked off the rook pawn with his two smaller fingers while installing the bishop in its place.

This was inexplicable. In playing Bxh2—bishop takes the king rook pawn—Fischer had fallen into a standard trap. At first glance, the undefended white rook pawn looks as though it can be safely pinched by the black bishop. At second glance, one sees that if the pawn is taken, white's knight's pawn will be advanced one square, leaving the black bishop helplessly stranded. White can capture it with nonchalant ease. Even for the average club player, the recognition of such a danger is instinctive.

Inexplicable.

Fischer was the chess machine who did not commit errors. That was part of his aura, part of the "Bobby Fischer" legend, a key to his success. Newspapers reported a gasp of surprise spreading through the auditorium. Spassky, who had trained himself not to betray emotion, looked momentarily startled. Those who later analyzed the match were equally dumbfounded. "When I saw Bobby play this move," wrote Golombek, "I could hardly believe my eyes. He had played so sensibly and competently up to now that I first of all thought there was something deep I had over-looked; but no matter how I stared at the board I could find no way out." Nor could Robert Byrne and Ivo Nei, who analyze the game in their book on the match: "This move must be stamped as an outright blunder." The British chess player and writer C. H. O'D. Alexander's verdict is similar: "Unbelievable. By accurate play Fischer had established an obviously drawn position . . . now he makes a beginner's blunder." A television pundit on the U.S. Channel 13 reckoned it would go down as one of the great gaffes of all time. *The Los Angeles Times* thought it could be explained only as a "rare miscalculation by the American genius." In Moscow, the correspondent for the Soviet state newspaper *Izvestia,* Yuri Ponomarenko, located the move's source in sheer greed. Bondarevskii commented that the move was "a vivid example to smash the myth of [Fischer] as a computer." Anatoli Karpov, the twenty-one-year-old Soviet star in the making, had a psychological theory involving both players: Spassky was afraid of the American and had sought to prove to himself that he could always draw with the white pieces. Fischer, annoyed, attempted to disprove this. "So he sacrificed a piece without rhyme or reason."

Years later, in twenty pages of exhaustive analysis, British grandmaster Jonathan Speelman concluded that even after Fischer captured the h pawn, totally accurate play could have earned him a draw. And to be charitable to Fischer, perhaps he recognized this intuitively. But that is hardly an explanation. For such a gambit had only a downside, offering no chance of victory. At best, with extreme care, it gave him the same result—a draw—that he could have achieved without any effort at all—indeed, probably by simply asking for one.

The game was adjourned after five hours, with Fischer's position in a hopeless mess. Only *The New York Times* could conjure up a spirit of generosity: "Even if Fischer does lose the first game, he has achieved the respect of every player here by rising to Spassky's dare and throwing away a sure draw for a speculative attack." In 1992, when Fischer and Spassky played a rematch, a journalist, still intrigued by the move two decades earlier, asked Fischer whether he had been trying to create winning chances by complicating a drawn position. "Basically that's right. Yes," he replied.

At the time, however, he offered a different explanation, claiming to Lombardy that he had reacted too fast because the cameras distracted him. Soon after his first move, he protested ferociously to Schmid about the noise coming from the camera towers and repeated his complaint several times as the game wore on. No one particularly approved of the towers Chester Fox had constructed, ugly contraptions designed to conceal the film cameras and cameramen. They had been wrapped in black hessian, under which the cameramen sweated in saunalike conditions. But overnight the problem appeared to have been resolved when the two camera towers were removed from the hall. A third camera remained, looking down on the game from the back of the set.

Viktor Ivonin had arrived during the first day of the game and had gone straight to the hall, attempting with relish to predict the moves. (In his notebook, he jotted down that at the thirty-fifth move, when Spassky captured Fischer's bishop, the American left the stage with "his trousers hung under his stomach.") Despite the intellectual stimulation, he had a number of anxieties. There were some irregularities, some abnormalities, he noticed. There was Fischer's luxury black leather American chair. The Soviet embassy had told him they were uneasy about it, without explaining why. Ivonin thought that the way the challenger constantly swiveled and threw himself around in it must surely distract the world champion. Spassky's chair, by contrast, was a regular office model, firmly upright, with arms. Another worry was that when Spassky wrote his sealed adjournment move, his action was picked up by the closed-circuit camera and displayed on the big screen at the back of the stage. (At the end of a session, if a game was ongoing, one player was required secretly to seal the next move.) Ivonin later told Spassky that he had seen him write "pxp," pawn takes pawn, and warned him in the future to make sure he concealed his move from the camera before committing anything to paper.

However, at dinner the mood was positive. Victory the following day looked assured. Ivonin quoted the Soviets' first astronaut, Yuri Gagarin, to Spassky: *"Poekhali!"*—"Let's go!" meaning "We have lift off!" At some point, Spassky took a call from Lothar Schmid. Was he happy with everything? "Yes," replied Spassky, "everything is fine." Schmid said that there was something Fischer did not like, but he was not at liberty to say what.

As the experts had foretold, the next afternoon Fischer quickly capitulated; he struggled on for only sixteen more moves. A player other than Fischer might not have bothered to see it through that far. Geller remarked that if Fischer was doing so petty a thing as continuing with the game—not resigning when he was definitely going to lose—he was not that strong. It showed how the Soviet team had failed to understand the American's character: that he would never give up, so long as there remained even a glimmer of a chance.

Spassky was not fooled by his victory, describing Fischer's blunder as "a present to the Sports Committee." When he and Fischer parted at the adjournment, Fischer had spoken to him in Russian, saying, *"Do zavtra"* ("Till tomorrow"). The Russian interpreted this as a mark of Fischer's resilience, understanding immediately that he had a fight on his hands and that this was merely an opening skirmish for the battle ahead.

On stage for the adjourned first game, Fischer had appeared satisfied. But after thirty-five minutes and three moves, he leaned far back in his swivel chair and caught sight of the camera. Incandescent, he hurled himself off the platform, pursued by the chief arbiter. Schmid, he spat out to the arbiter's face, was a liar for telling him the cameras had been removed. Unless the backstage camera was ejected at once, he would leave the match. Crushed by the force of the challenger's vehemence, Schmid complied, ordering the camera to go. The cameras, the cameramen, and their producer, Chester Fox—all had become the object of Fischer's rage.

Chester Fox was already an isolated and unpopular figure. The Icelandic camera team thought him unprofessional and his planned approach ludicrous, using miles and miles of film on a visually static scene when the action, and the profits, were outside the playing hall. (Of course, it is the traditional role of film cameramen to dismiss the director as being risibly ignorant and incompetent and for wasting their talent and time.) There were also cultural barriers. Fox was the New Yorker's New Yorker. Thirty-one-year-old Icelandic cameraman Gissli Gestsson, who supplied the crew and equipment, took against him:

> He was a funny character—a typically New York Jewish character. I didn't trust him because after a time I realized he promised more than he could deliver. He was noisy, and he and his colleagues had some odd ideas about Iceland. They complained that everything was primitive. I think they expected the atmosphere in Iceland to be like that in Manhattan.

Nor did the Icelander have much sympathy for Fox's problems inside the hall:

> He could claim he didn't have the access that he was promised, but he had access to so many other things that gave him a good

source of revenue. For a few weeks, this was the biggest event going on in the world. I think his loss in the auditorium was compensated for by what he was able to sell from outside the
auditorium to all over the world.

In fact, Fox could have been right. With the *longueurs* edited out,
a move-by-move film of the match would still be selling today.
Gestsson was under tremendous stress, and perhaps this partially
accounts for his impatience with Fox. The Icelandic film and television industry was negligible, and the cameraman made his living by representing two of the biggest British worldwide film
agencies. They had pressed him to cover the match for them; he
had to bar his regular customers from the hall.

The Icelandic Chess Federation also faced a dilemma. They
were contractually bound to Fox, and he was now in conflict with
Fischer's representatives, the very people who had suggested him.
Gudmundur Thorarinsson remembers that although the Americans had been so keen on granting Fox exclusive rights, "once the
problems started, they came to me and said, 'You have to tear up
the agreements with Chester Fox.' I said, 'We don't do that in
Iceland. Here we make an agreement and it's an agreement.' "

Like Gissli Gestsson, Thorarinsson was struck by the
"Jewishness" of the New Yorkers. (The number of Jews in Iceland
was negligible: historically, they came and went as traders or mer-
chants, and the Icelandic word for Jew, *Gyoingur,* was used to
mean cunning or sharp.) "Fox was one of the Jews—they were all
Jews around him," notes Thorarinsson. "I think he was rather a
simple guy, and he had nobody to support him; he seemed quite
alone." In a fight between Fischer and Fox, saving the match was
always going to come first.

In any case, the legal position was not clear-cut. From Fox's
viewpoint, the Icelandic Chess Federation had sold him all picture rights. Film and video exploitation was permitted under the
match rules and was a significant part of the budget. But the
rules also stated that the players had the right to demand the end
to any disturbance. And Fischer complained that the cameras disturbed him.

The Amsterdam agreement, in which all the rules were laid

out, was not drafted to be watertight. Edmondson had done his best to cover Fischer in all eventualities. Approached by Schmid after the adjournment of the first game and handed a copy of the Amsterdam agreement, Paul Marshall demonstrated the approach that had brought him success and riches in New York legal combat: "I dropped them on the floor, saying, 'They're written in English: Do not quote rules that you can't read.' Almost as an afterthought, Marshall adds, 'Because the rules were clearly in Bobby's favor, and his complaint was absolutely right.' "

Through Marshall, Fischer demands that the ICF underwrite a document giving him complete control over filming. Believing it could not favor one player over another, the federation says no. With only one game over, the match reaches another impasse. Fox has his rights. Schmid and Thorarinsson have the match to safeguard. Fischer has his rage. Behind the walls a space is discovered in which the cameras are hidden yet can still see the board. Has the problem been finessed? On learning that the cameras are still there, Fischer refuses to come to the hall for the second game.

The game is scheduled to begin at five P.M. on Thursday, 13 July. Schmid presses the clock on the dot. Rule five states, "If a player does not appear within one hour of the start of the game, he loses that game by forfeit." The road is cleared between the hall and Fischer's hotel. Engine running, a police car stands ready to bring him. All the traffic lights are held at green. From New York, Andrew Davis intervenes, calling Richard Stein, one of the lawyers for Chester Fox Inc., and proposes that the cameras be removed for this game only, pending further discussion. Stein takes the call at 5:30 P.M. while Fischer's clock is ticking and immediately agrees. He calls Lombardy on a hot line that has been set up from Fischer's room to the playing hall. Thorarinsson orders the cameras to be removed completely. Fischer adds one more condition: His clock must be restarted. Already bruised by Fischer, and now distraught, Schmid refuses. The rules are the rules. He has Spassky to consider; the world champion has been waiting for forty minutes.

German chief arbiter and grandmaster Lothar Schmid with Spassky. When duty's to be done, an arbiter's lot is not a happy one. ICELANDIC CHESS FEDERATION

Unwillingly, finding the whole affair "vulgar," grandmaster Fridrik Olafsson steps in at the request of the Icelandic Chess Federation. Within a few minutes, he has arrived at the Loftleidir hotel on a mission to mediate. His reward is a second dose of rudeness. Having ignored the Icelandic grandmaster at Keflavik, Fischer now submits him to a verbal tirade. Again and again he tells him that the ICF is a communist front. Olafsson phones Schmid. The only hope is to ask Spassky to agree to a restart. Schmid cannot. "There has to be a limit." In one of the worst moments of his life, he goes onto the stage at six o'clock and announces that Spassky has been awarded the game. That night, Schmid wakes up with tears in his eyes "because I thought I had destroyed a genius by my decision." Spassky now leads by two games to zero; it seems extraordinarily difficult for Fischer to surmount that—the champion needs only twelve points out of twenty-four to retain the title. *The Washington Post* reports that Americans are voluble in references to Fischer's "disgraceful behavior." Some are observed apologizing to Icelanders in the name of the United States.

A new round of crisis meetings begins. Andrew Davis jets in from New York, dropping everything to mastermind the predictable protest against Schmid's decision. It will be based on what he claims has been a guarantee by Iceland that all television equipment would be "invisible and noiseless." Seeking a way out for his client Chester Fox, Richard Stein tries schmoozing Fischer. He writes: "I can only express my admiration and appreciation for the elevation of chess in the eyes of the people of the States, through your Herculean efforts. As a folk hero of the Americans, you must permit millions of Americans to share this experience with you in their homes, through television." Stein points out Fox's investment and notes that the Icelandic Chess Federation's entire financial structure depends on video and film proceeds. For all the impact this letter was going to have, he might as well have put it in a bottle and thrown it into Iceland's famous Blue Lagoon.

Meanwhile, conscience-stricken, Schmid tries to reach Fischer to discuss matters. He makes it plain to the match committee, which will hear the inevitable American protest, how ready he is to have his decision overruled. After receiving a note from Cramer, he tells Darrach to write an official letter of appeal to reach him before the deadline under the rules, midnight (six hours after the forfeit). According to Darrach, Schmid comes to Fischer's suite just before time runs out, hoping to obtain the appeal. He is shown some scrawled pages and feels that they might count as delivered on time if he but touches them—which he does, then leaves them to be typed.

Why did the chief arbiter show such solicitude for the challenger? "I tried to give Bobby a chance. I had to be fair to both players. Bobby was unusual. He wasn't protesting just to protest. He thought he was right even when he was not. I knew Bobby was not easy, but I knew also that he was not a bad boy. We had to save the match."

Schmid is still in his pajamas, though with his hair neatly combed, when Fischer personally delivers the letter. Jumping up, the arbiter accidentally bangs his head on a lamp hanging low over a coffee table. According to Darrach, "Bobby grinned" at the sight of Schmid's discomfort. In the letter, Fischer writes that he had been told the cameras would be silent and invisible and that "nothing could have been further from the facts." "The bungling unknowns who claimed to be professional cameramen were clumsy, rude and deceitful. The only thing invisible, silent and out of sight was fairness on the part of the organizers. I have never compromised on anything affecting playing conditions of the game itself, which is my art and my profession. It seemed to me that the organizers deliberately tried to upset and provoke me by the way they coddled and kowtowed to that [camera] crew." Spassky sniffs, "The letter is about everything except chess."

That same morning, Friday, 14 July, the match committee meets. It consists of one American, Fred Cramer; one Russian, Nikolai Krogius; and two Icelanders, the assistant arbiter, Gudmundur Arnlaugsson, and a member of the ICF and head of the FIDE match committee Baldur Moeller, who is the Icelandic minister of justice.

Before the substantive issues can be thrashed out, a prior question must be addressed: Did Fischer's appeal arrive on time? Schmid presents the facts. The previous night at 8:40 P.M., he had received a letter from Cramer, who said that it was not the formal protest: that would come later. At 11:50 P.M., Fischer had invited Schmid to his room and shown him some scribbles. At one A.M., Schmid had gone to the Russians in the Saga to tell them that there was a protest, but he did not yet have the text. They made clear that they did not accept Cramer's letter as sufficient: Fischer had not signed it, as the rules required. The official protest duly signed had finally been delivered to him at eight A.M.

Davis then intervenes. He attempts to persuade the committee that the written protest was a mere formality; they must get to the essence. Schmid should not have started the clock because Fischer had already protested against the presence of television cameras in the hall. They had not been withdrawn. Thus, the conditions were not in order, in accordance with his demands. Ergo, Fischer was not late.

At this point, Geller interjects a counterargument. The rules said that players must be at the game on time. Now that the match was under way, it was too late to protest against the general conditions—there could be complaints only about specific games, and they must be made at the game itself.

As it is his judgment that is under question, Schmid withdraws. That same day at a news conference, Arnlaugsson announces the committee's ruling. The protest is accepted as delivered in time, but Schmid's decision to start the clock is affirmed. The cameras would be discussed later with the participants. Fischer's loss is approved.

Everything to do with Fischer now goes into reverse: in place of the question "Will he come?" is "Will he leave?" Lombardy, Cramer, Marshall in New York, all scurry around, organizing telegrams from fans in the States beseeching him to stay put. But in the event, an equal number of people, unprompted, send telegrams of condemnation.

While all this is going on, Henry Kissinger is on duty in California, helping to entertain the Soviet ambassador Anatoli Dobrynin at Nixon's western White House, Casa Pacifica, on the beach at San Clemente. It is a considerable honor for Dobrynin as well as an opportunity for long, informal conversations with Kissinger on U.S.-Soviet relations. They sunbathe on the beach, and Kissinger takes the ambassador and his wife to Hollywood to mingle with the stars. There is no record of them meeting the Marx Brothers, though Hitchcock proposes a suspense film set in the Kremlin. "The time is not yet ripe," intones Dobrynin. At some stage, Kissinger is said to have found time to put in a call to Reykjavik 22322, the hotel Loftleidir.

Fox's chief cameraman, Gissli Gestsson, tells the story of how he, Gestsson, was in Fischer's suite when the telephone rang: "That is the strangest call I ever witnessed in my life. I could hear Henry Kissinger giving him this pep talk like a coach, saying, 'You're our man up against the Commies.' It was unbelievable." Quite. Bearing in mind that the whole problem was caused by Fischer's wrath directed at the cameramen, being admitted to Fischer's side and hearing him take a call from the U.S. president's right-hand man must have been the scoop of the match.

Fischer's mind is unchanged, and again the match has descended into Marx Brothers burlesque. There are scenes involving flight reservations, plots to detain Fischer in Reykjavik to prevent his escape, and aborted drives to the airport. Marshall recalls:

We mainly communicated by telex. But one guy with a telephone would occasionally get through to us. We kept receiving messages about Fischer being booked on various planes; a plane to New York, a plane to Greenland, every flight that went out of Reykjavik had Fischer on the flight list. And we were getting these wonderfully droll messages from an Icelander about how Fischer had booked himself on these flights and that Cramer had gone to the airport to try to dissuade him. And there were all these exciting car chases going on.

Fischer off-stage continues to command almost all the attention. In the press, much of it makes for uncomfortable reading. *The Washington Post* agonizes that "Fischer has alienated millions of chess enthusiasts around the world." All the expectations of him have "turned to ashes, with Bobby Fischer himself as arsonist." The correspondent of Agence France-Presse writes that Fischer has crossed the boundaries of all proper behavior.

In contrast, the front pages of the Icelandic press are adorned with pictures of the well-mannered and apparently carefree world champion walking, fishing for salmon, or playing tennis. No doubt these help reassure the organizers that they can focus their efforts on keeping Fischer in the match and let the world champion await the challenger's decision. It is difficult to resist the conjecture that their attitude is also influenced by the cold war. The West-East, us-them relationship is instrumental in what follows. The Americans and the Icelanders, partners in NATO, both with free market economies and democratically elected governments, are "us," the Soviet chess delegation is "them." Not being a true "them" is to prove Spassky's undoing.

13

BLOOD IN

THE BACK ROOM

Spassky was a gentleman. Gentlemen may win the ladies,
but gentlemen lose at chess.   —VIKTOR KORCHNOI

Whatever the impression given in the press, the champion was in deep dismay. He had no wish to retain the title by default. To calm him down after the forfeit was announced, Viktor Ivonin took him on a long walk. Nothing was turning out as the champion had anticipated. He had wanted the focus of the combat to be on the aesthetic creations at the chessboard. "I was very patient with Fischer, but he is impossible to understand. And the organizers are making concessions to him. Remember how they said, 'Bobby Fischer is ill and in hospital. . . .' "

Ivonin had watched Spassky's expression as he waited for Fischer for that one hour. By the end, the deputy minister was fervently hoping Fischer would not arrive, his champion looked so empty and overwhelmed. All the uncertainties of the preceding days had returned in greater measure. Spassky had gained a point but with a pyrrhic victory. Ivonin noted that in conversation, Spassky talked obsessively about Fischer. The deputy minister found that disturbing. The sensitive Spassky was unable to switch his thoughts to more relaxing matters.

At four in the afternoon, after the forfeit was confirmed, Icelandic officials, Schmid and Moeller, the head of the match committee, representatives of the two sides, Fox, the cameramen, some journalists, and diplomats all met in the hall to reexamine the conditions and check Fox's cameras. No one had any queries.

Iceland's chief auditory expert, Curt Baldursson, conducted an official test of the noise made by the cameras. These were brand-new American models and were what was called self-blimped—constructed to be soundless during filming. Baldursson received no pay for his labors but was given, instead, free entrance to the rest of the match. For his experiment, he brought along a state-of-the-art sound-level meter. "The meter didn't register anything close to levels that could have been picked up by a human ear, so either Fischer had extrasensory faculties or this was part of a poker game." The noise level was measured at fifty-five decibels with the cameras running and fifty-five decibels with them turned off. Baldursson wrote out a report that Fischer peremptorily dismissed. The cameras were moved behind the walls of the set, looking through tiny windows. In Ivonin's judgment, they were unnoticeable.

The American millionaire chess fan Isaac Turover joined the group. He played a game on the official board with Ivonin. The Soviet politician took the opportunity of probing and trying out Fischer's chair, taking pains not to be noticed.

Someone wondered aloud whether it would be the last game there. Turover said that if Fischer was not given the point back, the match was over. An Icelandic journalist asked Ivonin for his opinion. He replied that the Soviet side had not breached the rules and was not going to breach them. Nor were they going to allow anyone else to.

The next day, Euwe telegraphed from Amsterdam to spell out FIDE's position. If Fischer did not appear for the third game, he would be defaulted on that one, too. And if he did not come to the fourth game, the match would be declared over; Spassky would retain the championship. At least that laid to rest Schmid's fear that he would have to stand on the stage game after game, starting the clocks, waiting out the empty hour, and pronouncing forfeits until Spassky had the requisite twelve points for victory.

However, if the match officials thought the forfeit was history, they were mistaken. The challenger was now observing his Sabbath and had unplugged the phone. (That Fischer could not play between sundowns on Friday and Saturday was the cause of amused speculation in Reykjavik, where in July the sun does not set until nearly midnight and it is never completely dark. Fischer solved his theological dilemma by choosing an arbitrary time and sticking to it.) His cudgels were taken up by Paul Marshall, who arrived on Saturday, 15 July, like a legal tornado, replacing Davis and insisting on a rehearing of the appeal. The committee's decision was not final—it could always be changed in the light of new evidence or deferred, said Marshall. He argued on and on; the committee listened until three in the morning. Then they confirmed their original decision, announcing that they found the conditions in the hall to be in line with the rules of the competition.

At last there was good news. Although Fischer had booked another return flight to New York, someone had persuaded him to stay. Perhaps it was Marshall, accusing him of cowardice. Perhaps it was the thin, gray-haired widow Lina Grumette, his intermittent surrogate mother, with whom he had had supper after emerging from his Sabbath.

Fischer's decision to remain in the match came with strings: He would play game three only in the separate, private room at the back of the stage and without cameras, not in the hall.

Lothar Schmid had to find a way forward. But what possible rationale could the organizers have for moving the game when the appeal committee, the sound engineer, and the mass visit to the hall had established that it was a wholly appropriate site?

He tried reason. "I said, 'Let's start in the main hall. If the noise disturbs us, then we can move.'" Reason was not enough. Marshall, says Schmid, preferred unreason. If there were no current disturbance in the hall, he promised Schmid he would create one. "'If you, Mr. Schmid, will not remove the third game into the separate room, I will go to the stage and take a big hammer and smash down the table and you won't be able to play there.' And I said, 'In these circumstances, I have to think it over.' "

This was a world turned upside down. The normal response to Marshall would have been, "In that case, you will be arrested and charged with criminal damage while we use another board." Instead, Schmid went to the champion. "I asked Boris if he would allow the third game to be played in the separate room. He said, 'Pozhaluista,' 'That's fine by me.' "

The Soviet team had not been involved in this decision. Spassky had capitulated without consulting his seconds or the deputy minister of sport, Viktor Ivonin. They discovered this only on taking their seats in the hall. Ivonin and the Soviet television and radio chess correspondent Naum Dymarskii exchanged startled comments.

Spassky had behaved like a sportsman, Schmid said later. Today his rationalization is less generous. "Of course, Spassky was in the lead. For him, it was worth agreeing to move the game to get Bobby back. So he was easy and friendly." With Schmid and Thorarinsson frantic to save the match, one to safeguard Fischer, the other to safeguard his reputation and all the hard work and money that had gone into the championship, not to speak of his political future, the Soviet player became the sportsman or, rather, the pawn. The Americans broke the rules, and the ICF colluded with them. For Iceland, continuing the match was simply too vital; comparatively, too much was at stake. A larger country might have shrugged off Fischer's wayward behavior and his lawyer's aggressive gambits—"It's his loss, not ours." Iceland could not afford that, and the Americans knew it.

 ·•·

For Spassky, as for Schmid, worse was yet to come.

The board had been reset in the unwelcoming, bare back room behind the stage, used normally for table tennis. It was small, about seventy-five feet by thirty feet, with a sloping roof. On one side were windows that looked out over a grassed area toward the main road. The noise of passers-by and children frolicking could be heard.

Spassky arrived in time for the start and sat down at the board. Lothar Schmid was opening a window. Anxiously, Spassky looked around for Fischer. The challenger arrived and was immediately possessed by rage. Wrapped in blankets, a closed-circuit television camera had been installed to carry the action to the thousand-strong audience in the hall and the journalists and commentators in the press room. Fischer roared at Schmid: "No cameras!" He prowled the room, turning switches on and off. Schmid protested that Spassky was being disturbed. Fischer yelled back at him to shut up.

White-faced, Spassky stood. Lothar Schmid recollects, "When Bobby started to fight again, Boris became upset and he said, 'If you do not stop the quarreling, I will go back to the playing hall and demand to play there.'" With the challenger turning the World Chess Championship into a verbal brawl, Schmid, panic-stricken, pleaded with the champion to continue the game. "Boris, you promised." He turned to Fischer. "Bobby, please be kind." Schmid remembers: "I felt there was only one chance to get them together. They were two grown-up boys, and I was the older one. I took them both and pressed them by the shoulders down into their chairs. Boris made the first move, and I started the clock."

So on 16 July 1972 at nine minutes past five in the afternoon, the World Chess Championship match was finally saved.

Schmid is unrepentant about his unorthodox tactics. "I could have said to Bobby, 'If you're disputing the conditions, you don't have to stay here in this closed back room. You are within your rights to lodge another complaint.' But I thought—and I think that's how it would have been—he would have gone away and never come back. This was the decisive moment in the match."

Fischer was two down to the champion. He had never beaten Spassky, and now he had the black pieces. Nonetheless, early in the game he went into furious attack; at last the spotlight was where it was meant to be, on the chessboard. "This is wild stuff," exclaimed a spectator. Fischer's eleventh move, Nh5, was a shock; it left his pawn structure in a mess and removed a pawn from the defense of his king. One expert in Reykjavik described the move as "an entirely new conception"; Spassky spent half an hour studying it.

Grandmaster Reuben Fine, a psychoanalyst, thought Fischer's ambiguous feelings toward women could be read off from moves like Nh5. Fischer, he maintained, liked to attack his opponent's center from the side. Applying his professional insights, he concluded that Fischer's tendency to hug the edge was "most likely the chessic equivalent of the running away that he was always threatening" and that this running away had to do with his apprehension about females.

Another grandmaster marveled, "Bobby's attacking as though his life was involved." Spassky was being outplayed. At the adjournment, Fischer wrote a move that, according to Frank Brady, left him exultant. " 'I sealed a crusher!' he crowed, smashing a fist into his palm. 'I'm crushing him with brute force! Haaaaaa!' "

Following a night's analysis of the position, and assisted by grandmaster Isaac Boleslavskii, a new arrival on a brief visit, Spassky opened the sealed move—B-Q6 check—thought for five minutes, and resigned. Schmid apologized to the audience for the brevity of the show. They had paid the equivalent of a dollar a minute and seen one move. Ten minutes after Spassky had left,

The contestants in the back room. Normally it was used for table tennis, not psychic bloodletting. ICELANDIC CHESS FEDERATION

Left to right: Geller, Spassky, Fischer, and Lombardy. And Spassky had acted to save the match. HALLDOR PETURSSON

Fischer rushed in to claim his victory. He had beaten Spassky for the first time.

This second session of game three—that single move—was held on the stage in the main hall. Overnight, Spassky had written a letter to Schmid, a not quite official protest, delivering it just before midnight. He said that the back room was unsatisfactory: there was too much noise, from the air-conditioning, the traffic, children. (Curiously, the children had not disturbed Fischer.) The rest of the games must take place in the auditorium, in accordance with the match rules. Fischer, no doubt buoyed by victory, agreed to return to the auditorium provided there was no filming. Thorarinsson went along with this, leaving Fox stranded and muttering about legal action. It was not a difficult decision for Thorarinsson. "The filming is not the first priority. The chess match is the first priority. If this is the only way the match can go on, then we must take it."

Because of Spassky's letter, the organizing committee and representatives of the delegations met the next morning—a little late, under the circumstances—to discuss the legality of moving the game into the closed room. Golombek, an elder statesman of the chess world, told the committee that he could recall only two

occasions when games were transferred to an alternative site because of a problem in the original venue: in the matches between
Botvinnik and Smyslov and between Botvinnik and Tal. In both
cases, the substitute venue had held spectators.

Schmid then spoke. He said Spassky had shown admirable
sportsmanship in agreeing at such short notice to move to the
back room. For future reference, the chief arbiter added: "I saved
the match, but I'm not going to take this sort of decision again."

Schmid's praise for Spassky's sportsmanship provoked bitter
comments in the Soviet camp. Ivonin noted in his diary that
Fischer's behavior had taken a heavy toll on the champion.
Spassky told him that his previous image of Fischer was shattered: "I idealized Fischer. The third game broke my idealism."
He had also seen something deeply disturbing in Fischer that he
described as "an animal."

That evening, the Soviet delegation held a meeting with the
ambassador Sergei Astavin. They agreed there should be no more
"charity" toward Fischer; the Americans did not go in for charity.
The group believed that the Americans had acted deliberately to
drag Spassky down and distract him—and that they had succeeded.

Later, Anatoli Karpov remarked that Fischer's game two forfeit
was "a stroke of genius, a stroke tailor-made for Spassky. It proved
that Fischer knew Spassky inside out. Had it been Petrosian instead of Spassky, he would simply have licked his chops and swallowed the extra point."

It was not the Soviets alone who recognized how destructive
these events were for Spassky. Brady wrote that Fischer's win
brought the challenger's gestalt into place—he had drawn blood,
and it would become, says Brady, "a torrent of energy streaming
out of Spassky's psyche."

In all this, what motivated Fischer? Many Fischer observers, including a few in the Soviet chess establishment, believed he was
frightened of the chessboard. For Fischer, leaving Iceland proved
as difficult as arriving. Marshall believed that when it came to a

decision, "he was less afraid of playing than he was of the unknown. But make no mistake, he was terrified of playing."

The Icelandic grandmaster Fridrik Olafsson, who was a friend and admirer of the challenger, also located the source of his behavior in that fear. "Why did Bobby not turn up? I tell you one thing. He had something really sick inside him. He had a terrible fear of losing." Losing was for other players; "Bobby Fischer" could not afford to lose.

14

EYEBALL TO
EYEBALL

. . . and the other guy blinked.

— SECRETARY OF STATE DEAN RUSK,
AFTER THE CUBAN MISSILE CRISIS

How does one negotiate with a Fischer, a man who is apparently prepared to risk everything rather than accept a compromise? Most people would not consider that to be rational. Yet there were few occasions when the challenger did not get his way with FIDE, the Icelandic Chess Federation, and other tournament organizers. The board and pieces, the lighting, the chair and table, the noise level, the proximity of the audience, the visibility of the cameras—all had to be just so. The prize money or appearance fee had to be increased. The games had to be played at specific times. Fischer's exasperated opponents would capitulate in the face of these demands, sometimes after putting up a perfunctory, halfhearted fight. But with other competitors, the tournament regulations were always strictly interpreted. So why with Fischer did the rules take on this remarkable plasticity?

Game theory, a branch of mathematics that analyzes complex

human behavior through simple models, offers some insight into Fischer's success to those perplexed by the apparent weakness of officials. Game theory has been used to revolutionize the study of intellectual disciplines from economics to international relations and from evolutionary theory to philosophy. Its proponents have won Nobel Prizes, and one of its key exponents, John Nash, has been the subject of a best-selling book and Oscar-winning Hollywood blockbuster, *A Beautiful Mind*.

"Games" come in various kinds. There are, for example, games of perfect information, such as chess, where at each stage of the game one knows all the opponent's steps to date, and games of imperfect information, such as a sealed auction, where one can only speculate about the sum of money a rival has bid. Then there are games of cooperation (where, as the name implies, players cooperate to achieve the best possible outcome) and games of noncooperation (where individuals act only in their own self-interest, irrespective of what other players are doing).

One reason Person A may not cooperate with Person B is that Person A's gain is Person B's loss: this is a zero-sum game. In non-zero-sum games, both sides can benefit. Compare chess to the usual form of charades, in which there are no teams and individuals take it in turns to act out the title of a book, movie, play, or song in front of the rest of the group, who try to guess it. In chess, your defeat is my victory. In charades, we all win or lose together.

So how would a game theorist explain the conundrum of Fischer's apparent bargaining imprudence and his negotiating success?

In bargaining, theorists have long recognized that there are rational advantages to irrationality, or at least to the appearance of irrationality. One purely academic illustration of this has a woman returning home to discover a dangerous-looking burglar in her house. She recognizes that the burglar has a motive to kill her because she can describe him to the police. If she could swallow a tablet, making her, for a short period, wholly and transparently mad, the burglar might believe she will not be able to identify him later and so might leave her unharmed.

Some game theorists even go so far as to say that we are biologically hardwired to be irrational—say, to want vengeance even when by hurting others we will only suffer further ourselves. It is possible that we have evolved to be partially vengeful; if my enemies know I will come after them, even at considerable cost to myself, they are less likely to inflict harm on me in the first place. The evolutionary drawback of such hardwiring is that once violence begins between individuals, factions, or nations, it becomes tough to stop, as evidenced by the generations of warring families in Sicily wiped out by the vendetta.

James Dean, in his 1955 classic, *Rebel Without a Cause,* made famous the deadly game of "chicken." In one variant of this suicidal game, two drivers hurtle toward each other from a distance of several hundred meters. The first driver to swerve away from the line of contact is "chicken" and the loser. If neither swerves, there will be a devastating collision. Now, as the driver of one of those cars, if you can convince the other driver that you are not worried about the consequences of a crash or want death, then the battle is half won. When your opponents realize that you have no fear, that victory (or not being defeated) is all that matters to you, that you do not value your life, then they will see no point in trying to test your courage. One game theorist, Herman Kahn, wrote, "The 'skilful' player may get into the car quite drunk, throwing whisky bottles out the window to make it clear to everybody just how drunk he is. He wears very dark glasses so that it is obvious he cannot see much, if anything. As soon as the car reaches high speed, he takes the steering wheel and throws it out of the window."

Bertrand Russell said that "chicken" was played by two groups: juvenile delinquents and nations. During the Fischer-Spassky match, the preeminent concern of the U.S. administration was the conflict in Vietnam and how to end it. Earlier, in 1969, President Richard Nixon had explained his madman policy to his chief of staff, H. R. Haldeman, as they strolled along a beach in Florida. As Haldeman recounted it, "He [Nixon] said, 'I call it the madman theory, Bob. I want the North Vietnamese to believe I've reached the point where I might do anything to stop the war. We'll just slip the word to them that "For God's sake, you know Nixon is obsessed about communism. We can't restrain him when he's angry, and he has his hand on the nuclear button," and Ho Chi Minh himself will be in Paris in two days, begging for peace.' " When Nixon ordered the bombing of Cambodia with B-52s, the intention, in part, was to signal to the North Vietnamese the potential deployment of the bombers in a nuclear role.

Henry Kissinger, Nixon's national security adviser, had also reflected on the madman theory. In 1959, he had attended two lectures given by Daniel Ellsberg titled *The Political Uses of Madness,* in which Ellsberg had explored the diplomatic value of extreme threats by an apparently reckless leader. He instanced Hitler's bloodless invasions of the Rhineland, Austria, and Czechoslovakia. One of Ellsberg's conditions for success in the political application of madness was that the demands should be limited in scale and the threat so extreme that the mere possibility of its being carried out would be enough to persuade a foe to yield.

Fischer could no doubt have won the world championship "chicken" contest—he always appeared ready to crash his career. When he stated his all-or-nothing terms for his participation in a match or tournament, it was transparent to those who met him both that he imbued each of his conditions with immense significance, and that his threats were totally credible. He had a record of inflicting financial and career damage on himself on failing to win concessions: when organizers turned down his demands, he had refused to play in tournaments, even withdrawn midtournament. With his all-or-nothing threats, he was not taking up a negotiating position. The threat was not a tactic; he meant what he said. Even as an adult player, Fischer was seen—by officials and friends alike—as an adolescent, capable of viewing everything as a zero-sum game. At the Palma Interzonal in 1970, the distinguished British chess official Harry Golombek asked a rhetorical question: "How had the organizers achieved the minor miracle of getting Fischer to play through the entire tournament?" He himself supplied the answer: "By acceding to all Fischer's demands."

Playing "chicken" when you have no intention of swerving may be a way of repeatedly winning the game, but it is a perilous path. For eventually such a contestant will come up against an opponent unaware of his reputation, or who believes his reputation for recklessness is inflated, or who thinks he has been having things his own way for too long and is prepared to tough it out, or who himself takes a similarly cavalier attitude to death. During one of Fischer's tournaments, an official implicitly recognized the danger. "Sure, Bobby's a genius. But what happens if we have three or four geniuses with their own phobias and demands?" Sousse—as we have seen—was an instance of Fischer pushing his demands too far.

In his description of the inebriated "chicken" driver who chucks out the steering wheel, Herman Kahn put the hazards of playing "chicken" another way. "If his opponent is watching, he has won. If his opponent is not watching, he has a problem."

Happily for Fischer, his negotiating partners had been watching every step of his career. Several times he took his match against Spassky to the brink of destruction. He provoked not just the Soviets, but the Icelanders and FIDE to the very limit of their tolerance. Almost each time they caved in.

With his "madness" established and his demands, if not reasonable, then at least, with considerable effort, manageable, Fischer proved at Reykjavik to be a hugely effective player of "chicken" as well as of chess. A condition for success was that the threat should be extreme—and for the Icelanders, Fischer's threat to walk out was precisely that.

15

A LOVE-HATE
RELATIONSHIP

What have you found in Iceland? What have we found?
More copy....

—W. H. AUDEN AND LOUIS MACNEICE,

LETTERS FROM ICELAND

Fischer could have faced tougher "chicken" opposition if the match had been held in a major city, Belgrade, Amsterdam, Paris, Moscow, New York. Another chess federation might not have felt obliged to concede ground.

During the contest, practically the entire Icelandic population had to be mobilized—the police, the hoteliers, the restaurateurs, home owners with a room to spare, technicians, the print media. The Icelandic papers gave up most of their front pages to the chess match (splitting broadly along ideological lines: of the dailies, the conservative favored Fischer, the center and left of center tried for balance, and the radical left backed Spassky). Conversation among the Icelandic public was dominated by chess. On park benches, in cafés, locals and tourists could be seen bent over their pocket sets. The shop windows displayed posters of the two contestants. There were decorations around town in the shape of chess pieces. On sale were memorabilia of all kinds, including postcards containing the final position of each game.

At one time or another in that July and August, more than 15 percent of the world's grandmasters came to Reykjavik. As well as the three grandmasters among the Soviet and U.S. teams and the German arbiter, Schmid, eight other grandmasters were present, reporting, or simply watching the match—Olafsson, Najdorf, Larsen, Byrne, Evans, Gligoric, Dragoljub Janosevic, and Lubomir Kavalek.

For this island on the edge of Europe, here was a golden moment: pride, their chess tradition, an invasion by chess tourists and the world press, the sound of cash registers tinkling nonstop—all came together in a national event never seen before.

But the scale of the operation and the effort involved also demonstrated clearly a fundamental weakness in the Icelanders' negotiating position. Goodwill, patriotism, love of chess, hard work, hospitality, and decency were not sufficient. With the whole island involved, Iceland could not risk Fischer's departure and the premature ending of this most intensely important of affairs.

⁂

Part of the pressure was that with the match, Iceland was international news, although foreign journalists' interests were strictly parochial. They acted like a small-town tour party jotting down pleasing facts and anecdotes for their readers' delectation: the place, the people, even the pets. There was a fascination with Iceland's canine population; in the countryside, if a dog barked at a stranger, the owner would be considered guilty of bad manners. In Reykjavik, dogs had been forbidden since 1924, and a campaign was now under way to have the relevant legislation revoked. The Association of Dog Friends threatened to take their case to the European Court of Human Rights at Strasbourg.

Happily for members of the press, Icelanders were too good-natured to take offense as the visitors focused on what were, to them, the quaint and the bizarre. Yes, many Icelandic homes have an "elves rock": elves are said to live underneath, and woe betide the person who moves the rock—he or she will be afflicted with boils. Yes, there are hardly any trees in Iceland, no reptiles, and in July golfers tee off at midnight. Yes, it really is true that in the phone book subscribers are listed by first names only and the cabbies do not accept tips. Yes, because of the small, tightly knit society, intermarriage is not as problematic as in more populous countries and genealogical records allow people to track their ancestors back a thousand years. (Hence, today, Icelanders are the focus of research into DNA.) Yes, Iceland boasts the oldest parliament in the world, the Althing. What is more, the country has a near 100 percent literacy rate, there is almost zero crime, and according to international polls, Icelanders are the people most likely to sacrifice their lives for others.

Back in the United States, Richard Milhous Nixon was embroiled in ending the Vietnam War and preoccupied with his dramatic breakthroughs to China and the Soviet Union; the leader of the free world was simultaneously preparing to run for a second term in the November presidential poll. A comparison with the president of Iceland was the cause of some merriment in the U.S. press. Dr. Kristjan Eldjarn held this largely ceremonial post in part because nobody else could be persuaded to take it off him. It paid only $12,000. Eldjarn was an archaeologist whose principal hobby was traversing the country hunting for birds' nests—he was an eiderdown plucker.

There was particular incredulity at the heroic capacity of Icelandic men to consume alcohol. Spirits were the liquor of choice, since the purchase and sale of beer was banned. Correspondents reported how, over the weekends, respectable citizens could be seen staggering out of bars in the middle of the night, near insensible from drink.

In the U.S. papers, there was some disparaging comment from the big-city writers about the tranquillity of Icelandic life, which seemed to be conducted at the leisurely pace of grandmaster chess. "Not much happens around here most of the time," began a dispatch from Joe Alex Morris Jr. for *The Los Angeles Times,* though he says things perked up in July with the arrival of a Scandinavian dentists convention. Amazement was expressed at the television station's closing as usual for the whole of July despite the fact that Iceland was hosting an event generating headlines worldwide. "The nightclubs never close," wrote Joe Alex Morris, before adding his sting: "There are none to close up."

How did the locals view this invasion? On the whole, with remarkable good grace. They were even accommodating, slowly, to Fischer. Before arriving in Reykjavik, Fischer had vowed, "I'm going to teach these Icelandic creeps a lesson." And when he failed to appear for game two, Icelanders returned the compliment. A voice from the auditorium shouted, "Send him back to the United States!" The Icelandic press were uniformly hostile: one paper called his action "the chess scandal of the century"; another printed a cartoon showing Fischer's hotel room and a DO NOT DISTURB notice, under the caption "Come Out and Fight, Bobby Fischer, Or Are You a Coward?" Fischer was labeled "the most hated man in Iceland."

Ordinary Icelanders had been baffled and hurt by his behavior. The struggle for survival on this barren island has bred into its citizens a high sense of responsibility for one another. The Reverend Pitur Mannusson called on his congregation to turn the other cheek: "I urge those who have been offended . . . to hold their heads high if they meet [Fischer] on the street. That is what I am going to do if I meet this sharp-tongued genius." Fischer's incessant demands became the butt of local humor. The joke doing the Reykjavik rounds was that Fischer had demanded the setting of the sun three hours earlier.

Meanwhile, Spassky was quietly winning admirers. Unfailingly courteous and diplomatic, he would chat with those who sought his autograph, and was shown in newspaper photographs enjoying the Icelandic wilderness on rest days. Soon after his arrival, the champion tried his hand at catching fish. Spassky loved the serenity and seemed not to mind how many (or how few) salmon he hooked.

Everywhere Spassky went, he was greeted warmly. When he went to a sports shop to buy sneakers, the shopkeeper refused to take his cash. When he went to the cinema, they let him in free. The champion could have been forgiven for believing he had arrived in a socialist utopia.

Ever popular Spassky. MORGUNBLADID/OLFAR MAGNUSSON

He made friends with several Icelanders, such as Sigfus Sigfusson, the vice president of the Hekla car dealership. Each night Spassky would take a stroll around the Saga, and each night he would walk past Sigfusson's house on the seafront, where a British Leyland Range Rover stood in the drive.

One evening, Sigfusson spotted the world chess champion admiring the car. He went out to greet him; the two started chatting and hit it off. A dealer to his fingertips, Sigfusson offered him a car for the duration of the match. From that moment on, Spassky was often photographed driving in his Range Rover to and from the match. "It was free advertising."

In the small, close-knit community of Reykjavik, news that Spassky was a gentleman quickly became common knowledge. But as the match settled in, the number of Fischer's fans also began to grow. Once the challenger got to work and ceased insulting Iceland, Icelanders began to reconcile themselves to his idiosyncratic ways. In sport, the bad boy has always exerted a powerful allure, especially when boorish behavior is accompanied by skill and glory.

He could not have had a more totally appreciative audience for

Now they love Fischer, too. (On the left) his Icelandic bodyguard, "Saemi-rock" Palsson. MORGUNBLADID/OLFAR MAGNUSSON

those skills. The local chess club, the Glaesibaer, bustled between match games; foreigners were allowed to join in, and masters, including David Levy, invited to give simultaneous displays.

> The Icelanders loved chess, and you couldn't move an inch without seeing some symbol of the world championship match. I remember, while I was there I was asked to give a simultaneous display against some schoolchildren. Well, there were probably 100 people in the country at the time who were stronger than me, but they roped in anybody they could because there were so many chess fans from the Icelandic population; everybody wanted to take part in something.

With the match now rescued, chess fans could look forward to a titanic struggle at the board.

16

SMASHED

I would not care to be the man who allows the championship to go to another nation. It would be a serious matter in many ways. . . .

— BORIS SPASSKY, QUOTED IN
THE WASHINGTON POST, 2 JULY 1972

The first phase of the match had ended with a fearful outcome for the champion. In Karpov's judgment, Spassky's confidence had been smashed.

Game four was played out in the main auditorium, now a camera-free zone. Thorarinsson hinted, tantalizingly, that the camera saga might soon be resolved since there was "one solution [Fischer] will accept"—however, he gave no details. The game itself was a desperately tense encounter. In a display of admirable, even bold, self-assurance, Spassky opted for the Sicilian Defense, a counterpunching opening seen routinely on the grandmaster circuit, but one he himself rarely played; Fischer knew it better than anyone on earth because he had relied on it countless times with the black pieces. Now Spassky was deploying Fischer's trustiest tool against its master: a bravura psychological stroke.

The opening, a specialty of the seventeenth-century Sicilian named Gioacchino Greco, is mentioned in the 1925 Soviet movie

Chess Fever, which actually featured the real-life world champion José Capablanca. A marriage is on the rocks because of the husband's obsession with chess. Eventually the couple do find happiness, through the wife coming to recognize the charms of the game. Her last line, just before the closing kiss, is, "Darling . . . let's try the Sicilian Defense."

On move sixteen, Fischer unwisely accepted the sacrifice of a pawn—after which Spassky's two bishops grandly commandeered the board, gaining between them a sweeping control of the long diagonals. Had the champion in the complex middle game found room for an apparently wasteful rook move, he could have forced white (Fischer) to advance a pawn. This pawn would subsequently have blocked the maneuver by which Fischer escaped. In the end, Fischer was lucky to crawl out with a draw. Later, the experts all concurred that Spassky had chosen the wrong order of moves and thrown victory away. Spassky and his coaches had plotted the development of the game right up to move nineteen. However, Fischer's responses were so quick that as the game wore on, Spassky was increasingly tormented by the idea that there had been a leak and that his rehearsed line had somehow been conveyed to the American. Believing in any case that he had found a stronger continuation, at the nineteenth move he deviated from his team's homework.

Off the board, even though several of Fischer's grievances had been resolved, the American camp was still unsatisfied. But their next attack, launched before the following game, was a public relations disaster. Fred Cramer issued a list of fourteen fresh demands on Fischer's behalf, a list that mysteriously found its way to the press. The outrageous nature of some of the items made Cramer look foolish and Fischer seem more than ever the prima donna. He, Fischer, wanted: a different car (something superior to the two-year-old Mercedes he had been allocated), exclusive use of the hotel swimming pool, smaller squares on the board, more pocket money ($10 a day did not suffice), another hotel room, and a wider choice of magazines in his hotel. Since several of the points mentioned concerned the Loftleidir, the manager issued a sharp statement: "Mr. Fischer is a treasured guest, but he does not own the hotel." Cramer was furious that the debate went public—"I have been stabbed in the back," he moaned.

🁢🁢🁢

Game five took place on Thursday, 20 July.

Pawn to queen four, knight to king's bishop three, pawn to queen's bishop four, pawn to king three, knight to queen's bishop three, bishop to knight five—the Nimzo-Indian, an opening in which black develops his pieces quickly and often exchanges bishop for knight. It frequently results in highly unbalanced positions. Spassky proceeded slowly—taking an hour and three-quarters for the first twenty moves, leaving him barely two minutes a move for the rest of the session. On move eleven, Fischer found an ingenious and unorthodox knight maneuver that most players would have rejected without a second glance, for on its new square the knight can be captured, leading to the kind of unsightly, disjointed pawn configuration beginners are warned to avoid. Pawns tend to be at their most robust, most difficult to pick off, and most useful as a defensive shield, when they are adjacent and can reinforce one another. In the Napoleonic wars, the British infantry usually fought in line abreast, the French in deep columns; in pawn terms, the British strategy is far superior. But Fischer had seen deep into the position and suddenly went on the offensive, his "weak pawns" transmogrifying into a potent force.

Although the challenger now had the better of the position, the widespread expectation was that to convert it into victory, to capitalize on his small advantage, he had a long slog ahead, two dozen more moves, a few hours' more concentration. And even if he played with great precision, the outcome was by no means a foregone conclusion.

In the event, no such chess toil was required. On move twenty-six, Fischer attacked Spassky's queen with his knight. The Russian had several safe and honorable retreats. He chose none of them. Instead, disastrously, he withdrew his queen a single square. It was a catastrophic error. Fischer whipped off a pawn with his bishop—and the game was simultaneously over. Spassky recognized immediately that Fischer's bishop was immune from capture, thanks to a simple trap.

He had committed the sort of gross mistake all chess players, duffers and masters alike, have experienced at least once in their careers; realization dawns and the heart sinks at the very moment the fingers relinquish the moved piece. Chess is the most unforgiving of sports; there is no comeback, no second chance, from such a careless gaffe.

Icelanders are not an expressive people; equanimity is a national trait in which they take pride. But now the crowd erupted, breaking into a rhythmic chant: "Bobby! Bobby!" They stamped their feet and clapped their hands. In the canteen, the predominantly north European audience had a Greek moment, hurling plates and glasses into the air. With the match level at 2.5 points each, suddenly the talk was of the pressure on Spassky. Fischer left the auditorium looking smug. The American camp began to brief the media: The Russian was on the edge of a breakdown. He was clinging by his fingertips to sanity. By now, Viktor Ivonin had returned to Moscow and was present at a review of the match in the office of the sports minister, Sergei Pavlov. Present were three former world champions, Petrosian, Smyslov, and Tal, and at least four other first-rate grandmasters, Keres, Korchnoi, Semion Furman, and Leonid Stein. "Why on earth did Spassky permit the Nimzo-Indian in game five?" Petrosian wanted to know. The champion was hopeless in Nimzo-Indian-type positions, both as white and black. Their meeting, they understood, was futile. There was little they could do to assist Spassky several thousand miles away and at this late stage. Anyway, they could not tell him what to do. But the apparatchiks wanted to be kept abreast of the opinions of the experts—as a prime minister would want expert military opinion on the progress of a distant campaign.

Meanwhile in Reykjavik, daily discussions about the cameras continued among the ICF, Fred Cramer, and the television executives. The Icelanders' budget had assumed major profits from television. Given the sums involved, the organizers and TV producers wanted and needed to believe that Fischer could still be brought round. But in an effort to circumvent Fischer's antipathy to Fox, the American network ABC was brought in.

The network sent a thirty-six-year-old, Chet Forte, to salvage a deal, even though he was supposed to be overseeing their coverage of the Munich Olympics in September. He was a celebrated sportsman in his own right: only five feet seven, he had nonetheless been a basketball star for Columbia University.

In Fischer's hotel room, the challenger told Forte, "I definitely want it filmed, but I cannot have it filmed when it bothers me." Chet Forte was emollient. Later he told the press, "Bobby is immature about a lot of facts of life . . . but once you sit down with him, you can change your opinion of him." On Saturday night, 22 July, they spent over two hours together in the auditorium with Forte patiently explaining how they would ensure the cameras were noiseless and invisible.

The stand-off lasted two weeks. At one point Fischer demanded Fox's expulsion from Iceland (he remained). Fox himself responded furiously to rumors that he had been sidelined, pointing out (rightly) that he still owned the exclusive rights. "I am not out of it," he said. Thorarinsson was sympathetic to Fox's plight. "This is not a question of money. There are principles involved. We are fed up with Fischer making impossible demands. This farce cannot continue." Another ABC executive, Lorne Hassan, became involved. After more talks with Fischer's lawyers, Hassan believed permission had been granted to place one camera discreetly on the main floor of the exhibition hall, right at the back, and two more at the side.

The very first move of game six on Sunday, 23 July, stunned the chess world: Fischer advanced his queen's bishop's pawn two squares. Known as the "English" (historically, its first recorded use was in 1843, when it was adopted by an Englishman, Howard Staunton), it ran counter to Fischer's direct style and formed no part of his supposedly narrow opening repertoire: he had used it only twice before. That confident remark of Spassky's about Fischer, "He plays one kind of opening, and he [will] not be able to find another," had returned to haunt him. The scale of such a surprise is difficult to exaggerate. It was as if a normally right-handed boxer suddenly switched to southpaw, leading with his right hand and not his left, as his opponent expected.

Krogius insists he had labored on detailed contingency plans in case Fischer deviated from the opening habits of a lifetime. Fischer had played only a few professional games with the white pieces in which he had not opened with e4, the two-square push of the king's pawn. "Spassky did not want to spend time studying the material that I had prepared. When, in particular, Spassky was asked what he would like to get ready in reply to 1. c4 or 1. d4, he told me: 'Don't spend time on this nonsense—Fischer would never play that.' "

The game itself was majestic, by far the best to date. Harry Golombek described it as "a masterpiece through and through." Fischer was able to create and then remorselessly exploit vulnerable spots in Spassky's barricade, prizing his defenses apart before battering him with the rooks and queen, and without once leaving his own position at risk. Spassky was virtually in *zugswang*—a term referring to an unusual position where a player would prefer not to have to move, since all possible moves will only make his position worse. Black's resignation position was quite pitiful, the king humiliatingly exposed to the world, like a naked man caught in the shower after the rest of his house has collapsed about him. The packed auditorium rose as one; a bemused, crushed Spassky joined in the applause, clapping for his opponent in recognition of the artistic creation to which he had fallen victim. Fischer had seized the lead. Outside, even the grandmasters were whispering in hushed tones about the possibility that Spassky was a broken man; his chess might never recover. In chess such a thing can happen.

Throughout this period, Spassky's team dutifully reported back to the Sports Ministry that the champion's problems arose from his departing from carefully worked-out plans. In Moscow, the grandmasters were also critical of Spassky's theoretical unreadiness and of his improvisation. Nevertheless, they felt that all was not yet lost. Ivonin, it will be recalled, had thought Spassky was put at a disadvantage by having to sit in an upright chair while Fischer swooped and twisted in his fancy black leather executive model. Game seven saw that disparity corrected. The audience filing early into the hall caught sight of two apparently indistinguishable swivel chairs. At least the championship was proving to be profitable for Herman Miller, the Michigan furnishings manufacturer; the Soviets, through the ICF, had ordered another of his chairs. Cramer protested—though he had no real justification for doing so—and had to be physically restrained by the exhibition hall staff from removing the imported item.

This was not the only change. Fischer had been at work again, asserting control, dictating the playing conditions. Now the table and the board were altered. Fischer had objected to the dimensions of the table—too wide; this made reaching for the pieces awkward. As for the lovingly prepared marble board, there was in-

ICELANDIC CHESS FEDERATION

sufficient contrast between the light and dark squares. So a simple wooden board was put in its place, as in the back room in game three.

Swiveling seemed to suit Spassky. The seventh game began promisingly, with the champion taking an early initiative. Fischer had steered the opening down a sharp line of the Najdorf variation of the Sicilian Defense. In this line, the black queen captures a white pawn (the "poisoned pawn") deep in enemy territory—"poisoned" because of the risks associated with the foray. Black has to extricate his queen before it is surrounded and captured.

Fischer, however, successfully soaked up the pressure, retaining his extra pawn. Spassky, now rocking gently to and fro in his chair, ended up clinging to an embattled draw after rescuing the game with a saving move just before the adjournment. It had taken him forty-five minutes to work out his response. (According to the Western press, help with overnight analysis had even come from a mysterious hot line to two former champions, who were watching developments thousands of miles away: Mikhail Tal in Latvia and Tigran Petrosian in Armenia.) Lovers of chess curiosities noted that Fischer's king's rook had remained on its home square throughout.

For Spassky, the draw proved only a temporary respite. Before the next encounter, game eight, Fischer had declared that he was still unhappy with the shading of the squares—worse than the marble board, he thought. But when, with only an hour to go before the game, Spassky was told about this, he refused to have it changed back. The rule was that any alteration in the equipment had to be sanctioned by both sides.

The Soviet's newfound resolution did not sharpen his concentration. In game eight, he made another blunder. It occurred early, on move fifteen, when Spassky overlooked Fischer's none-too-subtle bishop move targeting the champion's rook, which had nowhere to run. The champion thus lost a rook and got only a bishop in return. The repercussions were not as serious as the colossal howler of game five, but as an illustration of so-called chess blindness, this lapse was even starker—for he had missed not a combination of moves, but one simple move.

Normally priding himself on his inscrutability, the champion began to display signs of psychological wear; he clenched his hands between his knees, flickers of worry crossed his face. On move nineteen, he made another terrible mistake, a retreat of the knight, allowing white a neat little combination (Larry Evans called it "witty") that simultaneously gained a pawn and forced the exchange of queens. The ending was never in doubt. After his resignation, Spassky remained sitting for a few minutes, staring at the board, punch-drunk. Grandmaster Gligoric described this as the worst game of his career.

Fischer had been unaware that during this game his movements were being captured on film. Believing ABC had finally been granted permission, Lorne Hassan had shot the match from cameras surreptitiously placed far back on the balcony. When Fischer subsequently found this out—from a radio news report—he fell into a rage. He had been deceived. How dare they? He wanted apologies, lots of apologies, apologies all around. He wanted a daily veto power on the use of cameras.

Hollywood film producer Jerry Weintraub and the U.S. promoter of the Beatles, Sid Bernstein, had arrived in Iceland to try, among other things, to buy the TV rights, but Fischer refused to see them. Chester Fox was also reported to be holding out for $250,000. Exasperated, now even ABC threw in the towel. ABC president Roone Arledge sent a telegram announcing the company's withdrawal: "Obviously the cameras must have been unobtrusive since there had not been an objection either during or immediately after the game, and we are sorry that you were unaware of their placement." From this moment, not a single move would be filmed until the final day, when the Yugoslav journalist Dimitri Bjelica would sneak a camera into his bag and secretly shoot some footage.

The sign that greeted spectators on 30 July read SPASSKY VEIKUR (SPASSKY IS ILL). Run down by his opponent's chess and antics, thought the experts. Taimanov, Larsen, Petrosian—and now Spassky. Two thousand spectators were left disappointed; this was a Sunday, when a full house was always guaranteed. Spassky had produced a note from the physician. Cramer gloated: "We expected Spassky to adjourn a week ago. That's what the Russians normally do when their man is below par and is losing rapidly." In fact, in Moscow after game six, a meeting of grandmasters, strongly critical of the champion's performance, had recommended that Spassky should play one more game and then take a three-day break.

When the champion returned in full health two days later, he played out an uneventful draw in which the heavy artillery was quickly exchanged, leaving an inert rook ending. Like apathetic guards at a tranquil border crossing, four pawns apiece faced one another in a tedious standoff. The players called it a day, shaking hands shortly after eight P.M.

In game ten, on 3 August, for the first time in the match, Spassky allowed Fischer (white) to open with his beloved Ruy Lopez. No individual in the world knew it better than Fischer or had deployed it to such lethal effect. The key move was the twenty-sixth, bishop to g3, in which the challenger nonchalantly gave up a pawn. Suddenly Fischer's inactive troops sprang to attention. Each major piece was brought into the action with exquisite timing, arriving neither too early nor too late. Bent Larsen, the second-highest-rated player in the West, was electrified by the game's unfolding, with its pure, relentless logic: "I bow to Bobby's brilliant combination." The ending, with white ahead on material, was a display of technical mastery as Fischer coldly and clinically finished off his opponent.

Among Spassky's seconds in Reykjavik and the despondent official onlookers in Moscow there was concern over the champion's psychological state and talk of possible "outside influences" affecting his play.

On 31 July, the deputy chairman of the Russian Federation Sports Committee, Stanislav Melen'tiev, was sent to Reykjavik for ten days. Melen'tiev was on friendly terms with the champion. His instructions were to watch Spassky and his relations with the team. But the committee's vacillation and sense of impotence is clear in the contradictory advice Melen'tiev received just before he left. On the one hand, he was to inform Spassky (yet again) that from this moment on there was to be no "charity"—no more concessions—to Fischer's whims, and he was to remind the

A low point for the champion. ICELANDIC CHESS FEDERATION

Russian to take a firm stand. The match "was not just a personal matter; he [Spassky] bore a duty to society." On the other hand, Melen'tiev was not to force Spassky to act against his will or intimidate him by quoting "a higher authority as saying he should do this or that."

The score was Fischer 6.5, Spassky 3.5. Spassky was being steamrollered. In that context, game eleven represented the most challenging in the champion's professional life: a challenge to which he rose with great courage. Once again, Fischer played the poisoned pawn variation of the Najdorf, gobbling up white's sacrificial offering. He had brazenly captured the pawn in the same position against many other players and had always escaped unscathed. The great eighteenth-century player (and composer) François Philidor described pawns, the foot soldiers of the chessboard, as "the souls of the game," and Fischer certainly never underestimated their worth.

However, Spassky's team had had over a week to search for ways to enrich the venom. The toxicity of the swallowed pawn was exposed on move fourteen, when Spassky made a highly counter-intuitive retreat of his knight to its original position. He insists he conjured up this move at the table. Byrne and Nei describe it as "a diabolical withdrawal" and "the most interesting move in Reykjavik." Fischer soon found his queen short of squares as the hunt closed in; eleven moves later, she was finally trapped. There were whisperings and murmurings through the audience, prompting Schmid to spring nervously from his chair and to press down furiously on the "silence" button. The game was now effectively over, though Fischer limped on for a few more moves. When he eventually conceded, cheers and shouts of "Boris!" resounded through the hall. The champion visibly relaxed. "The rest of the match will be more interesting for me," he said.

Fischer rarely lost, and the historical evidence was that when he did lose, he was psychologically knocked off balance. What impact would defeat have on him this time? Around the world there was excited talk of "turning points," of the match being "at a crossroads." In *Izvestia*, grandmaster David Bronstein wrote, "The world champion has at long last retrieved the key to offensive play and will now probably be able fully to display his many gifts."

In the event, game twelve was a quiet game—plain-speaking grandmasters called it "tedious": manifestly drawn a good twenty moves or so before the result was sealed with a handshake, it was prolonged apparently through pure obstinacy. The only amusement to be had was watching the beads of sweat break out on the brows of the two contestants. For once it was a warm day, but Fischer had insisted the air-conditioning system be switched off because of its gentle hum. Throughout the game, he made constant complaints to the arbiter about disturbances in the audience. This time, he had unmistakably good grounds. Some local lads had managed to sneak into a basement room and were screaming into the ventilator pipes that led directly to the hall.

Later, Schmid received a Fischer missive, insisting that the first seven rows in the hall be cleared: "The spectators are so close, and so noisy, and the acoustics are so poor, that I can hear bits of conversation, as well as coughing, laughing, and so on. This is not suitable for a world championship match, and I demand that you and the organizers take immediate action to ensure full and complete correction of these disgraceful conditions, and furnish me a full report of what is to be done." "It was just a normal letter by Bobby's standards," Schmid said, trying to ignore it. However, for Fischer and thus for the organizers, noise was an irritant that would not go away.

Complaining seems to have been cathartic for Fischer. Game thirteen certainly suggests so. Just to replay the seventy-four moves of this nine-hour marathon is to sense the tension. For much of the time, the position was mind-bogglingly complex, and it was unclear who was ahead. C. H. O'D. Alexander described it as "a struggle of heroic proportions." Fischer gave up a piece but retained and then activated a phalanx of pawns on the wing; they marched, slowly, inexorably, and menacingly, up the board. Several times, under intense pressure, Spassky found just the right saving maneuver. But then on move sixty-nine, exhausted, he slipped up, making the wrong check with his rook; the Soviet press called it "the fatal check." After that, he could not stop one of Fischer's pawns from queening. "Bobby poured more into the endgame than he ever did in his life," said Lombardy. When the victorious Fischer left the stage, Schmid—disregarding U.S. allegations of bias—sat with a demoralized Spassky and rehearsed the latter stages of the game. His mistake and his fatigue apart, Spassky could have taken comfort from his part in such a tour de force. David Bronstein went through the moves countless times and wrote of the game's delightful intricacy, "It's like an enigma titillating my imagination."

Larisa Spasskaia, together with the wives of the other Soviet team members, had now arrived in Iceland. "I hope I can make him relax and think," she said. Following his titanic and ultimately futile exertion, Spassky needed time to recuperate. On the morning of the fourteenth game, a second postponement was announced. Ulvar Thordarson, a keen chess player and eye specialist who had been asked to be the official doctor shortly before the Fischer-Spassky match began, issued a statement confirming that he had "today at this time [10:20 A.M.] examined Boris Spassky, who does not feel well. I have on medical reasons advised him not to play the scheduled game today." The exact nature of the illness was not disclosed at the time. Thordarson now says that it was not serious—a cold, no doubt brought on by stress. When the doctor went to see Spassky in the hotel Saga, the champion was well enough to joke with him. "He challenged me to a game of chess. I said, 'You stick to chess, I'll stick to medicine.' "

Cramer was less than sympathetic. "Poor Spassky. The Russian bug has struck again because I'm sure there is nothing wrong with the Icelandic climate. Perhaps he wants a couple of days to talk with his wife and get his mind off chess." Then Cramer approached Thordarson, demanding to see the medical report and receiving instead a stern rebuke. "Before I threw him out, I explained the ethical code between a doctor and a patient." Thordarson handed the report over to Schmid, forbidding the arbiter from making it public. Cramer next tried it on with Schmid, too, earning him a second scolding. "Spassky does not feel well. That is enough," the German grandmaster said. The widespread perception in the Western media was that Spassky, behind in points and mentally drained, would now capitulate without much of a fight.

17

MIDDLE

GAME

Now I have nothing but my wife. — CHESTER FOX

After the trauma of the first phase of the match, the organizers and contestants settled into a familiar routine. The shock of Fischer's approach had worn off. Like inhabitants of an occupied town, they accommodated to a new way of life. There was the certainty of a complaint or more each day by letter, sometimes signed by Fischer, sometimes by Cramer; there were threats, tantrums, ultimatums. But there was also a built-in momentum arising out of a comforting regularity—the game, the day(s) off, the familiarity of the proceedings. As under occupation, the citizens could never let down their guard: there was always the danger that a Fischer complaint would escalate out of control. Some of the protests, however, began to lose their edge; indeed, tension levels among the organizers peaked when no objections were lodged. What was Fred Cramer planning now?

This self-made millionaire from Milwaukee and former president of the U.S. Chess Federation was a tiny man with a giant ego who had made his fortune in the lighting industry. Brad Darrach described him as five feet five "with a little help from his shoemaker" and added that, depending on his mood, he "looked like any of the seven Disney dwarfs." When Cramer was encircled by the press, his lack of height rendered him invisible and all the journalists on the edge of the group could make out was a squeaky voice somewhere in the void.

Cramer was then in his late fifties and held the official title of vice president of FIDE, responsible for Zone 5 (the United States). He became Fischer's unofficial spokesperson after Edmondson was summarily fired. Two men more different than Edmondson and Cramer would be hard to imagine. U.S. Air Force colonel Edmondson had a dignified military bearing and a calming influence. Former captain Cramer was excitable and self-important. However, he was highly regarded for his work as president of the USCF—bringing in the Elo system, named after its inventor, professor of mathematics Arpad Elo, which rated the strength of chess players. Cramer also left the USCF a substantial legacy.

Cramer regarded himself as a man of many key roles: gatekeeper to the American genius, main organizer, strategist, and spokesman—someone equivalent to the U.S. president's chief of staff, barring the way to the Oval Office. In reality, he was little more than chief gofer, in charge of a coterie of lesser gofers, all tensely awaiting Fischer's barked orders and sweating in case they failed to meet their fickle master's whims at any hour of day or night. He once even admitted as much: "I am authorized only to complain." Complain he did. Barely a day passed without a volley of his discourteous notes. He would also complain in person to officials—sometimes rather conspiratorially, by whispering to them in a public place. "Ear-shattering whispers from six inches," according to the British *Guardian* newspaper.

He was in the habit of holding impromptu press conferences in the antechamber to the main playing hall or in the lobby of the Loftleidir hotel, oblivious to how comical or portentous the journalists found them. He reveled in the attention and would dramatize the latest developments using an idiosyncratic vocabulary consisting predominantly of warring metaphors such as "The

Russians are supporting their frontline troops with a paper barrage." Not being blessed with the spokesman's qualities of wit, tact and diplomacy, he was a journalist's godsend, always to be relied on for a quote. In public relations terms, he was twenty years ahead of his time, defending Fischer's behavior by launching verbal counterthrusts rather than by apologizing. The more outlandish Fischer's conduct, the more vociferous Cramer's defense. The Russians were always talking "nonsense," "garbage." The officials were "stupid" or "incompetent" or "biased."

Reporters aside, he was not popular in Reykjavik. Spassky accused him of acting as though Fischer were the champion and "I was nothing." The officials disliked him, too. Today, Schmid dismisses him with a laugh as "Bobby's servant," simply carrying out his wishes in a way Edmondson might not. He found fault so often, says Schmid, "that I was well trained." Following his early attempt to have Schmid removed as chief arbiter, Cramer had aired doubts about the German grandmaster's impartiality when he played bridge with the champion on a day off and when on a separate occasion he was observed dining with Ivo Nei. Schmid dismissed the accusations robustly: "Whenever I see Mr. Cramer, he tries to hide behind a big man."

The big man was the key to Cramer's frenetic activities. In Don Schultz's phrase, "He was a 100 percent 'yes-man' for Bobby: Cramer did not want to be fired, like his predecessor, Edmondson. So he did literally everything Fischer wanted. Whatever Fischer would say, he would respond, 'Yes, sir. I agree with that, let's do it.'" It is easy at this distance to mock Cramer's submissiveness to Fischer's every wish. But he was far from alone: most of those serving Fischer accepted that there was a line not to be crossed if his wrath was to be avoided.

Cramer's press conferences were his—often desperate— means of proving to Fischer that he was faithfully executing orders. Schultz believes it was not the most effective strategy. "A better way would have been to go to the authorities behind the scenes. Instead, Bobby would say something and there would be a press release." Frank Skoff, who became president of the U.S. Chess Federation in August 1972 and was one of Fischer's aides in Reykjavik, is more generous: "Fred would have been a good guy if he'd just tempered himself a bit, but he was one of these people who bubble over, and when he gets going he shoots in all directions."

Fischer's bodyguard in Iceland, and one of the few to achieve some sort of rapport with the challenger, Saemundur—"Saemi-rock"—Palsson recalls how if Fischer needed to be woken up for a game, Cramer would "knock on the door and then say to me, 'You stay there.' Then he would run off."

The close relationship that developed between Fischer and Saemundur Palsson, between the chess megastar and an Icelandic policeman, is one of the curiosities of the match.

In Iceland, the thirty-five-year-old Palsson was as much a celebrity as Fischer. An avuncular, regular-guy, he had won the gold medal in the Icelandic Judo Championship (middleweight), had taken first place in a Reykjavik rock-dancing tournament, and was the ex-goalkeeper for the national handball team. He had one other fateful attribute that put him on guard outside Fischer's house the evening the contender finally arrived: His superiors knew he spoke some English, enough to communicate with the challenger.

On that night, at around midnight, Fischer poked his head out of the window to check whether the road was clear. When he saw that it was, he went out, asked Palsson, who was sitting in his police car, for directions to the city center, declined a lift, and loped off into the night. Palsson radioed his headquarters for instructions. "Don't let him out of your sight," he was ordered.

The chess player was now heading due west—away from the city. They pulled up alongside him. "Good evening, Mr. Fischer," Palsson said. "How about coming with us? If you like, we can show you around and escape this jungle of much concrete." The American agreed to an excursion. The night was chilly; Fischer had ventured out without a sweater. After picking up some warmer clothing, they took off for the mountains. Palsson contacted headquarters again, naturally briefing them in Icelandic. Sharply, Fischer demanded to know what they were talking about. Palsson was suitably mollifying.

In the country, they found a flock of sheep and chased them "like children." It was the beginning of a firm friendship—some say Palsson was the only real friend Fischer ever had. "I need a tailor," Fischer said that night. "Do you know where I can find one?" Palsson knew everybody in town—he promised to introduce Bobby to the finest tailor in Reykjavik, Colin Porter, an Englishman married to an Icelander. "My TV aerial is broken. Do you know anyone who can repair it?" "I'll make sure it's fixed," said Palsson.

For the next two months, Palsson and Fischer were nearly inseparable. Fischer always called him "Sammy." The policeman became the dependable elder brother that Fischer never had. They played tennis, they swam ("I was a little faster than him, but to keep him in a good mood I would lose"). Palsson would take Fischer to his house by the sea, where Bobby would lounge on the sofa while Mrs. Palsson cooked up colossal helpings of Icelandic cuisine. Fischer grew attached to Palsson's son, Asgeir, then seven years old. Bobby could not understand why, when they went out in the middle of the night, Mrs. Palsson would not let her son accompany them.

Palsson even looked after Fischer's finances. He remembers Fischer as being naive to the point of ignorance on issues of money, and especially on the foreign checks he received from various sources in Reykjavik. "He only wanted green [cash]. I said, 'I can prove to you that these checks are real money.' And I took a check for six or seven thousand kronur and we went down to the bank, where I said, 'I need to change this check.' And Bobby signed and got his money. Thank God he didn't throw all those checks in the wastebasket."

Meeting Palsson today, one understands instantly why Fischer found him easy to get along with. The Icelandic police inspector is immensely likable, transparently trustworthy, and unaffected. In Iceland, he is a national icon. "Oh, you must meet 'Saemi-Rock,' people say when talking about Fischer, and their eyes twinkle as they tell you about his exploits and how close he was to the strange American. The tone is affectionate, if a touch mocking.

His reputation for irrepressible amiability was enhanced a few years ago in an episode with which everyone in Reykjavik seems familiar. At a drunken and rowdy party, a brawl had broken out and neighbors called in the police. Palsson duly arrived, and within a few minutes he had deflated the situation and was teaching the partygoers how to dance. "I said, 'Hey, everybody, let's all be in a good mood. Shall we try a few steps?' "

During Fischer's two months in Reykjavik, Palsson's devoted attendance on the challenger was rewarded with shabby treatment from the police, the ICF, and particularly Fischer himself. Paid for a shift of eight hours, sometimes he worked eighteen. For the first fortnight, he had obligations during the day, and then, because of Fischer's unorthodox sleeping habits, he would be on duty half the night as well. Later he was released by the Icelandic police force to be with Fischer full-time—but this still involved long hours. When Palsson complained, the Icelandic Chess Federation promised him some overtime, which he never received. Paul Marshall suggested to Fischer that they recompense Palsson, to which Fischer replied, "Offer Sammy money? He's my friend. He would be offended." "Whether he was very clever or very mean, you never knew," says Palsson. "I would never have asked, but if he had offered, I would not have said no."

Financial rewards might have been lacking, but Palsson had privileged access to the entire drama, even to the games themselves. Fischer wanted Palsson to stay backstage, to bring him orange juice and provisions; as Spassky did not protest, he was there for almost every match. At least once he served Spassky as well, not wanting to leave him out.

Palsson confesses to not being the brightest star in the firmament. But he has an emotional intelligence that allowed him to read Fischer's moods. "You had to play Bobby like a violin. Sometimes it was best not to talk at all." His attachment to Fischer remains touching, though he badly overrated Fischer's attachment to him.

By late July, a diurnal rhythm has taken hold of the match. The games are supposed to begin at five in the afternoon on Tuesdays, Thursdays, and Sundays, but Fischer is always tardy, at times by just a few minutes, at other times by up to half an hour. Palsson is under strict instructions not to rouse him too early from his slumber. It is a short drive from the hotel Loftleidir to the coastal road and then to the Laugardalur, the municipal sports center consisting of an open-air athletic stadium, a swimming pool, and the giant fungus-shaped exhibition hall where the match is taking place.

Fischer's car pulls in at the back entrance. Ignoring the animated, smiling faces of the young autograph hunters, the challenger, head down, strides through the door, along the narrow corridor, and left onto the stage. He barely glances into the auditorium. His clock is already ticking; if he is black, he now catches sight of Spassky's first move. A quick handshake with his opponent, who only half rises, and Fischer slumps down into his chair. For a minute or two he surveys the board. Then, once he makes his move, several more are fired off in quick succession in response to Spassky's.

Both players are well turned out. For game one, Spassky chose a formal suit, but by now he usually opts for smart casual: sports jacket, white shirt and tie, light-colored slacks. Sometimes he sports a cardigan, too. (Moscow and Los Angeles are suffering under heat waves, but in Reykjavik the weather is unusually miserable for this time of year, cold, cloudy, and wet.) The champion's jacket goes on the back of the seat. Fischer's wardrobe of suits spans the rainbow, from blue to an unfortunate maroon, the latter tailored locally. He has gray and black suits, too. A brown cardigan worn below his jacket combats the chill. His shirts also come in a range of garish colors, including canary yellow.

Both players have startling powers of concentration. In each session, which can last up to five hours, they leave their seats only for short periods to stretch their legs. When Spassky rises, he does so carefully and deliberately, eyes still on the board; Fischer bounds up in one movement. Nikolai Krogius identifies two typical Fischer poses at the table: "in one of them he would lean back in his armchair and swivel it slightly (his arms on the armrests), his gaze seeming to bore into the board from afar; in the other, his armchair would be moved as closely as possible to the table and his head, supported by both his hands, would be bent over the board." Occasionally he picks at his nose. He has been seen putting his fingers in his ears. Krogius observes how Fischer covers his eyes with his hands but leaves chinks through which to observe his opponent.

Spassky too has a variety of postures. One is sitting upright, chin in hand, elbow on table; another is head in hands, blocking out extraneous sound and vision. What to do with those fingers? He might drag them through his thick mane of hair, place the tips in his mouth, or cup them on the bridge of his nose. There are times when he stares, not at the game, but at the rear wall— though it is clear that he is still computing permutations. After making his move, he jots it down with, in the words of one reporter, "the air of a man penning a note to a secretary." The inscrutability into which he has long since trained his otherwise expressive features is a tremendous asset. Fischer once described what it was like facing Spassky across the board. He has "the same dead expression whether he's mating or being mated. He can blunder away a piece, and you are never sure whether it's a blunder or a fantastically deep sacrifice." The only giveaway for those fluent in body language is an almost indiscernible compression of the lips in complex positions.

Energy levels must be kept high during such sustained periods of mental effort. During the match, Spassky sips at a glass of orange juice or pours himself a cup of coffee from one of two thermos flasks he brings in. Fischer has ice water, tomato juice, or cola. There is food behind the curtains, backstage, out of sight of the spectators. Fischer's aides bring in supplies especially for their man, which they wrap in tinfoil. It is a smorgasbord of cheese, fresh fruit, cold meat, and herring. Before game fourteen, Cramer announces that they have added an extra foodstuff— hard-boiled eggs. Spassky has sandwiches.

The platform is carpeted green, with an extra rug under the table and chairs. There are a few unassuming potted plants on stage. The hall can hold around 2,500 on its deep purple seats. It varies from half-full to full to capacity. Sundays are busiest. Most of the spectators are male. They have paid the equivalent of $5 to watch—or, for the dedicated, $75 for a season ticket. Some have high-powered binoculars that they train on the two contestants, trying to read clues to their thoughts.

Lothar Schmid is positioned at the back of the stage. He has started the clock; he will take in the sealed move at adjournment, and open the sealed envelope at the beginning of the next session. But his principal task becomes policing the noise in the auditorium, which he does like a teacher in charge of a remedial class.

By now, Schmid has developed several ways of pleading for quiet. He might deliver a short speech before the game: "Do not even whisper," he begs. Once the game is in motion, he will walk to the edge of the stage, placing a finger to his lips. He presses the button that lights up the neon sign, which is in English and Icelandic: SILENCE, PÖGN.

Noise prevention sees the hinges of the doors oiled regularly to keep them from squeaking. Carpenters construct soundproof boxes at the entrances to the hall: the aim is to muffle the sound of clinking crockery from the restaurant. The sale of cellophane-wrapped food or candies is banned, though the Icelandic Chess Federation refuses to ban children, too, as Fischer wants. The place, Fischer charges, is "being turned into a kindergarten."

But the hall is still, by championship standards. The highly chess-educated audience is as well behaved as any chess audience anywhere in the world. Inevitably there are disturbances and mishaps. Fischer complains that a man is snoring; Schmid immediately dispatches the ushers to rouse him. On another occasion, someone drops what sounds like a hefty piece of metal—the sound bounces off the walls, echoing around the auditorium. The audience do not resent Schmid for his admonishments—indeed, his predicament earns him sympathy. "What do [the Americans] expect him to do?" asks one. "Use nerve gas?"

Understandably, many spectators prefer to watch the match not in the hall—where they may be the target of a Fischer glare—but on the television monitors in the cafeteria. There they can sit chatting over the moves, eating hot dogs and pastries, drinking beer. They can also wander downstairs and sample the boisterous atmosphere of the analysis room. Here one of the visiting grandmasters will be explaining the nuances of the position and trying to predict what comes next. Bent Larsen, in town for a short period, is the punter's favorite. Blunt and droll and voluble, his comments are sometimes greeted by applause—the rumble filters through to the auditorium, leaving Schmid at a loss.

At the end of a game, a pack of enthusiasts waits by the side entrance. Fischer ignores them all. He straps on his safety belt, as his driver—normally Palsson, occasionally Lombardy—slowly tunnels an exit through the crowd. Back in the auditorium, Spassky is more leisurely in his departure. A disappointing game may find him staring at the board for some minutes, lost in thought, contemplating how, where, why it went so wrong. Lothar Schmid comes to join him, the consolation of company. The champion puts on his jacket and slowly walks out. The auditorium is emptying now. Schmid collects up the pieces and stores them away.

Look skyward and you can see a man climbing across a platform just beneath the roof of the hall. He is smuggling out the closed-circuit video of the match. Chester Fox is determined to take possession of this, but the person responsible for closed-

The champion alone with his seconds, (left to right:) Ivo Nei, Nikolai Krogius, Efim Geller. CHESTER FOX

circuit TV, Gunnlaugur Josefsson, believes the American producer has no right to it. It is Josefsson who arranges the video's
thrice weekly escape.

* * *

Nonmatch days have also developed a more reliable tempo. The
Icelandic Chess Federation committee gathers almost daily to discuss the latest crisis. The treasurer, Hilmar Viggoson, has the task
of devising ever more ingenious schemes to compensate for the
loss of film revenue. Some suggestions come from the public, after
he placed an advertisement in a newspaper appealing for ideas.
The most successful venture is commemorative gold coins. They
sell out quickly. "We made a fortune from this," says Viggoson.

Preparation for the next game remains the priority for the
two contestants. Between periods of analysis with his seconds,
Spassky relaxes with tennis—when it is not raining or too
windy—or by seeing a movie. (When Larisa arrives, the TASS
correspondent accompanies her to a film that would never reach
the screen in Moscow, about a priapic monk who takes charge of
a nunnery.) During the course of the two months, a number of
close supporters of Fischer's arrive to cheer him on. There is his
early mentor, Jack Collins, his sister, Joan Targ, with her family,
and his friend from Los Angeles, Lina Grumette.

Fischer works alone until late at night to the accompaniment of
rock music; then he swims at the hotel, plays table tennis or tennis, or goes bowling at Keflavik. Archie Waters, a second-rate
chess player, is Fischer's favored table tennis partner. As for tennis, he has a number of opponents to choose from, including
Svetozar Gligoric and Robert Byrne, both of whom are quite a few
years older than Fischer. Byrne says they walked onto the court at
eleven o'clock at night: "He saw that I could only play for twenty
minutes, and for all these twenty minutes we merely warmed up.
Then, noticing that I was already panting, he said: 'Okay, that's the
end of the knock-up. Now we'll start playing.' "

Fischer's favorite leisure activity, however, is bowling. Even this
is a means to a chess end, as Victor Jackovich from the U.S. embassy recalls. The most junior diplomat, Jackovich was assigned
to take Fischer to the bowling alley in the American air base:

ÉG Á NEFNILEGA ENGA SUNDSKÝLU ! ! !

Fischer demands sole use of the pool. "The point is, I have no swimming costume." HALLDOR PETURSSON

Bowling was partly a physical exercise and partly a mental distraction. That's all it was. Bowling as a sport had no interest for him. He would always bowl out of turn. I would bowl, and his second, the Reverend William Lombardy, would bowl, and Fischer would bowl, and I would bowl, and Fischer would stand up. And if I went over and said, "No, it's not your turn, it's the father's turn," Lombardy would signal me to say no, no. And he told me later, 'It makes no difference. It's just throwing a ball at a bunch of pins, it's not real bowling here, it's not a game.' And I remember a person at the base coming up to Fischer and with the best of intentions trying to tell him, "Look, let me show you what you're doing wrong with your hook," or whatever, because his balls were going all over the place. Fischer very curtly, very abruptly, told him, "Look, I throw this heavy ball in order to exercise my arm, in order that I can be in better physical shape, in order that I can sleep better, in order that I can play better chess. That's it." He wasn't impolite about it. I think the American was a bit taken aback because he thought this was his opportunity to show Fischer something, help him out. But Fischer didn't care.

Fred Cramer compiles a timetabled daily duty roster, which he writes on Loftleidir stationery and sends to Frank Skoff, with a copy for Lombardy. They are a reminder to Skoff of his numerous tasks, though these vary from day to day. He must regularly comb the playing hall for cameras. He must chase up the Mercedes-Benz automatic-shift car, as promised by the Icelandic organizers. He must arrange the laundry. He must ensure there is a tennis or table tennis or bowling partner for Fischer, available at all times, and that the facilities are unlocked and ready for Fischer to walk straight in.

```
In general, have each activity so set up that
Bobby can be doing it on thirty minutes notice
or less. Don't leave any blank spots. Don't
leave anything to anybody else, even Sammy. (Of
course, we count on him—and various others—
heavily, but you must, in all cases, be so set
up that Bobby can go, regardless of any other
individual. Always have at least three of four
backup men at each point.)
```

Skoff should always have suitable clothing ready for Bobby's activities. He should try to ensure the facilities are not used "for other persons or other activities." He should always be looking to add to the list of potential playing partners for Bobby. "Bear in mind that people do other things. Some even leave Iceland."

As the sun sinks on a Friday night, the mood lifts in the American camp and among the championship organizers. For twenty-four hours, Fischer is locked away, observing his Sabbath. There is a temporary armistice between Fischer and the organizers. It is all quiet on the Loftleidir front.

In the Fox tragicomedy, it was far from quiet. The central issue now was not whether the cameras would be permitted in—most of the parties concerned had reluctantly abandoned any such hope—but whether Fischer could be made to pay. Chester Fox maintained he had so far spent up to $200,000 on setting up the film coverage and estimated his lost earnings at $1.75 million. He wanted compensation and threatened to sue Fischer "for every cent we can lay our hands on." To cover himself, Fischer asked the Icelandic Chess Federation to deposit $46,875—half the loser's share of the prize fund—in his bank account. The ICF refused.

Legal proceedings continued apace, with Fox going to the U.S. federal court to claim that Fischer had intentionally inflicted upon him "grave financial harm."

On Fischer's behalf, Cramer shrugged off the impending court action: Fox was merely trying to upstage Fischer—as usual. Fox's lawyers obtained an order from a federal judge, Constance Baker Motley, to freeze a portion of Fischer's prize money. "All we really want is to make sure that this historic game is preserved on film for posterity," explained Fox's attorney, Richard Stein. He would rather serve the order on Fischer privately, but if Fischer refused to meet him, he might have no option but to do so publicly, even if that meant walking onto the stage during the game. From this point, four helmeted policemen stood backstage to protect the challenger in case someone tried to thrust the papers on him.

On 27 August, the ICF came to a settlement with Fox. In return for Fox's agreement neither to block the prize money nor to bring a lawsuit in Iceland against Fischer, the ICF gave up its share of any profits he had made from the film rights so far (and still hoped to make in the future). Not for the first time, Fischer was absolved of responsibility for his actions. Once again, the Icelanders had lost out. Eventually Fox would abandon the legal fight; it was only throwing good money after bad.

18

CHESS CONTAGION

You know that creativity and money accompany each other. The question is which is more important: money in order to play chess or chess in order to earn money.

— MIKHAIL BOTVINNIK

To the rest of the chess world, Fischer's conviction that the game's elite could and should command the same respect and rewards as screen idols, boxing stars, golfing celebrities, or Formula One racing drivers was in the realms of fantasy. Up to the 1970s, chess was Western sport's poor cousin, never quite shaking off its character as a strictly cerebral game for passionate amateurs, inevitably bespectacled and boasting bad haircuts, playing in the smoky back rooms of tenebrous, sequestered clubs or on the bare boards of dank church halls.

A decade before Iceland, Fischer complained, "Reshevsky and I are the only ones in America who try to make a living. We don't make much. The other masters have outside jobs. Like Rossolimo, he drives a cab. Evans, he works for the movies. The Russians, they get money from the government. We have to depend on tournament prizes. And they're lousy. Maybe a couple of hundred bucks." Thousands enjoyed the game, but nobody could make a living wage from it. There was little prize money in tournaments, little demand for books and coaches. In 1962, when Donald Schultz, later president of the U.S. Chess Federation, was setting up a tournament in a small town in upstate New York, he thought of inviting the teenage superstar, Bobby Fischer. "I contacted the chess federation office in New York and they put up $500—which doesn't seem much now but was a lot then, and certainly no one else was doing it. And we brought Fischer to our tournament."

For those U.S. players whose life was chess, old age could be tragic. In December 1971, a stalwart of the American chess world, then in his seventh decade, Hans Kmoch, wrote to the mayor of New York, John Lindsay, with a desperate request for financial assistance for himself and his crippled wife. Kmoch had labeled the thirteen-year-old Fischer's match against Donald Byrne "the Game of the Century." He was at the time earning $1,000 a year from his chess, which even in 1970 was barely subsistence level. The letter to Lindsay ends, "We would greatly appreciate it if you could tell us to whom we could apply to get the necessary assistance to keep us alive."

Yet nine months after that plea, chess was featured daily on the front page of the nation's newspaper of record, *The New York Times*. All three major U.S. TV networks dispatched crews to Iceland. To the astonishment of television executives, when Channel 13's afternoon show broadcast the games as they were relayed by a special telegraph hookup from Reykjavik, it was soon drawing over a million viewers, the highest ratings public television had ever achieved. The thirty-five-year-old presenter, Shelby Lyman, a Harvard dropout and former sociology lecturer, provided move-by-move analysis, often performing for five hours at a stretch. A guest would join him, and in between moves they would chat about various aspects of chess. "But the move was the most important thing. Whenever there was a move, a tiny desk bell would ring and I'd announce, 'Okay, we have a move!' A woman would come in and hand it to me, and I'd say, 'You won't believe it. Fischer has done something we didn't even consider!' It was very dramatic."

One reporter did a tour of twenty-one bars during a game, to discover that eighteen of them had their televisions tuned to this program and only three were showing the New York Mets baseball game that drinkers would normally have demanded. When, on one occasion, Channel 13 TV executives chose to show the Democratic presidential convention rather than the chess, they were quickly forced to reverse their decision when hundreds of people rang in to complain, some threatening to burn down the station. So successful were the broadcasts that Lyman began to command huge appearance fees for promotional campaigns. As the match moved into its second half, the multinational computer giant IBM stepped in with a $10,000-a-week grant to fund a nationwide broadcast of the Sunday game.

Some preferred to follow developments in the company of fellow enthusiasts, in clubs and other venues. At the Marshall Club, chess expert Edmar Mednis puzzled over the moves on a large demonstration board. He would be wearing the club tie adorned with blue-and-yellow pieces. You had to arrive early to guarantee a seat. Mednis described being in front of that audience as "an electrifying experience; when Bobby won a game, the place would erupt in cheers."

In London's West End, aficionados gathered at Notre Dame Hall just off Leicester Square. The venue seated 200 to 300 people. Moves would be relayed from Iceland over the teleprinter. There were two large magnetic boards, one showing the actual position, the other available for analysis. In Geneva, diplomats at an international conference on disaster relief followed the action in breaks between negotiations.

BBC editors initially vacillated over whether the match justified its own television slot. Producer Bob Toner recalls, "What sold it as a news story was the cold war. The single U.S. figure pitting himself against the Soviet chess machine." The corporation eventually decided to broadcast a weekly show from its Birmingham studios in the English West Midlands; like its American counterpart, this rapidly gained popularity, pulling in a million viewers. Leonard Barden was the regular chess expert, although the young and articulate international master Bill Hartston often co-commentated: the BBC regarded him as steady in a crisis (the show went out live on a Sunday night).

Around the world, the contest captured headlines. The prime minister of Bangladesh, Sheikh Mujibur Rahman, courted popularity by professing a fascination for chess to local journalists. *The Bangladesh Observer* says he became so absorbed by a game of chess at the National Press Club that he pulled up a chair and began to watch it—there is a photograph to prove it. Egypt's official paper *Al-Ahram* reproduced a photograph of Fischer swimming in the pool at his hotel, the Loftleidir. The Yugoslav grandmaster Svetozar Gligoric reported daily for Radio Belgrade. In Belgrade itself, the games were replicated on a large display screen in Republic Square. During the weekend, a thousand people would be there to watch. In the main Argentinean newspaper, *Clarin,* the match was front-page news for almost two months, until it was superseded by a massacre of political prisoners in a jail in Patagonia. Grandmaster Miguel Najdorf was covering the event for the popular radio show *El Fontana.*

In the Italian daily *La Stampa,* a doctor made a neurological analysis of Fischer's and Spassky's brains. The more conservative Milan-based *Corriere della Sera* carried an exclusive interview with Fischer—after their correspondent had bumped into him at a restaurant. For journalists in Britain, where headline writing had long been turned into an art form, the match provided fertile subject matter. After one Fischer victory, the mass circulation tabloid *Daily Mirror* bellowed, SPASSKY SMASHKI.

⋯

Chess moved out of dilapidated back rooms to become part of consumer and commercial society. Advertisers and marketing managers called on it as a brand image to add allure to their products. To anyone wanting to identify the match as one between two political systems, the gleeful speed with which capitalist America responded to the business possibilities of the game should have been proof enough.

In New York, just up the road from the UN, the Metropolitan Museum put on an exhibition of chess pieces collected from all around the world. Department stores like Macy's placed full-page advertisements in the press for chess courses as well as for chess books. Chess was now in fashion—and, like glamorous models, could be used to sell. An upmarket men's clothing store encouraged custom with a picture of a board and the slogan YOUR MOVE,

GENTLEMEN. The Dime Savings Bank also had a chessboard in its advertisement, this time with the slogan SMART SAVERS MAKE THEIR MOVE TO THE DIME. A sports shop used a picture of chess sets with the headline NOW IT'S AN AMERICAN SPORT!

And it was. With the transformation in the visibility and appeal of chess, there was a sudden thirst for information on the game—articles appeared on other grandmasters, on former world champions, on chess terminology. There was a bonanza in the sale of chess sets; in Britain, shops sold out of traditional wood sets, and plastic sets had to be imported from abroad. Booksellers reported with astonishment that chess books, once the slowest-selling items in their stores, were now leaving their shelves faster than romantic fiction.

Across the United States, during lunch breaks and after work, boards would be set up in public squares. The chess epidemic infected all generations and classes: the old played the young, business suits looked across the board at blue collars. An article appeared about two construction workers who had played each lunch break since the Fischer-Spassky match began. A photo shows them concentrating on the game, still wearing their hard hats. African Americans took up the game in increasing numbers—a lasting legacy of Reykjavik. Kibitzing decamped from the obscure club to the park bench: "Come on, *patzer*, even Fischer would resign in your position."

In bars and saloons, people who barely knew the moves began to place bets on the outcome of the Reykjavik games. The bookmakers Ladbrokes of London established official betting odds, with Fischer as favorite at six to four. In Atlanta, the owner of a basement snack bar, Anita Chess, discovered that misled chess fanatics were swamping her café, the Chessboard. A composer of politically inspired songs, Joe Glazer, found he had caught the mood with his seven-minute paean to Robert Fischer. The lyrics, composed well before Reykjavik, opened presciently enough:

He studied all day
and played all night.
But he wouldn't play a match
unless things were just right.

Inevitably, chess metaphors spilled into other items in the news, most particularly into politics. In *The New York Times,* an opinion piece by Tom Wicker described President Nixon's decision to choose Spiro Agnew as his vice presidential running mate in the forthcoming election as a sort of "king's pawn opening." Why a "king's pawn opening" as opposed to a "queen's" or "queen's bishop's pawn" was unclear and unexplained.

Predictably, diplomatic correspondents called on chess to describe negotiations between Washington and Moscow. One such article satirized the recent superpower summit, imagining it as a chess contest between Bobby Nixon and Boris Brezhnev. Far from shunning publicity, à la Fischer, Nixon courted it. "Nixon has insisted from the start that the match be held in as large a place as possible, that television cameras be turned on and kept on well before and after each game, that either he or his second be interviewed daily, and that all games be scheduled between 8 P.M. and 11 P.M., Los Angeles time. . . ."

In Britain, a broadsheet daily *The Guardian* wrote, "Getting President Nixon and Mr Brezhnev together [in May 1972] was child's play compared with the Fischer-Spassky chess summit." The editorial assumption was that readers on both sides of the Atlantic had followed the chess drama. "Mugs sell mags" is the rule, and the tall, besuited genius made a compelling picture, while his personality and behavior could be relied on for a peg or angle to hook the reader.

⬛⬛⬛

The press attention given to the match was all the more surprising in the light of the competition for space.

Most important, there was Vietnam. As Kissinger shuttled between Washington, Saigon, and Paris in search of a peace agreement, Nixon pledged that there would be no letup in the bombing of North Vietnam without substantial progress in the negotiations, though he continued to withdraw American troops. Meanwhile, jury selection had begun for the trial of Daniel Ellsberg on charges of conspiracy, theft, and espionage of the top-secret *Pentagon Papers,* the seven-thousand-page study of America's involvement with Vietnam.

The conflict in Southeast Asia was not the only fissile issue preoccupying the president: the election was looming. At 2:30 A.M. on 17 June of that year (Iceland's Independence Day), five burglars wearing rubber surgical gloves had been arrested at the Democratic National Headquarters in Washington's Watergate complex. The police found they were carrying electronic eavesdropping equipment, cameras for photographing documents, walkie-talkies, and large sums in consecutively numbered $100 bills. As the match went on, two young journalists, Bob Woodward and Carl Bernstein, were on the trail, their articles slowly forcing their way from the inside to the front pages.

Nixon was already involved in attempts to conceal the White House's role in the break-in and continued to be at the center of the cover-up as summer turned into autumn and his thoughts were occupied with preparations for the Republican convention in late August (he was renominated by 1,347 votes to 1). The Watergate film *All the President's Men* has the radio reporting Fischer's forfeiture of game two as Woodward finds his first message from the secret source "Deep Throat" hidden in his breakfast *New York Times.* With the growing involvement of Congress and the courts and daily fresh evidence from the press, as the match ground on, Nixon became engaged in his own desperate game of chess, making move after move to save his presidential skin.

Chile was the scene of increasing anarchy (fueled, as we know now, by the United States) under the divisive and ultimately doomed government of the democratically elected socialist Salvador Allende.

In Northern Ireland, it was a summer of dreadful riots, paramilitary killings, and bombings. The psychopathic ruler of Uganda, Idi Amin, expelled the country's fifty thousand Asian citizens on 5 August, accusing them of "sabotaging the country"—in fact, the Asian community was at the heart of Uganda's business and commerce, as the country discovered to its cost after the expellees had grudgingly been given refuge in Britain by the Conservative government.

Readers seeking relief could turn to the sporting pages. Billie Jean King beat Evonne Goolagong in the Wimbledon women's final, while Stan Smith defeated Ilie Nastase in the men's. In golf, Lee Trevino won the British Open, and Belgian cyclist Eddie Merckx took the Tour de France for the fourth time. And as the chess match was drawing to a close, attention was shifting to Munich and the Olympics: Soviet hearts would beat faster when tiny Olga Korbut rippled her way to gymnastic gold. Among other American triumphs, Mark Spitz would capture seven swimming gold medals.

Munich would be remembered for the spilling of blood. A few days after the closing ceremony in Reykjavik, the Black September Palestinian terrorist group took eleven members of the Israeli Olympic team hostage and then murdered them.

If amid all these events, Fischer-Spassky found its way on to the front pages, it was not just because of the challenger's personality, the chess itself, or the off-board antics. In the United States there was much more to it than that. The country was undergoing a fit of cultural pessimism, mainly because of Vietnam, but also because of social and racial cleavages at home. Now, in the words of George M. Cohan's bouncy lyrics, here was "a real live nephew of [his] Uncle Sam, the kid with all the candy"—in other words, here was an undisputed, unalloyed world-class player who (once he started to play) appeared to be a kick-ass winner. When Americans bought into chess, they were affirming the American way. Fischer appeared to be a guarantee that can-do America could do it at a time when it was profoundly in need of that reassurance.

19

TO THE
BITTER END

In a contest for the nicest guy in chess, Bobby Fischer would finish out of the money. But he is definitely the best chess player in the world. —ISAAC KASHDAN

The match was following a path familiar from Fischer's blitzkrieg to the final. Spassky appeared to be crushed. And experience told that once down, Fischer's opponents never bounced back. The challenger was the master of the kill. In the face of weakness or injury, while others might ease up, he only raised the pressure.

Would history be a guide to this match?

Fischer opened the fourteenth game, again with the English. The realization must surely have dawned on Spassky that much of his opening preparation—such as it was—had been wasted. But the champion's demeanor had improved. Maybe it was the arrival of Larisa that lifted his spirits, maybe leaving the hotel for its dachalike annex in which they could enjoy family life.

His more positive state of mind became evident in this game. On move fourteen he played a knight retreat (Ne7), turning down the opportunity to simplify the position and exchange knights.

Chess books on the match give Ne7 an exclamation mark, meaning it is strong (a weak move is branded with a question mark). Perhaps taken aback, Fischer gave away a pawn. Six moves later, Spassky blundered disastrously in return, pawn to f6 (double question mark), in what should have been a hard but ultimately won ending.

Now it was down to rook, bishop, knight, and five pawns against rook, bishop, knight, and five pawns. The knights and bishops were soon exchanged, and the game petered out to a draw.

"Oh, no!" ICELANDIC CHESS FEDERATION

"Oh, yes!" ICELANDIC CHESS FEDERATION

The players were no doubt still both fatigued by the exertions of game thirteen. The grandmasters in the audience, while admiring Spassky's doughty character, were unimpressed by the quality of play. Referring to a hangover-inducing Icelandic schnapps, one joked, "It's like they're playing on brennivin."

Fischer's only complaint in the game came after move one, when he objected to the lack of lighting. It was followed up later by a telegram to Euwe from Cramer in which the arbiter and the Icelandic Chess Federation were slated for being both "arrogant and inconsiderate." Fischer's demand to empty the front of the auditorium did not go away. The Icelanders, who had already lost the television revenue, pointed out to Cramer that vacating the first seven rows would halve the downstairs capacity to 475, seriously denting box office returns.

Harry Golombek described game fifteen, on 17 August, as "one of the most thrilling I have ever seen in a world championship match." It was a Sicilian opening, and Fischer was offered the chance of taking it down the poisoned pawn variation, the same line in which he had been so humiliated in game eleven. Would he rise to the challenge, show that he had not been cowed, seek his revenge? In other words, would he bring his queen out to b6? The clock ticked on: in the analysis room they were willing him on. He had had nearly a fortnight to work on improvements and identify where it had gone so wrong before.

The queen stayed on its square. Fischer moved his king's bishop one diagonal, to e7. He had played this several times in his career, but for Spassky it still represented a minor psychological triumph. It seemed to put the Russian in an optimistic frame of mind: he prematurely advanced a pawn on move twenty-five, setting Fischer a simple trap, into which the challenger was never likely to tread. Byrne and Nei call Spassky's idea "a silly stunt." Then the champion confidently picked off one pawn and then another, but his rapacity only left most of the attacking possibilities to Fischer. In the end, after the adjournment, they settled for a draw—with black finding nothing better than to repeat moves with the same checks on the white king. So quickly were the postadjournment moves made that those manning the display board became confused, losing track of the position.

That day, Fischer's complaint to Schmid was couched more personally. Referring again to the noise, Cramer fumed that Schmid must "do something better than piously wave [his] hands from time to time." The Americans reiterated their demand that several more rows of seats be emptied. The riposte from the Icelanders was that the gap between the dais and the first row of spectators was already greater than at any previous chess match.

Game sixteen was played on a Sunday and witnessed by a full house. By move nine, the middle game had already been bypassed with the exchange of queens and they were into an endgame.

For several moves, Spassky maintained triple isolated pawns—three pawns on the same column with no pawn on either side. This is a most unusual chess formation, and to a chess player its strange architectural structure has a visceral ugliness. Eventually, all three of these defenseless pieces were lost, and by move thirty-two the position had become lifeless, devoid of genuinely alternative strategies. It did not end there. Perhaps pure stubbornness kept them going for another thirty futile moves, when ordinarily they would have settled on a draw far earlier. Was Spassky exacting his revenge on Fischer, forcing him to stay put at the board? Did Fischer see offering a draw as a humiliation? Whatever the reason, they carried on until move sixty, in what Larry Evans and Ken Smith in their match book, *Fischer-Spassky Move By Move*, describe as "a marathon of nonsense." The audience became restless. Golombek wrote, "It is a sad confession to make but the last thirty moves . . . bored me to tears." Byrne and Nei are equally dismissive: watching these two geniuses in such an elementary position was like observing Frank Lloyd Wright "playing in a sandbox."

Fischer might not be on the attack over the board, but he showed no compassion to the officials away from it. With his demand to remove the first seven rows ignored, he delivered an ultimatum. He would withdraw from the match unless conditions were improved. "I do not intend to tolerate them further." From the seventeenth game onward, he said, the match would have to be played behind closed doors in a private room until the venue had been altered "completely to my satisfaction." Cramer, naturally, backed him up; the sixteenth game, he said, was played in a hall "as noisy as a ball game in Milwaukee."

Cramer met Thorarinsson over lunch on 22 August, the day of game seventeen. The Icelander agreed to clear three rows of seats from the front; two were added at the back. This increased the distance between the players and audience by seven or eight yards, to a total of twenty yards. "To save the match, we shall remove some rows of seats, although it is with a bleeding heart, because we will lose revenue," said Thorarinsson. The consent of the world champion and his team was not even sought.

But now came a Soviet bombshell. Spassky's second, Efim Geller, issued a statement to the press in which he accused the Americans of using "non-chess means of influence" to weaken the champion. Here it is reproduced as written:

The World Chess Championship Match now taking place in Reykjavik arouses a great interest in all parts of the world including the United States. Mr B.Spassky, the other members of our delegation and I have been receiving many letters from various countries. A great number of the letters is devoted to an unknown in the chess history theme, i.e. a possibility to use non-chess means of influence on one of the participants.

It is said that Mr. R.Fischer's numerous "whims", his claims to the organizers, his constant late arrivals for the games, his demands to play in the closed-door room, ungrounded protests, etc have been deliberately aimed at exercising pressure on the opponent, unbalancing Mr. B.Spassky and making him lose his fighting spirit.

I consider that Mr. R.Fischer's behaviour runs counter to the Amsterdam Agreement which provides for gentleman behaviour of the participants. I believe that the arbiters have had enough facts to demand that Mr. R.Fischer should observe the provisions of the match in this respect. Furthermore, it must be done immediately now that the fight is approaching its decisive stage.

We have received letters saying that some electronic devices and chemical substance which can be in the playing hall are being used to influence Mr. S.Cpassky. The letters mention, in particular, Mr R.Fischer's chair and the influence of the special lighting over the stage installed on the demand of the US side.

All this may seem fantastic, but objective factors in this connection make us think of such seemingly fantastic suppositions.

Why, for instance, does Mr R.Fischer strongly protest against filmshooting even though he suffers financial losses. One of the reasons might be that he is anxious to get rid of the constant objective control over the behaviour and physical state of the participants. The same could be supposed if we take into consideration his repeated demands to conduct the game behind closed doors and to remove the spectotors from the first seven rows.

It is surprising that the Americans can be found in the playing hall when the games are not taking place even at night. Mr. F.Cramer's demand that Mr.R.Fischer should be given "his" particular chair, though both the chairs look identical and are made by the same American firm.

I would also like to note that having known Mr. B.Spassky for many years, it is the first time that I observe such unusual slackening of concentration and display of impulsiveness in his playing which I cannot account for by Mr. R.Fischer's exclusively impressive playing. On the contrary, in some games the Challenger made

```
technical mistakes and in a number of games he
did not grasp the position.
     In connection with the above said our
delegation has handed over the statement to this
effect to the Chief Arbiter and the Organizers
of the Match which contains the urgent request
that the playinghall and the things in it should
be examined with the assistance of competent
experts and that the possibility of the presence
of any outsiders in the place allocated to the
participants should be excluded.
                                    E.Geller
```

On 3 August 1972, the next actor to play James Bond had been announced; henceforth Roger Moore would star as the British secret service agent 007, licensed to kill. Iceland might have been his first assignment. There was a gentle wave of sniggering through the audience when the Soviet allegations were publicized. "We will get 007 to investigate the hall," quipped a member of the Icelandic Chess Federation.

In an explanation of why Reykjavik so ignited the public imagination, the rich stream of chess influence, allusion, and archetype in literature and film must play a part. Democrat against totalitarian, individual against machine, plot and counterplot, the images of chess player as alone and without feeling, insane but brilliant, scheming and utterly devoid of morality—some or all of these shaped (particularly Western) perceptions of the match. No doubt some of the Reykjavik jesters remembered the 1963 James Bond film, *From Russia with Love,* based on the earlier novel. *From Russia with Love* takes the plotting theme straight into the cold war. It reinforces our apprehension that the skills needed to control events on the chessboard are transferable—in this case, to a diabolical Soviet plot against the British secret service and its star agent, 007: Bond, James Bond.

The film opens with the final game of an international grandmaster tournament. Kronsteen, all high forehead, heavy eyelids, and intense, unblinking eyes, is competing against a Canadian called MacAdams.

"Kronsteen" is close in sound to "Bronstein," and the game in the movie is in fact a variation of a brilliant match from Leningrad in 1960 between two Soviet grandmasters, the then world title challenger David Bronstein and Boris Spassky. In the movie, Kronsteen is victorious, having risked defying an order to break off the match and report to the clandestine international criminal organization SPECTRE (Special Executive for Crime Terror Revenge and Extortion), where he is Director of Planning. In real life, Bronstein lost when Spassky made a dazzling rook sacrifice, setting up a spectacular twenty-three-move victory. The other difference is that in the film, two of the pawns have been removed—the speculation is that the director, Terence Young, felt that aesthetically they ruined the shot. Without these pawns, Spassky's combination would have failed; in cinemas worldwide, chess players shook their heads.

In Reykjavik, chess players shook their heads at Geller's statement. But if, when the laughter stopped, audience and officials had read the statement in detail, they would have had an unprecedented glimpse into the tensions within the Soviet camp. Although on the surface the statement was aimed at Fischer, it was also born of a deep frustration with Spassky and what Geller describes as his "impulsiveness," his "slackening of concentration," his not taking advantage of the challenger's "technical mistakes" and failure "to grasp the position." Then there is Geller's view that the fight, now at game seventeen, was approaching its decisive stage. Ivo Nei later wrote that game seventeen was for Spassky practically the last chance to change the course of the match. In Moscow, they were saying, "The train has left the station."

The timing is also curious. The reference in Geller's statement to Fischer's "repeated demands" suggests that the real trigger for the letter was Fischer's latest ultimatum, coupled with the aggrieved feeling that the organizers always surrendered to him.

The chief arbiter said Geller's allegations would have to be examined. "From the American side, we have had fantastic things, so why not from this side also?" Guards were positioned at the hall around the clock to prevent any nocturnal espionage. The American delegation offered a sophisticated explanation for their insistence that each player retain his own chair; Fischer was four inches taller than Spassky, and his chair had been adjusted accordingly. Cramer called the allegations "garbage. What experts do they want to examine the hall? The KGB?" He was nearer the truth than he knew.

As for the seventeenth game itself, once again Fischer unpacked a shock opening: a Pirc Defense (named after Slovenian grandmaster Vasja Pirc)—Fischer had never used it before in tournament play. In the Pirc, which has always been considered mildly eccentric, black concedes the center in the expectation of eventual counterplay. The main talking point, however, was the manner of the end. A player can claim a draw if the same position is repeated three times. On move forty-five, Fischer summoned Lothar Schmid and they conferred for a short period while examining the score sheet. Then Schmid nodded and the clocks were stopped. If Fischer moved his rook to e1, the same position would indeed have occurred three times. Spassky afterward remained in his seat; the draw by repetition appears to have taken him by surprise. He was rook for knight up and was expected to battle on, though whether he could have achieved a breakthrough is unclear.

The game over, the Icelandic organizers approached two local scientists to examine the scarcely veiled charges of electronic and chemical chicanery. One was Dadi Augustin, an electrical engineer; the other was Sigmundur Gudbjarnason, a U.S.-trained professor of chemistry who had returned to his native Iceland from Detroit two years earlier. Augustin would investigate the lights, while it was Gudbjarnason's job to inspect the chess table and the chairs: "When I returned from America, I brought back with me a state-of-the-art gas chromatograph. It enabled me to analyze chemicals. We put on disposable gloves and took smear tests by wiping the table and chairs with a special tissue." He also took samples from the walls and the stage. All were carefully placed in plastic bags marked "Fischer's chair," "rear wall," and so on. They agreed to conduct their investigations gratis. Says Gudbjarnason, "It was our contribution to the match; *we wanted to ensure that it would continue.*" Had the Soviets known that, they might well have questioned the objectivity of the evaluation.

Gudbjarnason then set about comparing the profile of the chemicals on the one chair with that of the other and examining the surface swabs from both sides of the table. Throughout this period, the chemistry professor refused to answer the question put to him by journalists: Was it indeed possible surreptitiously to infect someone, in the way the Soviets had alleged? In part, he was silent because he did not want to spread alarm, but "I knew it was feasible, and I'm sure the Russians and the Americans knew it could be done. I'm sure they have used this kind of technique in the past."

The study took several days to complete; they wrote up their findings in a short report, only a few pages in length. This was then handed in to the Icelandic assistant arbiter, Gudmundur Arnlaugsson. The Icelandic Chess Federation said Soviet charges of tampering were unfounded. The bottom line was that Gudbjarnason had found nothing wrong—the chemical composition of the chairs and either side of the table was identical and, as one would expect, consisted mainly of the materials used in polishing. Augustin had more luck—in the huge lighting fixture he found two dead flies, prompting much press hilarity.

However, that did not settle the matter: something unusual was observed. X-rays were taken by the Icelandic Maritime Administration (they routinely took X-rays to check the welding of shipping). The X-ray of Fischer's chair appeared to show a long, tubelike object with a cylindrical loop at one end. It did not appear in Spassky's chair. A second X-ray was taken. This time there was nothing. The chair was later dismantled. Inside they found some wood filler, apparently there because of a crack in the plywood seat. Loftily, the organizers took it to be the item seen in the first X-ray (though they never explained why in that case it did not show up in the second).

***

If game seventeen was seen by the Soviet camp as Spassky's last chance to alter the course of the match, with his failure to break through defeat now loomed large. Tenaciously, he fought on. However, game eighteen also ended in a draw through repetition. Spassky's king had been exposed throughout; by contrast, Fischer's king spent much of the game locked away in a corner, a state of affairs with its own sort of frailty—if attacked, it had nowhere to run. This time, it was Fischer's willingness to accept a draw that surprised the experts—he was a pawn up. For anybody else in the same position, the draw would have been understandable; with every half point, Fischer was edging closer and closer to victory. But Fischer, as Gligoric put it, "was reputed never to gun for a draw," whatever the score. Was he now showing a human side? A psychological infirmity? Pragmatism?

The score was Spassky 7.5, Fischer 10.5, leaving the American only two points away from the title.

Prior to the eighteenth game, Geller had issued a protest about the removal of the front rows of seats, for which the Soviets had not granted permission. Schmid now negotiated an ingenious compromise which would have made that consummate dealmaker Henry Kissinger proud. The seats would go back to their original place, but they would be roped off and thus remain empty. Fischer entered the hall for the next game and appeared not even to notice the change. But Schmid's patience was finally running out. When Cramer reiterated his demand for the removal of the first seven rows, accusing Schmid of bias toward the Soviets, the chief arbiter fired off a barbed letter, its tone entirely out of character. Cramer's letter, Schmid said, [is] "no doubt meant to be helpful, but if so, then unfortunately is deprived of any opportunity of being useful by its largely inaccurate contents." It concluded, "If you have any complaints or protests to make, please, and I must underline the importance of this, please make them in accordance with the rules of the match."

Game nineteen was a clever little game, with both players producing the unexpected. Fischer came up with a startling defense on move twenty-one. Spassky had just sacrificed a piece—when he did so, one grandmaster said, "Hold on to your seat belts." Brazenly ignoring his opponent's undefended rook, Fischer forced instead the exchange of queens; it left the American with a drawn game. He was absolutely right: to have taken the rook—indeed, any alternative move—would have spelled disaster. Spassky had brilliantly and daringly taken risks, but to no avail. "That Bobby," said Gligoric, "he always escapes."

Before game twenty, the Icelandic Ministry of Finance made a goodwill gesture. It announced that the government had decided to ask Parliament in the next session to make the prize money tax-free. Normally, the winner would have to pay government and local income taxes of $28,000 and the loser about $16,000.

The game itself was a long, tough struggle that lasted through the five-hour session. The advantage moved from one player to another and then back again. At the adjournment, they were well into an ending, but one that was not clear-cut. The following day, when the game resumed, Geller was seen in the audience barely able to stay awake. The night had been spent buried in analysis. Spassky too looked gaunt and fatigued; they had been searching for a win that patently was not there.

It was the seventh draw in a row. There had not been such a consecutive run in the world championship since the marathon contest between Alekhine and Capablanca in 1927. Far from being dull, lazy games, several of these had been desperate, protracted, bare-knuckle brawls, exciting if not always pretty. Fischer, who normally moved much more quickly than his opponent, was now taking just as long on the clock. Spassky prodded and probed and took gambles; Fischer, on untested ground, clung on. While the commentators had predicted a Spassky collapse, the champion had instead dug in, held the line, and, incredibly, fought back. This had required more than just skill and concentration; above all, the champion had had to draw upon cavernous reserves of psychological strength.

The twenty-first game took place on 31 August. Since game eight, not a single move had been filmed. But on this day, the Yugoslav journalist Dimitri Bjelica smuggled a Sony videocamera into the hall and sat in the back row. On one occasion, as the ushers wandered up and down, looking for the slightest disturbance, Bjelica covered up the camera's hum with a fit of coughing. He realized this could be the last game, and so his last chance to film.

Fischer had 11.5 points and thus needed only one more for the title—a win or two draws. With tickets at a premium, the auditorium was packed for what was potentially the culminating moment. After two months of farce, mystery, and tragedy, of edgy strain and petulant anger, of showbiz and high jinks, of bluff and double bluff, of demands and climb-downs, of genius and blunder, the people of Reykjavik—even those ignorant of the rules of the game—wanted to be there to witness the climax.

As usual, Lothar Schmid started the clock. As usual, Fischer was late. The game opened with a Sicilian. On his second move, Fischer, black, played pawn to e6, yet another new line for him. Spassky was fueling himself with cup after cup of coffee. It may have been the surprise of Fischer's seventh move—a pawn thrust tried before but considered somewhat dubious—that unsteadied the Russian's hand, causing him to spill his drink. With his clock ticking, he went in search of a cloth. Fischer watched the cleanup operation as though his opponent were crazed.

The queens came off early, leaving Fischer with the advantage of two bishops against bishop and knight, but with the disadvantage of double isolated pawns. "[When] Fischer obtained an edge," Spassky said later, "I felt everything was finished." On move eighteen, the champion sacrificed a rook for a bishop and pawn in a reckless bid to create complications and perhaps winning prospects. Move thirty was the turning point. Rather than retrench, set up an impregnable fortress, and settle for a draw, Spassky pushed his knight pawn two squares to g4, allowing his opponent to create and exploit deadly weaknesses in white's flailing defense. Fischer played out the ending with unremitting, nerveless accuracy.

Adjournment came at move forty-one. Spassky seemed exhausted. He invested only six minutes' thinking time on his last move, which was then committed to paper and handed over to Schmid, who carefully sealed it in the adjournment envelope. Fischer signed the flap, a standard security check. Now the audience could relax and chat, and as they rose from their seats, the conversation was of who held the positional edge. Fischer had by now sacrificed back a pawn, so with his rook and two pawns against Spassky's bishop and four pawns, the combatants were in theory evenly matched. But Spassky's pieces were tied down, going nowhere. Meanwhile, Fischer's rook's pawn was "passed" (that is, it had a clear view to the eighth rank, with no opposition pawns on its file or the adjacent files). Every pawn has the potential to be reincarnated as a higher being, a more powerful piece, normally a queen, but a passed pawn is a particularly potent threat. And Fischer's rook and king were well stationed to shepherd its advance.

Most amateurs would have rated the prospects for either side as about even. However, the experts realized Spassky's struggle to retain the title was over; his doughty fight back had collapsed and the grandmasters were predicting a Fischer victory. In Moscow there was already an acceptance that their man had lost: the champion had told Geller that there was no point in fussing over the analysis. Spassky knew he had not sealed the best move.

⁂

The following day, there was an audience of 2,500 people, some of whom had arrived early to guarantee a good seat and all of whom had paid $5 in the expectation of witnessing an exciting denouement. Fischer bounded in late, looking confident but, surprising for one who normally took care to appear impeccable, dressed in a hastily selected and still unpressed blood-red suit. For a change, Spassky's seat was the one empty.

Two hours earlier, at 12:50 P.M., the champion had put in a call to the arbiter Lothar Schmid. He officially informed Schmid of his resignation; he would not go to the adjourned session. Schmid had had to phone Euwe: Could he accept a resignation by telephone? Euwe ruled this was permissible. Fischer was not informed and might not have found out until later, had the *Life* photographer Harry Benson not bumped into Spassky at the Saga hotel as the now ex-champion was on his way out for a walk. There followed a flurry of calls. Benson rang Fischer, who rang Schmid, insisting that, if true, this resignation must be put in writing. Schmid wrote something out himself but said Fischer would still have to show up at the scheduled hour for the adjourned session.

The match was over.

This was no grand finale, no knockout punch sending the

champion to the mat, no winning hit into the stand or breasting of the tape. There were no hats thrown into the air, no stamping or cheering. This was the way the crown passed, not with a bang but a formal announcement. Once Fischer had arrived, Schmid walked to the front of the stage and addressed the hall: "Ladies and gentlemen, Mr. Spassky has resigned by telephone." Polite applause broke out around the room. The spectators had seen no action for their entrance fee, but they were witnesses to chess history. The new world champion gave a gawky wave but rejected Schmid's proposal to take a bow. The Italian daily *Corriere della Sera* severely disapproved of Spassky's nonappearance: "He missed the salute he deserved. But he no longer deserves it. One should fight until the end. It is the law of sport, and he has betrayed it."

Icelandic government cars were parked in front of the hall alongside the U.S. ambassador's car. Victor Jackovich was also waiting there.

It was all a ploy, because Fischer did not want to talk to anyone or be accosted by the press. So the plan was that he would come out of the side door and hop into my car—a pretty nondescript yellow and black Ford Maverick. I had been told, "Don't stop for anybody. As soon as he gets in, just take off for the base." So I drove him to the base, where he had a celebratory steak and a glass of milk, it was always a glass of milk. I don't recall him being jubilant; he was a bundle of nerves, still high like a sportsman at the end of a game. It was the same Fischer I'd always taken to the base.

In victory, Fischer was at least magnanimous about his defeated opponent. Spassky was "the best player" he had met. "All the other players I've played crumpled at a certain point. I never felt that with Spassky." President Nixon sent Fischer a telegram of congratulations. Spassky himself gave some interviews. He looked exhausted and said he needed to "sleep and sleep and sleep."

The New York Times deployed Nietzschean rhetoric in their investigation of what they called "the aura of a killer." "Basically the Fischer aura is the will to dominate, to humiliate, to take over an opponent's mind." It was uncanny, they pointed out, how players defeated by Fischer never fully recovered. A loss to another opponent could be excused away, put down to a bad day or a rare oversight. "But a loss to Fischer somehow diminishes a player. Part of him has been eaten, and he is that much less a whole man." Fischer was guilty of serial "psychic murder."

For their part, the Soviets were asking whether Fischer was guilty of other crimes.

20

EXTRA-CHESS
MEANS AND
HIDDEN HANDS

Sniff out, suck up, and survive.

— KGB MANTRA, CHRISTOPHER ANDREW AND
OLEG GORDIEVSKY

It is striking how, to this day, some Soviet participants believe dirty tricks played a part in Spassky's defeat.

On arrival in Iceland on 10 August, Larisa Spasskaia was conscious of the overwrought atmosphere in her husband's suite on the seventh floor of the Saga hotel. With the wives of his team members, she had left Moscow at a time when a heavy brown haze covered the city from the heathland fire that had been steadily creeping toward the suburbs for more than a month, engulfing thousands of acres. It had reached to within fifteen miles of the suburbs and had taken the military as well as firefighters to control it. So dense was the smoke that their flight had been switched to the domestic airport, Vnukovo, because planes could not depart from the international airport at Sheremet'evo.

The Boris she encountered in Reykjavik shocked her. That day, Spassky was defeated—a massive psychological knock after his victory four days earlier that finally seemed to have stalled Fischer's momentum. "He looked lost and strained, his nervous system out of order." The immediate problem was the accommodation. "For Boris, the whole atmosphere in the Saga was difficult. There was something unhealthy about it; it depressed him. He couldn't sleep and became very irritable. His mattress irritated him. Perhaps there was something in it." This had nothing to do with the champion suffering an allergy to its composition. The dark suspicion was of a substance planted to affect his nerves.

Larisa was not alone in suspecting mischief afoot. "Geller was sure that somebody entered their rooms in their absence. Someone from the American camp. Our team was very naive. Geller left his notes for the games in his suitcase—when he opened it, he saw that everything was in a different order. He had a sealed box with a special medicine from bees, Royal Jelly. Once when he came back, the box was open. Someone had taken a pinch."

On returning to Moscow ten days later, Geller's wife, Oksana, reported her husband's worries to the authorities, telling them that the score was not a reflection of Spassky's chess ability. "Their misfortune was not a chess misfortune." She informed them that her husband had lost eight kilos and that Spassky felt as though his mind was in a fog. Something was up with Nei, too. He had become inert, lethargic. Because of this lassitude, he had basically withdrawn from the preparations.

Mistrust was not confined to conditions in the hotel. According to Larisa, "Boris believed things were happening that were surprising and worrying. All of a sudden, in the first or second hour of the day, he would feel drowsy. At first, he thought he must have eaten too much. He cut down on the food and just took snacks, but still he was sleepy. Twice when he left for the game, his pulse rate was normal, measured at sixty-eight to seventy, and within an hour he was in a state of prostration. He couldn't drink the coffee or juice supplied to him for fear it had been spiked."

After spending a few days in the embassy, Larisa and Boris moved into a house in the country, ten kilometers from Reykjavik. The Soviet ambassador Sergei Astavin had arranged it for them.

"We managed to escape," is how Larisa puts it. Owned by the hotel, it resembled a dacha. There her husband slept well for the first time in weeks. His eyes became brighter and he started to talk in his normal lively manner. He also began to take more heed of Krogius and Geller, whose advice he tended to dismiss when he was wound up. Helped by the embassy cook, Vitali Yeremenko, a great admirer of Spassky as a man as well as a chess player, Larisa took care of the meals. "First I made them lunch, then a thermos of coffee and a flask of juice." She squeezed fresh oranges, a pleasing change from the sickly sweet ersatz version in Moscow. "With those two flasks, he went to the match." She adds, "He had never been this disturbed before. There was nothing like it in other matches. Nothing like it." Larisa Spasskaia has a technical background; she is highly educated, an engineer by profession. She is not a woman susceptible to idle speculation. Yet to this day she is convinced that psychotropic drugs were used against her husband. "I don't know how they did it, but I'm sure there was something. Maybe it was a special light; maybe it was in the hall, in the food."

The conviction that Fischer's team had taken stringent security precautions served to heighten Soviet paranoia that the champion was being got at—the only possible explanation for his not being himself, not being on form. Geller later remarked on the Americans' preparations for the match: "They had a technical team. What did they need this for? They had a psychological team, a security service, an information service." Larisa Spasskaia is not the only Russian who says she remembers Fischer's house being encircled by armed U.S. Marine guards.

This was not so. The American records reveal that Fischer's people requested marine guards and the request was summarily turned down by the U.S. chargé d'affaires in Reykjavik, Theodore Tremblay. He loathed Fischer's discourtesy, was embarrassed by it, could not wait for him to get off the island, and had deliberately kept embassy assistance down to a minimum in the face of Fred Cramer's attempts at intimidation. Cramer had warned that he would take matters all the way to the White House. Tremblay had prayed that the "damned thing" would not come to Reykjavik at all because of the trouble Fischer might cause for the Ice-

Larisa Spasskaia reunited with Boris. He feared his food was tampered with, but home cooking is safe cooking. TASS

landers. "I had no doubts they—the Icelanders—could handle it. But Fischer even before the match had quite a reputation, which even I as a non–chess player was aware of, and I could just see problems ahead." When Fischer's praetorian guard arrived and demanded that the embassy help financially, Tremblay had a cast-iron defense: "I wasn't inclined to be very cooperative with any of these people, and frankly it didn't matter to me what they threatened. Indeed, I had been instructed by the State Department not to spend one cent of American taxpayers' money on Bobby Fischer, since he had been so disrespectful of everything. So that was the way it was."

However, the Soviet "recollections" are significant, showing the depth of insecurity and suspicion that USSR citizens carried everywhere they went. The idea that extra-chess means were used against the team in Reykjavik runs like a threnody through the postmortem four months after the match, albeit in a minor key, perhaps because the participants had more immediate, personal scores to settle. Stalinism had left the people of the Soviet Union permanently on the lookout for conspiracy, internal and external, and for culprits, someone to blame. The KGB handbook for its employees, *The KGB Lexicon: The Official Soviet Intelligence Officer's Handbook,* states that "the political vigilance of the Soviet people is represented by their unfailing mindfulness of possible dangers threatening the country."

This vigilance existed even prior to the match, as evidenced in the official report to the Sports Committee on Spassky's preparation, drawn up on 16 October 1971 by Viktor Baturinskii. In the report, he warned that the Americans would try to hold the match on the American continent, conferring on Fischer "certain advantages." The report went on:

> Furthermore, in connection with the results of Fischer's matches against Taimanov, Larsen and Petrosian, there has been some conjecture about the influence on these results of non-chess factors (hypnosis, telepathy, tampering with food, listening in on domestic analysis, etc.).

In the wake of Taimanov's crushing defeat, his team manager, Aleksandr Kotov, raised the issue of external, non-chess influences on Spassky: "It appears that this has happened before. At the Taimanov-Fischer match, I had the feeling the whole time that people were eavesdropping on us."

Mikhail Botvinnik also mistrusted the Americans; he thought Spassky should not play in any country in which there was an American base. That was why he recommended against Iceland. An electrical engineer with an early and passionate interest in computer science, Botvinnik feared baleful computer manipulation of Spassky and help to Fischer—presumably controlled by U.S. military intelligence facilities. When Reykjavik was confirmed as the match site, some Sports Committee officials even suggested a Soviet ship should be moored there, on which the Soviet team could live in a security cocoon. That idea did not progress beyond the committee's offices, probably just as well for Spassky's blood pressure.

Then, during the match itself, otherwise rational Soviets were alarmed by the way Spassky was prone to error and threw away promising positions. Were there sinister explanations, hypnotic rays, parapsychology, chemicals?

Once back in Moscow, Spassky himself questioned his mental state over the chessboard. "Can it really be that my chess powers fell so sharply only as the result of some small incidents and confusion? Can my psyche really have been so unstable? Either my psychology was made of glass or there were external influences." Before we shrug our shoulders in amused disbelief, we should recall Soviet use of toxicology against opponents. When the KGB wanted to bug the apartment of Colonel Oleg Penkovskii, whom they suspected of spying for the British, they smeared a poison on his chair that sent him briefly to hospital. Why should others not have access to the same technology?

Of course, not all the Soviet insiders were disposed to blame Spassky's apparent loss of form on American dirty tricks. But even those who dismissed the possibility of an "outside agency" charged Fischer with using non-chess tactics—that is, psychological warfare. Spassky's trainer and second, Nikolai Krogius, was head of the Psychology Department in Saratov University as well as a grandmaster. Looking back, he gives this diagnosis:

> The psychological war waged by Fischer against Spassky and his (Fischer's) attempts at self-assertion (by crushing the will of the other player) were linked; they were two sides of a single process of struggle against Spassky. . . . Note that in the 1970s Fischer began to place great significance on the psychological aspects of the game. He would openly declare that he was trying to crush the will of his opponent. To this end, all means were justified. In Fischer's opinion, the psychological subjugation of the opponent inevitably led to a reduction in the strength of the opponent's game. Fischer carried out such a program consistently, both before and during the match.

In the Sports Committee, too, Fischer's mind games were seen to be at the root of Spassky's problems. The committee considered the possibility of hypnosis as early as the beginning of August but dismissed it. The former women's world champion, Elizaveta Bykova, claimed to Viktor Ivonin that Fischer had a telepathist among his lawyers. This was not true. In any case, the committee did not believe in telepathy.

From Reykjavik, the Soviet ambassador had complained to the Sports Committee that the press, Soviet as well as Western, misrepresented Fischer when they wrote of his "eccentricities." They were not such, he said, but deliberate, well-planned nonsporting techniques to undermine the champion. In Moscow, they analyzed Fischer and concluded that he was a psychopath, a personality for whom the norm was a conflict situation—something with which Spassky could not cope.

The crisis for Spassky was caused, they concluded, by his inability to manage the psychological pressure. This conveniently dovetailed with criticism of his refusal to accept a leader for the delegation. After the match, Viktor Baturinskii put his view roundly: "If we are talking seriously, then we should not regard external factors as the most important, especially since we have no proof." However, driving home his point that Spassky was wrong not to have had a proper team (in other words, one that might have included a KGB translator or doctor), he hedged his bets: "The question of whether certain chemical components were introduced into the food is another matter. The delegation was warned about this. We sent Comrade Krogius especially to Reykjavik for several days to explore the security issues. We offered to send a cook, a doctor. But all this was refused by Spassky."

Whatever the degree of incredulity in Moscow over external tampering, backs had to be guarded, appropriate action seen to be taken. For instance, to investigate possible interference with Spassky's food, a sample of the juice the Icelanders supplied to Spassky was carried to the Soviet capital for laboratory analysis.

The charge that the Americans were deploying psychological

warfare was also examined. Spassky's refusal to take a doctor to Reykjavik did not stop the Sports Committee from deciding on 10 August that certain specialists should go anyway. The Health Ministry was asked for help. So, somewhat to his surprise, an eminent psychiatrist, Professor Vartanian, received a request to meet Ivonin on 21 August at the committee's offices. He was invited to travel to Iceland with a colleague of his choosing, make observations, and then report back. Discretion was the order of the day: they would go as Ambassador Astavin's guests. "We didn't want to upset Spassky," says Ivonin, "so we arranged for the psychiatrists to go as the ambassador's friends." Their mission was to assess the personalities of each player and whether Spassky was being "influenced."

The late professor Vartanian was then general director of the Mental Health Center. He approached Professor Zharikov, a psychiatrist at the Medical Institute, where today he is dean of the Department of Psychological Medicine. The bait was the trip to Iceland, an exotic location they might otherwise never visit. Professor Zharikov is a survivor of the epic tank battle of Kursk, where he was wounded. Above the entrance to his office is a plaque recording his status as a veteran of the Great Patriotic War. Inside, a picture of Lenin dominates the room.

On arrival, Vartanian and Zharikov were immediately briefed by embassy staff; the allegations were repeated about hypnosis, parapsychology, and interference from a device in Fischer's chair. They leafed through the press, looking at cartoons of the match. Professor Zharikov was in a skeptical mood. He did not believe in parapsychology, and rumors were to be expected with so much at stake. Amusement flickers in the professor's eyes as he remembers sitting in the hall, observing the players through binoculars. He regarded the episode as a joyride. The trip made few professional demands. He had no opportunity to get to know the subjects of his studies, and given the stress of the situation, diagnosing their characters and distinguishing normal from abnormal behavior was nearly impossible. "Each person involved in such a difficult psychological situation would respond differently," Zharikov says. "There were no standards. You wouldn't say such-

and-such behavior is a problem and such-and-such behavior is not."

He considered the champion to be balanced. Their only meeting with Spassky came at an embassy reception, and Zharikov was impressed: "A very clever young man, maybe a bit solemn—a person in whom psychosis would not develop easily. He was very self-possessed and liked to show off, like to talk." The professors assured Ambassador Astavin there was nothing to worry about. They repeated that view in the official document to the Sports Committee: "We wrote a short report dismissing the speculations and confirming that the participants in the match were in an absolutely proper condition."

Soviet paranoia was by no means one-sided. The second secretary at the Soviet embassy, Dmitri Vasil'iev, has a recollection of Fischer complaining of KGB men in the hall trying to hypnotize him. It was the expression of what Victor Jackovich described as Fischer's anti-Soviet mind-set.

> Fischer was convinced the Soviets were listening in, were watching somehow. He thought they were playing with him in a variety of ways—that there were people sitting in the front rows of the audience somehow affecting his concentration, perhaps with electronic devices. His paranoia was pervasive. It was part of the reason why going to the U.S. base at Keflavik was such a comfort for Fischer—part of our trying to make him feel more comfortable in terms of "Look, this is a military U.S., NATO base. You're safe here." If someone would say something about the Russians, he would perk up immediately and would shoot a question about it. I just had the sense that if you really wanted to get his attention, you just mentioned the Russians.

The tension was such that it even got to the New York lawyer Paul Marshall. He recalls how his and his wife's passports were missing from their hotel desk and then suddenly appeared back in their room. "And we started to feel the same pressures, thinking, 'That's odd.' This and several other things made us believe that Bobby's idea of Russian trickery may have some merit." However, the atmosphere could also be used to provide some wholesome American fun. He and his wife, Bette, were in the public entrance to the hall when Nikolai Krogius was passing. Bette called out: " 'Grandmaster Krogius, friends and contacts in America wanted me to give you these papers.' And Krogius turned and ran."

With the probability of a KGB watcher loitering there, who could blame him?

However, Spassky and Geller were not completely mistaken. Outsiders did try to influence the proceedings.

What we now know is that the KGB was active during the match—active in investigating possible attacks on the world champion, active in attempting a preemptive propaganda coup against the Americans, working with the connivance of the Moscow chess authorities, perhaps active too in spreading a rumor that Spassky was planning to defect.

Soviet grandmasters of the era assumed that the KGB was involved in chess, as in all pursuits deemed important by the state. Chess players sized up one another. Which of them had a role beyond chess? Which of them was receiving an extra stipend—had a so-called side job? Which of them was informing? Who was holding a chess position while actually a KGB officer?

To this day, many in the former Soviet Union will contend that the KGB's work in defending the state was an honorable undertaking—so there was no dishonor in collaborating with them. The KGB was the real travel authority, lurking behind all the committees of Party faithful who had the task of initially vetting applications to travel. Through its informants, the KGB was tipped off as to what was going on in chess circles and would "suggest" to the authorities who should be encouraged, who should be discouraged, who should be banned from leaving the Soviet Union, who should be allowed to go abroad. It was a common practice to suggest to would-be travelers that their passports might be more readily available if they agreed to act as the eyes and ears of the organization.

Some even claim that the KGB had an office in the Central Chess Club in Moscow—though an officer is more likely. Yuri Averbakh professes ignorance of any such thing: "I had an office there, and if so, I did not know about it." Nonetheless, he fully understood how the system operated, even if his deeply embedded instinct—or perhaps superstitious habit—is to avoid speaking directly of the KGB. "In the Stalin era, usually if a team were traveling, an obvious representative of *this organization* was sent along. *This person* would observe the participants. In 1952, I played in the Interzonal tournament, and there was *such a person* there. In 1953 at the Candidates tournament in Zurich, there was *such a person*. In 1955, when Spassky traveled to the World Junior Chess Championship—I was his coach at the time—there was also a *representative of that organization* with us. After 1956, for about three years, no one was sent. This was the time of the thaw. Then, at the beginning of the 1960s, *such people* began to appear again. In Curaçao, for example, a KGB person accompanied us."

"Such people" were scarcely secret. Garry Kasparov's former coach Aleksandr Nikitin records, "From the first time Garry went abroad, he had a companion who was not a professional trainer. He was a KGB lieutenant colonel, Viktor Litvinov. Litvinov kept an eye on Garry and his mother wherever they went." Even Karpov was "protected." "From 1975, Vladimir Pichtchenko, a prominent KGB agent, followed Karpov like a shadow on all his foreign trips."

Nikitin wrote that these agents fulfilled a useful role: "Today everyone is in the habit of condemning this organization. We should not, however, think that people who worked in the KGB were monsters. Those with whom we dealt were cordial and competent, and of high intellectual caliber. The organization operated within all the sport federations. Sport as an aspect of culture had to reflect the success of our system. . . ." The high level of intellect is accurate: the KGB creamed off the brightest for its ranks.

Given the official view of Spassky's political "immaturity," given his earlier brushes with the KGB in Leningrad, given this was a U.S.-Soviet contest on an island with a major American air base, it would have been little short of a miracle if there had been no KGB operatives there. Nikolai Krogius allows the possibility: "As far as I know, official representatives of the KGB were not present. There were rumors that there were two or three KGB workers. But they simply watched, of course. Nothing more." Nei thought there were many. Now only recently retired from the Russian Foreign Ministry, then second secretary in the Soviet embassy, Dmitri Vasil'iev remembers two or three *such persons* inside the hall in Reykjavik, watching the match: "I can't be sure they were KGB, but they were a bit strange. You know, these people, CIA or KGB, they were always a bit strange." Members of these secret organizations—whether CIA or KGB—were dissimilar, of course, but something about them made identification easy. To an observer, in the Russian idiom, they were "men with identical shoes."

The Soviet embassy was already swollen beyond normal requirements for a sparsely populated island; during the two months of the match, there were an unusual number of Russian "tourists." Some reports name an embassy official, Viktor Bubnov, as the head of the KGB in Reykjavik. But he was actually from Soviet military intelligence, the GRU, and so had quite different priorities. We can assume no shortage of KGB officers and informants in Reykjavik. And we now have reason to believe that some among them were not there simply, as Nikolai Krogius would have it, "to observe."

In Moscow, at the end of July, apprehension over Spassky's performance was running at a high level.

On 27 July, when the champion played his worst game to date, game eight, Viktor Baturinskii was summoned to the Central Committee to explain what was going on and in particular why Spassky did not react to Fischer's late appearances at games. Present were the acting head of the Propaganda Department, Aleksandr Yakovlev; his deputy head, Yuri Skliarov; and the head of sports, Boris Goncharov—who apparently had not the least interest in sports. They discussed how they might help Spassky and how they might identify and neutralize the psychological pressures on him.

It was the beginning of a period that finds an array of senior KGB figures passing through Ivonin's office. (Of course, this was also the run-up to the Olympics.) They included Viktor Chebrikov, deputy chairman of the KGB and a protégé of Brezhnev's. Brezhnev had appointed him in 1968 under Yuri Andropov, following the Kremlin power struggle that saw Pavlov go to GosKomSport. Chebrikov would go on to become KGB chairman in 1982. Even more senior, the first deputy chairman of the KGB, appointed in the same reshuffle as Chebrikov, Semion Tsvigun, also turned up. There were visits from the deputy head of the KGB's Fifth Directorate (which dealt with ideology and so covered sports), Major General Valentin Nikashkin. One of his staff, KGB agent Viktor Gostiev, will come into the story. He too worked in the Fifth Directorate of the KGB. Later, while remaining a KGB officer, Gostiev became deputy chairman of the Dynamo Sports Society, which provided physical training for the KGB and those employed in the Interior Ministry.

The senior rank of the KGB participants has probably more to do with Ivonin's ministerial status than with the importance accorded Reykjavik. Viktor Ivonin is unable to recall anything of these visits. His normally unfailing memory for people and events lets him down when confronted with these KGB names. While his tone becomes decidedly more guarded, his mind is a blank.

What might they have discussed?

The theme of these comings and goings is less how to undermine Fischer and more how to prop up a rattled Spassky. (In this period, there is a proposal to send the champion *Kogitum*—a medicine against nervous tension—and some exasperation at his refusal to take it.) First, this requires investigating stories of possible interference with his playing. One report to have reached the KGB was that Fischer was being assisted by a computer (in Russian called an IBM—a Soviet tribute to American big business) and a device in his chair. (Whether the two are linked, a computer in Fischer's chair, is unclear.) There have already been reports in the Western press of Fischer being computer aided, reports derisively dismissed in Reykjavik by Spassky, Geller, and Krogius. Back in Moscow, the KGB does not believe silicon-based shenanigans are any more practical. A Comrade Lvov, a KGB technical officer and a constant caller on Ivonin at this time, explains to the deputy minister that Fischer would have needed a full year to develop the requisite computer program and would have to have a portable receiver and a membrane in his ear to receive the signals.

Lvov is also the bearer of other shadowy news: he reports the possibility that Spassky has had a letter threatening his family if he returns to Moscow a winner. This is investigated, and no proof of its existence is found. The provenance of this letter is unclear; today, Spassky says he had no knowledge of it.

Other means of defending Spassky are afoot. As July turns into August, an unnamed forensic psychiatrist takes part in a meeting with Lvov and Gostiev. Lvov is all set to organize a check for radiation from radio waves and X-rays "on the spot"—presumably in the hall.

Throughout this period, the possibility of Spassky's being the target of hypnosis and telepathy is being discussed. There is a hint that sending a psychiatrist to Reykjavik is Gostiev's brain-child. The psychiatrists Vartanian and Zharikov are primed, and Gostiev arranges the logistics of their visit.

Then there is the alarm over Spassky's refreshments—that on 15 August he drank some juice and was overcome with lethargy. Once more, the KGB and Gostiev are involved. Once more, Gostiev springs into action, ensuring a sample is sent to Moscow. KGB scientists check the sample. Later, Gostiev's superior, Nikashkin, tells Ivonin that nothing untoward was found.

However, the KGB is not content to play a purely reactive role. The organization's idea of a helping hand also involves taking the initiative, instigating its own rumor that Fischer is cheating through a device hidden in his chair—a device, so the rumor goes, that is impairing Spassky's performance and/or benefiting Fischer. This idea is canvassed toward the end of July. It must have sounded convincing. As Ivonin listens to the "comrades" talking, he finds himself wondering whether there might really be something to it. On 29 July, Boris Goncharov, of the Central Committee, reports to Ivonin that the rumor has been "launched." The rest is silence.

Given the launch date, it is a mystery whether there was any connection between this rumor and Geller's statement to the press three weeks later, on 22 August, protesting about dirty tricks being used to influence Spassky, though Geller asserted that "letters had been received." The story of the scenes that followed this statement has already been related. In Moscow, Major General Nikashkin informed Ivonin that the episode had received a lot of publicity; that Icelandic experts had checked everything and nothing had been found.

Was Geller obeying KGB orders? Had he been told the full details of the KGB plotting, or was he himself a victim of the plot, inveigled into believing and then publicly conveying the allegations of American high-tech machinations? Within Spassky's chess team, Geller, who was ultrasuspicious of the West, acted alone. Krogius did not sign the controversial declaration, and today he categorizes the action as "unsuccessful and clumsy." He attributes it entirely to "Geller's tendency to act spontaneously." Nei says he refused to put his name to the statement because it was evident to him that Geller had issued it under political instruction from Moscow. Ivonin declares that the first he heard of the letter was when news of it came from Reykjavik. Spassky now remembers that a letter before the match had warned about the chair and "this letter was fished out." Perhaps, nearing the end of the contest, desperate to account for his failure to find a breakthrough at the board, he and Geller consciously or subconsciously cast about for non-chess explanations. Still ignorant of the KGB scheme, Spassky continues to believe that Fischer's black leather swivel chair might have had something in it; he says he was not at all embarrassed by Geller's pronouncement.

It remains an open question whether a KGB operative actually planted something in Fischer's chair for the X-rays to pick up,

part of an inept attempt to rescue the champion's reputation, perhaps even to have Fischer disgraced and disqualified. Strikingly,
even the American Don Schultz, an IBM engineer by profession
and president of the USCF from 1996 to 1999, is suspicious.
During the X-ray process, Fischer's team sent Schultz along to act
as an observer. He still has the contemporaneous notes he took,
including a sketch of the object with the loop that he saw in the
first X-ray. At the time, in public, he laughed off the Soviet allegations. But later he too admitted to doubts: "Everything wasn't
fully explained." What puzzled him was the discrepancy between
the two X-rays. He was there as the second set of X-rays was developed and saw that the looplike object, the "anomaly," as he
calls it, had disappeared.

> I've thought long about this. The only plausible thing—and it
> really sounds radical, and I didn't want to mention it at the time,
> as I thought nobody would believe me—but I think there is a
> slight chance that some crackpot Russian agent—and this is really
> wild—some crackpot Russian agent had a plan to try to embarrass
> the U.S. by planting something in the chair and then making a
> complaint and having it found. And their security forces found
> out what he did and thought it was a crackpot idea, and somehow
> they got it out.

This, he says, is "a very disconcerting possibility. I am convinced
this is what had to have happened." Of course, once the alarm
was raised, the Soviets and the Icelanders might each have had
their own reasons for ensuring nothing was found. Don Schultz
was startled when Icelandic officials announced the all clear before the results from the second set of X-rays had been reported.

Whether or not the KGB did implant a device, what is clear is
that Krogius is right to call the entire exploit clumsy and unsuccessful. The Icelandic organizers dismissed the accusation, the
American media ridiculed it, and the Soviets were left humbled.

The possibility of a spy in the troubled Soviet camp also raised its
head. The challenger's unforeseen departure from a lifetime of

From Don Schultz's contemporaneous notes. DON SCHULTZ

opening predictability had thrown Spassky; that Fischer was the better prepared is indisputable. But Geller was convinced that Spassky's prematch analysis had been leaked.

To suspicious Soviet minds, if there were a fifth columnist, who was the likely culprit? In the written record of the post-mortem on the match, there is no direct accusation against any member of the Spassky team, but the wording of a comment by Viktor Baturinskii points a finger. Spassky had cited Ivo Nei as the weak link in his team. Evidently angry and on the defensive, the former prosecutor lashed out: "Here mention has been made of Nei, *who proved to be all but a spy.* I objected to the inclusion of Nei in the training group, but Boris Vasilievich [Spassky] insisted on it. To cite Nei now as one of the reasons for his own performance is at the very least unscrupulous."

In the minds of the Sports Committee, Nei had no real business in Reykjavik. From the moment Spassky's team was first assembled, Nei was referred to as the champion's "physical trainer."

Nei insists that he played a full part in the chess analysis, working at night alongside the rest of the team. He also spoke fluent German and some English, and in Reykjavik he interpreted for the chief arbiter, Lothar Schmid, and for Max Euwe, president of FIDE. He knew the president well.

No doubt it was a combination of Nei's command of chess and his position as an "insider" that commended him to Paul Marshall as the possible author of a book on the match. Marshall recognized the market for such books—especially one written from inside Spassky's camp. Nei says that as well as royalties, Marshall offered him anything he wanted from America. Nei then approached grandmaster Robert Byrne to be coauthor. This former U.S. champion was in Reykjavik as a commentator for a Dutch television station. Nei had been getting out and about, hobnobbing with match officials and the American visitors. The Soviet ambassador had not vetoed his extramural activities, but he advised Nei to be cautious in his contact with U.S. citizens. As Spassky's coach, says Nei, his meeting the Americans was beneficial for Spassky: He was able to give his team some insight into how the U.S. camp was thinking.

The book Marshall brokered is called *Both Sides of the Chess Board*. It includes an introduction by Euwe in which the FIDE president notes that Nei was privy to inside information, both technical and psychological. Just so, and from Nei's viewpoint a more apt title would have been *Farewell to Reykjavik*.

Immediately after game seventeen on 22 August, Nei left the match so abruptly that he had to kick his heels in Copenhagen waiting for an onward flight to Moscow. Today he says that his job was done and he was needed for the beginning of the academic year in Estonia, where he was head of the chess school. The match was as good as over. He was no longer engaged in serious analysis with Spassky's other seconds, and Geller thought it was pointless for him to stay. Spassky agreed.

Krogius's version differs. Certain Soviet embassy personnel informed him and Geller that "Nei is behaving oddly." The Estonian was spending a long time alone with Byrne. In turn, the two seconds told Spassky. The same evening, Nei was put under hostile interrogation. He did not deny his contacts with Byrne, that he

and the American were analyzing the match and that he was passing Byrne his comments on the games for future publication in
the United States. His dubious listeners pressed Nei: "Why was
he engaged in outside work of such a suspicious nature, and in
secret, without Spassky's permission? And in the material passed
to the American, what had he said about Spassky's condition and
his own assessment of Spassky's chess to date?" They were not
satisfied with Nei's responses. The conversation grew extremely
heated. Nei was told that his services were no longer required
and that he must leave. (Spassky says members of his team had
no right to engage in business.)

On the following day, the Estonian flew out. He changed
planes in Moscow, flying straight to his home city of Tallinn, thus
avoiding a visit to the Sports Committee, where he was due to
hand in his foreign travel passport.

Nei says that many people in the chess world were surprised to
see him return to Estonia; they thought he would end up in
Siberia or the West. But, he asks, why? He had not behaved in-
correctly. From Tallinn, he went on to send his final contributions
for the book to the States, in seven parts. He must have had some
trepidation about the project: he posted each of these sections to
separate addresses in Canada as well as the United States.

For transgressing the rules—he had not informed the KGB or
the authorities about the book—Nei had earned official displeasure. Upon his return, he was banned from foreign travel for two
years, a relatively light punishment signifying that the critical
charge of disclosing secrets was not taken seriously. It was highly
incorrect, says Ivonin, to talk about the match during the match,
but Nei could not be punished, as nothing was proved. "There
was only suspicion."

There was more than enough of that to go around. The KGB
was even focusing on Spassky himself.

As the match approached its climax, Reykjavik was swept by gossip that Spassky was about to defect. The American chargé
d'affaires, Theodore Tremblay, recalls how the Yugoslavs at the
match "kept coming to me and saying, 'Spassky wants to defect,

Spassky wants to defect.' Well, by that time, I had developed a rather close relationship with Boris. I kept telling them, 'Look, if Boris wants to defect, all he has to do is tell me. We'll see what we can do.' "

Tremblay had met Spassky at the reception following the official opening, and they had talked amicably over the champagne. According to Tremblay, they became good friends and "just kept running into each other." The American diplomat sometimes dined at Spassky's hotel, and when the world champion spotted him, he would come over to chat. Tremblay found the atmosphere around the Soviets much more relaxed than in his previous posting in Bangkok. No one circled around, keeping people away from Spassky—though if he spoke for any length of time in the hotel or on the street, somebody would deliberately break it up. Naturally, the American denies cultivating Spassky professionally, though without sounding wholehearted about it: "Actually, we could have got him out of the country in a hurry if he had wanted to, but I knew he had no intention of defecting."

The Soviet authorities did not share Tremblay's confidence. In Ivonin's office, there were expressions of unease and confusion over what would become of Spassky. The KGB was certainly aware of the rumors. Major General Nikashkin decided they needed a representative in Reykjavik and recommended to Ivonin that Spassky's friend Stanislav Melen'tiev should return to Iceland. Ivonin was anxious not to provoke Spassky into feeling he was distrusted and warned Nikashkin that the champion could misunderstand Melen'tiev's arrival. The Sports Minister Pavlov then intervened, ringing in to say that this was a lot of fuss over nothing and they simply had to rely on Spassky's loyalty. Nikashkin coolly pointed to press reports that Spassky had ignored Pavlov's advice at the beginning of the match, though all other sportsmen would have had to take it. (According to Ivonin, if they had thought there was a real danger of Spassky's defecting, they would have taken precautionary measures—for instance, having someone escort him back or offering him an inducement to return.)

Relief arrived on 4 September. Nikashkin informed Ivonin that Spassky had bought a car in Iceland and was planning to ship it to Leningrad. At first, he had wanted to transport it to Copenhagen and drive home, but he was persuaded that the journey would be too dangerous. More heartening news had come: He had attacked those journalists who had questioned him on whether he might defect. "This is a provocation," he told them. He said he was thinking of buying a dacha outside Moscow. In the Central Committee, Aleksandr Yakovlev was duly told: Spassky is coming home.

Tremblay's judgment about Spassky proved correct. Spassky's chess colleagues never doubted his patriotism—Russian, if not Soviet. Defection could not have been further from his mind, says Spassky today. So what was the source of the rumors, spread so assiduously by the Yugoslavs? With the match seemingly lost, could this have been another ham-fisted KGB operation—this time to discredit Spassky rather than bolster him, this time to explain why he seemed unable to make a breakthrough against the American?

21

ADVERSARY

PARTNERS

On the whole, in 1972 U.S.-Soviet relations were at their best in many years. —HENRY KISSINGER

Seen from the vantage point of the twenty-first century, was Fischer's triumph a cold war victory—at least symbolically—for the United States over its long-term adversary the USSR?

One flaw with a cold war interpretation of the match is immediately apparent. Fischer and Spassky had in common their sheer unsuitability to represent their countries' political systems. Spassky was not a *Soviet* patriot—and he made no secret of it. Fischer's idiosyncratic and asocial behavior marked him as un-American for many of his compatriots.

In the London *Sunday Times* on 2 July, Arthur Koestler, the author of the terrifying study of Stalinism, *Darkness at Noon*, understatedly warned, "Bobby is a genius, but as a propagandist for the free world he is rather counter-productive." *The Washington Post* ruminated that Fischer's behavior had caused the match to escalate "from a sport into a revival of the Cold War." One of the *Post's* readers wrote that "Fischer is the only American who can make everyone in the U.S. root for the Russians." In an article written in late July and passed around the Soviet embassy in Reykjavik, causing much merriment, *Washington Post* humorist Art Buchwald mused over a presidential dilemma: Would Nixon place a telephone call to Iceland if Fischer won? He foresaw the conversation:

> "Hello, Bobby, this is President Nixon. I just wanted to call and congratulate you on your victory in Iceland."
> "Make it short, will you? I'm tired."
> "This is a great day for America, Bobby."
> "It's a greater day for me. I won $150,000 and I showed these Icelandic creeps a thing or two."

Eventually the president hangs up and calls Richard Helms, the director of the CIA.

> "Dick. I'm sending the presidential plane to Iceland to pick up Bobby Fischer. Do me a favor. After he's on board, will you see to it that he's hijacked to Cuba?"

Victor Jackovich remembers the qualified rapture in the embassy when the match ended:

> When he won the crown for America, pride was not the first reaction in the embassy: our first reaction was one of relief that it was over. Our second reaction: we won. The U.S. has won. Our guy has won. An American born and bred winning—that was something. But our first reaction was one of great relief. This was quite an ordeal.

However, incontrovertibly, the common view was that the confrontation was an episode of the cold war. The new champion had certainly seen it this way. In April, the London *Times* noted: "Fischer believes that in some sense he is doing battle for the free world against the Soviet Union, in an atmosphere akin to the Berlin blockade of twenty years ago." Fischer would have deleted the phrase *in some sense*. He told a BBC interviewer, James Burke:

> It is really the free world against the lying, cheating, hypocritical Russians. . . . This little thing between me and Spassky. It's a microcosm of the whole world political situation. They always suggest that the world leaders should fight it out hand to hand. And this is the kind of thing that we are doing—not with bombs, but battling it out over the board.

The Western public too was convinced of the geopolitical significance of the battle, and there were letters to the local and national press to this effect. Donald Kurtis, from Connecticut, wrote to *The New York Times* to point out that "chess is far more important to millions of people abroad than in the United States. A victory by Mr. Fischer can be more positively impressive to these people than all the trade, aid, and arms treaties." A *New York Times* editorial makes a similar point, referring to the Soviets' space achievement, with relish: "Unquestionably, Spassky's loss of the title would be regarded as a major national setback; a Sputnik in reverse." Just before the first game, *The Washington Post* claimed, "A Fischer victory would strike at a basic claim of Soviet ideology." Decades later, many of the characters in our story concurred. For Icelandic cameraman Gissli Gestsson, this was not simply a chess match: "It was a battle for the minds of people all over the world; it was about the superpowers. I think it was a bit sad for chess, that it was used in this way."

Stereotyped contrasts between "us" and "them" abounded in articles and contemporary books by writers projecting the period through which they lived. The Soviet embassy interpreter Valeri Chamanin was used as an example of the Soviet lack of humanity. Francis Wyndham, coauthor of an instant account of the match, saw Chamanin as dummylike. (How animated should a professional interpreter be? In private life, Chamanin is warmly ebullient.)

According to Brad Darrach, Chamanin was "one of many quasi-official Russian bureaucrats of the island whose faces appeared to have been restored to almost human form after a fatal accident." The Soviet delegation, he noted, walked in single file, expressionless and uncommunicative, "like finalists in a self-effacement contest." All except Spassky, that is, and Krogius, who was expressive enough to Westerners to seem sinister and who was accorded the character of a horror movie psychologist plotting the hero's downfall through his cruel insights. However, to his Soviet contemporaries, let alone to Western reporters, Efim Geller seemed unusually paranoid about the West, and TASS correspondent Aleksandr Yermakov called him "Mr. No" for his unwillingness to share anything even with the Soviet agency. (In Icelandic, "no" was pronounced like "Nei," so to the local population another Spassky aide was Mr. No.)

The London *Sunday Times* perception of the two protagonists in Iceland revealed how, seen through the prism of ideological confrontation, reality was distorted: "Both are wonderfully cast for their roles. Fischer the rugged individualist, adventurous and occasionally reckless both in his life-style and chess style; Spassky the more benign type of Soviet bureaucrat, cautious, noncommittal, evasive."

GosKomSport officials would have greeted with incredulity the idea of Spassky as the benign bureaucrat. But for Moscow and the Soviet bloc, Fischer-Spassky was demonstrably a clash of systems. Naturally, red-clawed capitalism was held responsible for the American's undesirable obsession with money, though it is not difficult to discern a note of envy over the way in which Fischer grasped riches from the game. But there was worry, too, about how this could transform the financial weather for Soviet players, making them less amenable to state control, diverting them from socialist priorities.

Even so, once the match got under way, ideology vanished from the coverage. The turning point was Spassky's disastrous third game, when the Soviet press settled down into straightforward chess analysis, with increasing hints that the champion was the author of his own misfortune. The match itself took second place to the Olympics in the use of limited hard currency and journalistic resources. Aleksandr Yermakov's living expenses were severely restricted; he survived by finding student accommodations and cooking for himself. The TASS man's task was to send the moves to Moscow. His editors had next to no interest in the anecdotes, drama, and human stories preoccupying Western journalists, though the facts were reported.

Back in Moscow, commentaries in the press made clear Soviet grandmasters' dissatisfaction with Spassky's standard of play. Although there was little coverage of the Fischer sideshow, an American journalist in Moscow, Robert Kaiser, was struck by the freedom of the coverage of the chess itself.

> All Russia seems transfixed. . . . The self-centered, unpredictable American is a puzzlement here, but he is also the object of admiration. His moves as well as Spassky's are subjected to a rare form of public commentary—vivid, outspoken journalism. The grandmasters all write well, in a frank and lively style more like American political commentary than standard Soviet journalism. Phrases like "Then Spassky grossly miscalculated" may read like normal comment to an American eye, but it jumps out at a reader of the Soviet press.

There was freedom among park bench experts, too. Another American reporter overheard a note of gloom: "Spassky is playing like a shoemaker."

But some two-thirds into the match, its prominence in the state newspaper *Izvestia* steadily declined. After game seventeen, the FIDE logo was removed from its place beside the articles (whether as official disapproval of the federation or simply to make the match less prominent—or both—is unclear), and the byline of grandmaster David Bronstein, who had provided the analysis, also disappeared. The final report from TASS was tucked away on the lower-left-hand corner of the sports page, overshadowed by pictures of Soviet athletes and gymnasts. It was one column, eleven lines:

> Not arriving for the game, Spassky admitted his defeat in yesterday's adjourned twenty-first game of the chess world championship. This decision is explained by the fact that further resistance on the part of white, as analysis showed, was already

hopeless. Thus Fischer won the match with a score of 12.5–8.5 and earned the title of World Champion of Chess.

The newspaper *Sovietskaia Rossia* put the passing of the title from Russian hands in a black-bordered box used for an obituary. But the Munich Olympic games were now the lead story, and for good reason. As Fischer seized the title, a Russian sprinter, Valeri Borzov, took from the United States the crown of world's fastest man. Just as an American had never before been world chess champion, a Russian had never before won the Olympic 100-meter sprint. (Pavlov had chosen the right event to mastermind.)

A downplaying of the chess match was to be expected. The role of the Soviet press was to reflect official views and priorities, not to satisfy the appetites of readers. With the strength of Fischer's challenge to Soviet hegemony, the news media's response became pragmatically low-key.

Significantly, there were neither political allegations nor recriminations against the West. There were no attempts to couch the match in strategic terms. While the loss of the title was a blow, it was to be presented as an internal chess issue, not a matter of direct international or ideological importance.

But then this was not a time for unnecessary dissension toward the United States. Indeed, far from epitomizing East-West conflict, the championship took place in the high blossoming of détente. In Europe, the cockpit of the cold war, a postwar settlement had finally emerged, in effect the long-deferred World War II peace treaty. Though almost all Western accounts of Fischer-Spassky couch the match in geopolitical terms, they are, in this respect, curiously misleading. The encounter might have been seen by the public and written up in the press as a cold war showdown, but in the Kremlin and the White House, East-West showdowns were not on the agenda.

Thus, on the Soviet side, the political level of interest in Spassky's preparation was high, but not exceptionally so. One of the two secretaries of the Central Committee who ranked just below Brezhnev in authority, Mikhail Suslov was in ultimate charge of ideological matters and therefore chess. He apparently never officially discussed the match. The Soviet leader Leonid Brezhnev does not appear to have involved himself in the match, though the figurehead president of the USSR, Nikolai Podgornii, sent a telegram of good wishes to Spassky. (It would have been unthinkable for Brezhnev himself to put his name to such a message.) When Spassky was plainly in trouble, Lev Abramov, the former head of the Chess Department of the State Sports Committee, wanted a team manager sent to Reykjavik. He went directly to one of Brezhnev's aides, Konstantin Rusakov, to enlist his help. But Rusakov was abroad; there was no sense of urgency in the Kremlin, and Abramov's initiative came to nothing.

As for the Americans, we know that Henry Kissinger made two calls to Fischer, but his almost day-by-day record of his time as national security adviser, *The White House Years,* contains no reference to them. There is no mention of the match in Nixon's equally detailed *Memoirs.* The Soviet ambassador to Washington, D.C., Anatoli Dobrynin, told the authors that in his frequent contacts with Kissinger, the match never came up. Neither Fischer nor Spassky is cited in his book, *In Confidence,* even though Kissinger appears to have rung Fischer when he and the Soviet ambassador were the president's guests in California, working and relaxing together while Fischer was threatening to fly home to Brooklyn.

In an interview for this book Dr. Kissinger reflected, "It was not the biggest decision I had to make in those days, but I thought it would help create an atmosphere of peaceful competition." Indeed, what could be more competitive or more peaceful than a World Chess Championship? Yet the former national security adviser insists that, unlike most members of the public, he did not see the match as an aspect of the cold war or democracy versus communism.

᠉᠊᠊᠊

By the end of 1971, the London-based International Institute for Strategic Studies (IISS), in its *Strategic Survey* of that year, com-

In the White House Map Room (left to right), the president's national security adviser, Henry Kissinger, with the Soviet ambassador Anatoli Dobrynin. THE WHITE HOUSE

pared 1971 to 1947 in that it marked a point where "the international system as a whole formed into a visibly new pattern." One of America's foremost strategic thinkers, Samuel P. Huntington, summed up geopolitics of the early 1970s: "All in all, the skies were filled with planes bearing diplomats to negotiations, and the air was rich with the promise of détente." In its *Strategic Survey* for 1972, the IISS announced that the cold war was dead and buried.

The broad period of the championship saw three successful summits, when Nixon visited Beijing and Moscow in 1972 and when Brezhnev visited Washington in June 1973. A torrent of talks, suggestions for talks, the promise of future agreements, and actual agreements cascaded into the diplomatic desert. These included the U.S.-Soviet Strategic Arms Limitation Talks (SALT), the Interim Agreement on Certain Measures with Respect to Strategic Offensive Arms (SALT I), and the Anti-Ballistic Missile Treaty. Eventually, 150 agreements were signed and 11 joint commissions established. A handshake in space in 1975 could be seen as the culminating moment.

The essential difference between détente and the previous era, Dr. Kissinger argues, is that Nixon believed that negotiations were still possible and desirable with the Soviet regime as it was. Previous U.S. administrations held that any meaningful dialogue with the Soviets would have to await a fundamental transformation in the Soviet political system. Nixon turned this thinking on its head. He maintained that if international stability could be created over a long enough period, the monolithic Soviet system would be unable to resist change.

What was Brezhnev's view of détente? Essentially that it was a mechanism for dealing with problems between governments and that this foreign policy was distinct from and not applicable to domestic affairs. Or, if there was a connection, it was a matter of preserving the Soviet system, not liberalizing it. Indeed, in the Soviet Union, repression stiffened in the détente years.

For the Kremlin, importantly, détente also meant America's acknowledgment that the USSR was a military superpower and a political equal. As the Soviet foreign minister Andrei Gromyko said in 1971: "There is no question of any significance that can be decided without the Soviet Union or in opposition to it." To Brezhnev, recognition of equality was of greater consequence than SALT. The Soviet leader could reassure himself and the Soviet people that the so-called correlation of forces in the world was tilting toward communism; the Soviet Union was riding the wave of history that would wash capitalism away. An article in *Komsomolskaia Pravda* justifying the policy was entitled "A Triumph of Realism." Détente did not mark the end of global political competition. On the contrary, now was the time to step up the struggle; at this juncture in history, the circumstances were exceptionally favorable to the onward march of socialism. (Kissinger saw Brezhnev's sensitivity on political equality as showing his psychological insecurity: "What a more secure leader might have regarded as a cliché or condescension, he treated as a welcome sign of our seriousness.")

Détente also offered immediate practical and material payoffs for the adversarial superpowers. The Soviets wanted trade to avoid root-and-branch economic reform. The United States hoped détente would give the Soviets a stake in stability and temper their adventurousness abroad.

Thus, there was necessarily a contradiction at the heart of détente—between cooperation and competition. Rivalry between the two superpowers remained intense—as seen in the long list of Nixon's reactive measures against perceived Soviet threats. The administration took action to counter the construction of a Soviet naval base in Cuba (U.S. spy planes had photographed a football field being set out when the Cuban national game was baseball), the movement of Soviet surface-to-air missiles to the Suez Canal, the Soviet role in the Indo-Pakistan war, and Brezhnev's aggressiveness and apparent readiness for military intervention in the Arab-Israeli war.

Both sides worked on improving their weaponry and extending their influence. And both sides had problems with allies and client states whose interests did not align with theirs, or who felt their interests were subordinated to those of the superpower. For example, during the first days of Fischer-Spassky, the Egyptian president, Anwar al-Sadat, expelled the 20,000 Soviet advisers and technicians based in his country, together with Soviet combat and reconnaissance aircraft. Angered by Moscow's refusal to give him advanced weapons, Sadat initiated secret contacts with the Americans.

When the match was over, some of the press picked up these opposing themes—suspicious antagonism against peaceful competition. On the one hand, Fischer and Spassky represented their countries, and the match, according to the broadsheets, embodied East-West confrontation, particularly given the Soviet claim that its chess supremacy was the outcome of its superior ideology. On the other hand, no nationalist rivalry had been sparked off. Many Americans had supported Spassky, and many Russians had quietly rooted for Fischer. All in all, concluded *The New York Times*, the match had a unique political importance in terms of improved U.S.-USSR relations.

So Reykjavik *was* a cold war confrontation in this sense: It illustrated the tension within détente and the strains that led to the policy's breakdown within three years. Fischer-Spassky smacked of both the continuing divide in politics and society and the suspicion and enmity that infused relations across the Iron Curtain. The separate territory kept to by the Soviet team, with all their customary watchfulness and suspicions, their lack of experience in dealing with the press, the go-go aggression of the Fischer staff, the tendency of the Western officials and Americans to make unilateral decisions and then to present them to the Soviets, the stereotyping by Western journalists of the Soviet team—all these reflected the cold war and directly affected the match.

Our two heroes also dramatized the contradictions of the era. For Spassky, Reykjavik was supposed to be a feast of chess, a celebration to be shared with friendly rivals. As for Fischer, in victory he had no doubt about the implications of his win. He said he could crush anyone the Soviets threw at him: "The Russians are wiped out." He was delighted to have seized the title from the Soviet Union. "They probably now feel sorry they ever started playing chess," he told the BBC. "They had it all for the last twenty years. They talked of their military might and their intellectual might. Now the intellectual thing . . . it's given me great pleasure . . . as a free person . . . to have smashed this thing."

Of course, as it turned out, news of the cold war's death was greatly exaggerated. But if Fischer had not been so anti-Soviet and mercurial, if he had been as convivial as Spassky, the match might even have gone down in history as symbolizing détente.

22

UNEASY LIES THE
HEAD THAT WEARS
THE CROWN

Nothing except a battle lost can be half as melancholy as a battle won. — DUKE OF WELLINGTON

Fame is when you stop signing and start autographing.

— BILLY WILDER

With the match over and Fischer wrapped in triumphalism, the organizers were still unable to relax. His absence at the opening ceremony had been a catastrophe; now they worried that the new world champion would ignore the final dinner. Worn down by two months of Fischerism, Gudmundur Thorarinsson was almost reconciled to this. Fred Cramer fed the doubts. He thought his man should be crowned in his hotel room: "I cannot see Bobby sitting quietly through a load of speeches."

Euwe, Schmid, and Thorarinsson met for a drink at the hotel Esja before the ceremony. A journalist asked Schmid whether he would arbitrate another match. "I would have to have a long think about that," was the cautious response. Euwe thought the best thing about the match was that it was over. *Corriere della Sera* completed its coverage of Fischer-Spassky as though it had been a fairy tale: "Good night, Fischer; good night, Spassky; good night to the enchanted island of Iceland."

China's newly appointed ambassador to Iceland, Chen Tung, was one of many delighted that the match was finally over. Chen Tung had a long-standing booking of the presidential suite in the Loftleidir, expecting the match to have concluded. So as not to cause a diplomatic row, the hotel had approached Cramer, wondering whether, in view of Chen Tung's prior reservation, Fischer might be willing to move to another suite. "We are not prepared to discuss anything but chess at the moment," the panjandrum shot back. "Bobby cannot be bothered with the problems of the Chinese ambassador." For Chen Tung, there was always the option of the other main luxury hotel in town, the Saga. But that was where the representatives of China's ideological foe—the Soviets—were quartered.

For the closing dinner at the Laugardalsholl on Sunday, 3 September (price $22 a head), a Viking theme had been chosen. The waiters wore plastic Viking hats. Guests could feast on barbecued suckling pig and spitted mountain lamb, washed down with Viking's Blood, a potent concoction unknown to Vikings and containing wine, cognac, orange juice, and lemonade. The meal began on time at seven P.M. Spassky was there, as were Schmid, Thorarinsson, Euwe, the minister of finance Halldor Sigurdsson, and over 1,200 other people. In a reprise of the opening ceremony, Fischer's place was vacant.

Virtually an hour late, at 7:55 P.M., as the band on stage was striking up the chess federation's anthem, the guest of honor finally appeared, garbed in a violet velvet suit. Harry Golombek wrote that it "must have been made of samite, mystic, wonderful. . . ." A standing ovation greeted the new champion. He took his place to the right of Max Euwe; Spassky was on Euwe's other side. The FIDE president rose to deliver one of several speeches that night. Fischer promptly shuffled into the vacated seat, reached into his jacket, took out a pocket chess set, and showed Spassky the adjourned position from their final game. It must have been the last thing the weary ex-champion wanted to see, though he maintains today that he was unperturbed by Fischer's behavior. In any case, he dutifully followed the analysis, from time to time adding comments of his own.

At issue was whether Spassky could have survived with a draw by sealing an alternative move before the adjournment. Fischer thought not.

A crowd gathered around their table. Fischer finally noticed them and turned to his friend and bodyguard. "Hey, Sammy, get these guys outta here."

It was Thorarinsson's task to hand over the checks. For the victor, this was a sum of $76,123—two-thirds of $125,000. An equal amount awaited transfer from the United Kingdom—Jim Slater's money, the donation that had saved the match.

Fischer made no speech of thanks, no graceful comment on the hard work that had gone into the long contest, no tribute to his defeated opponent. Taking his prize, he immediately tore open the envelope and closely scrutinized the contents for several minutes, checking the figure. Satisfied, he then returned to his seat.

Chester Fox came into his own at last, filming everything in sight, probably motivated as much by one-upmanship as profit. There was dancing until one A.M. Fischer boogied awkwardly with two young Icelandic women, Anna Thorsteinsdottir, eigh-

You were lost whatever you did. CHESTER FOX

CHESTER FOX

teen, and her friend Inga, seventeen—the papers the next day called them "beautiful Icelandic blondes." Palsson had arranged their tickets. (He and Fischer had been eating in a restaurant when he had seen them gawking at Fischer and invited them to the banquet. The two women had even been back to the American's room late at night to listen to rock music.) They denied rumors that there was any romance. "He has been very nice to us, but there is nothing in it. You couldn't interest him in girls because he's married to chess."

To end the formalities, there was still one final reception, given by the government at the president's official residence. Palsson drove Fischer there: this time, amazingly, they were early. "When Bobby saw that the ministers were arriving after him, he took me to one side and said, 'Saemi, how did you manage to get me here on time?'" Iceland's rock 'n' roll policeman had cracked it. While Fischer was in the shower, he had put the wall clock, the clock on the table, and the champion's wristwatch all forward by an hour. "'Oh,' Bobby said, 'that was a great move!' Sometimes you could say or do anything. But if he'd been in a bad mood, he could have erupted, maybe left, maybe gone straight back to America."

At that reception, Fischer chatted amiably with officials from the Soviet embassy, and he and Spassky tentatively agreed to go swimming the following day. Spassky later rang to cancel: He was leaving for home early the next morning and he had to pack and so forth. Fischer was annoyed and told Palsson he would not bid good-bye to his opponent. Palsson recounts how he became angry in turn and told Fischer that he should at least write a farewell letter. The *Life* photographer Harry Benson had given Fischer a cheap camera. As Fischer did not want it, the Icelander suggested he present it to Spassky. Fischer replied that it was too cheap. " 'No,' I said. 'That's not the point, it's a token.' So I took it to the Saga to hand it over, and Spassky was so emotional. I've never seen a man so pleased. It was one of the best things I did during the match."

In 2000, looking back at his time as world champion, Spassky remarked to the *Irish Times*, "I was a king in Russia." Yet his period of office had been so uneasy that we can imagine his mixed feelings on watching Fischer, whom he had so admired, take his place. David Spanier of *The Times* sensed "that in some deep and hidden part of himself, he wanted Fischer to win."

After the debacle of the third game, Spassky had fought hard. When it was all over, he commented that Fischer had started the match as a sprint but instead it had become a marathon; he had expected the American to crack at any time. He met Fischer only once after the closing ceremony, at the presidential reception, and asked the new champion whether they could have a rematch.

"Maybe," replied Fischer.

"When?"

"Maybe in a year—if the money side is okay."

The former champion reflected on the fate that awaited his successor: "It will be a hard time for him. Now he feels like a god. He thinks all problems are over—he will have many friends, people will love him, history will obey him. But it is not so. In these high places it is very cold, very lonely. Soon depression will set in. I like him, and I am afraid what will happen to him now." These somber words were also about himself.

By the end, Spassky was far from the figure of radiant well-being who had arrived in Iceland so full of confident anticipation. Larisa Spasskaia remembers also being affected: the healthy woman who went to Reykjavik returned with stomach pains and was not herself for six months. Boris, she recounts, was in a bad way, drinking more than usual and needing psychotherapy to deal with the trauma of the contest.

Trauma was to be expected. "I do not know which is worse, before the match or after," Spassky said. "In a long match, a player goes very deep into himself, like a diver. Then he comes up very fast. Every time, whether I win or if I lose, I am so depressed I want to die. I cannot get back in touch with other people. I want the other chess player. I miss him. Only after a year will the pain go away. A year."

There were material compensations. Spassky had his share of the prize money, $93,750. The USSR chess authorities had made no provision for dealing with such staggering winnings, and Spassky simply kept the money for himself; the authorities never asked for it. In the Soviet Union, it made him at least the equivalent of a millionaire in the West. Tigran Petrosian remarked, "Normally you could buy a car with your winnings, but when you could purchase the whole car park, that was something else." (In future, Soviet participants in world championship matches would be obliged to hand over half their bounty.) He could also parade around in a new Range Rover four-wheel-drive car, sold to him at cost by his dealer friend, Sigfus Sigfusson, who had arranged for the latest model, in white, well equipped with spares, to be sent to Reykjavik and shipped on to Leningrad. Larisa's prize possession was a new Icelandic winter coat. (The car was sold after two years of hard labor on Soviet roads; the winter coat lasted much longer.)

After leaving Reykjavik on 7 September, Spassky and his wife stayed in Copenhagen for a few days before returning to Moscow to face the music. Was he not the Soviet who had surrendered the crown to an American, and with it Soviet hegemony? Would he not be seen as having failed to live up to the spirit of the great motherland? Perhaps visions of Taimanov's reception after his defeat by Fischer haunted his dreams.

In fact, the message had already gone out from Central Committee secretary Piotr Demichev that Spassky was to be received in a civilized manner. At Sheremet'evo Airport, the welcome party included a representative of the Sports Committee, a journalist, and some close friends. Nikolai Krogius remembers that "on the whole, Spassky's defeat was received calmly in Moscow. It was a pleasant surprise that the sporting leadership and the press did not seek to punish him and his team."

Nevertheless, it was hardly the hero's reception he would have expected had he been victorious. The Associated Press described it as "anti-VIP" treatment. He had to stand in the long line for passport control, queue up for his bags, fill out the customs forms. A battered gray-and-blue bus awaited them rather than an official Chaika limousine. Larisa was observed chewing gum: a "dirty habit" she had learned "over there," someone remarked. "Over there" meant outside the USSR. His bus stopped at all the traffic lights: triumphant, he might have sailed through as if he were Brezhnev.

And knives were out over his defeat. Mikhail Botvinnik commented later that Spassky lost because he overrated himself. The former world champion Vasili Smyslov chastised Spassky. In a creative sense, he said, Spassky went to the match completely empty. And he added that Fischer and Spassky both took home what they thought about: Fischer the crown and money and Spassky only money. Geller gave his views privately to Ivonin: that Spassky loved himself, that this defeat had taught him a big lesson, that he had underestimated the need for preparation and had not played enough, that he was still an idealist who "melted again" when he last talked to Fischer. Spassky was "very soft with his enemies and very ferocious with those trying to help him."

These were just the precursors to the official postmortem held on 27 December 1972 at the Sports Committee and chaired by Viktor Ivonin. Apart from Spassky, Geller, and Krogius, the top brass of Soviet chess was represented in the fifteen men gathered around the table. They included five grandmasters, two of them former world champions, as well as the senior officers of the

USSR Chess Federation. Their deliberations are recorded in near verbatim minutes.

The purpose of the meeting was to look ahead, Ivonin declared from the chair: "We must draw up plans for returning the championship to our Soviet family." But in opening the discussion as the official team leader in Reykjavik, Geller wasted no time in going for Spassky, laying on him all the blame for the lost title. He cited Spassky's decision "taken on his own" to play in the closed room, constant and incomprehensible departures from agreed tactics, and unbelievable blunders. The most damning accusation related to a psychological failure:

> We were unable to change Spassky's mind about
> Fischer's personal qualities. Spassky believed
> that Fischer would play honestly. Perhaps
> Spassky's views on bourgeois sport were
> important to his agreement to play in a closed
> room. He placed a naive trust in the honesty of
> this sport.

Geller had set the tone, although Krogius, in a much briefer intervention, couched his opinion more positively: Spassky's defeat was due to his treating people better than they deserved. He related to Fischer as to a comrade and an unhappy genius, but not a cunning enemy.

Then it was Spassky's turn—the speech for the defense. Like many such speeches, its strategy was to direct material guilt elsewhere while confessing to a human, eminently forgivable weakness. Thus he complained that because they had not been given an organizer, the team's energies had been diverted into everyday affairs. Pre-Reykjavik, "special work on technical matters" had not been satisfactory—a dig at Geller and Krogius. But the main problem was his being a very weak psychologist, "giving rise to a series of mistakes"—in other words, he admitted to being too trusting.

> I knew Fischer as a chess player, but perhaps I
> idealized him as a man. Bondarevskii's departure

```
was a strong blow. I found it difficult without
him. It is a big minus to be involved in
extraneous matters that you are not suited to
dealing with. Bondarevskii shielded me from such
matters. Our many sleepless nights . . . because
of the mistakes we made were extremely damaging.
It seems to me that I should have listened to
the advice of my comrades that Viktor Davidovich
[Baturinskii] be temporarily removed from the
match.
```

He also owned up to a failure to foresee that someone was required in Reykjavik specifically to handle "the prematch fever" and what he described as "a real war." He also offered his version of "the culminating moment," game three, after which, he said, everything turned against him. Through faintheartedness, he had met Fischer halfway, rather than forcing him to play in the hall or withdraw. Thus he had opened the way to Fischer's "colossal domination" up to game nine. Only from game ten did he begin to control his emotions.

There was no recognition of his own role in setting up the training routine and the other arrangements for Reykjavik. And the rifts with Baturinskii and Bondarevskii were scarcely as he described them.

Little wonder, then, that there is a note of suppressed wrath in Baturinskii's point-by-point reply. It covered Spassky's rejection of the grandmasters' counsel (Yuri Averbakh noted dryly that "when a person does not wish to listen, it is difficult to give him advice"), his passive attitude to the maneuverings of Fischer and Euwe in the run-up to the match, his failure to prepare effectively, and his refusal to accept the full team on offer. It did not escape Baturinskii that although Spassky complained about the absence of a delegation leader in Reykjavik, he had not consulted Ivonin over the move to the closed room. Finally, he protested that he had done everything asked of him to ensure victory for Spassky, and would always do all he could for the common cause of chess and chess players.

As the discussion went on, the question marks over Spassky's preparation and his inability to take advice were raised again and again—"superficial," "unsatisfactory." Mikhail Tal was particularly cutting: "It is not an embarrassment to have lost to a chess player like Fischer, but Spassky's game was simply shocking."

Spassky's politics and personality were also attacked. The president of the Leningrad Chess Federation, A. P. Tupikin, told the meeting that the Leningraders' love affair with Spassky was at an end, blaming what he called Spassky's arrogance, his alien views, and his failure to understand the political significance of the match.

A deputy president of the USSR Chess Federation and FIDE vice president, B. I. Rodionov was even more brutally direct. In effect, the world champion had ignored the fact that he was wearing a red shirt and was guilty of damaging the prestige of the state. It was incomprehensible how Spassky had given in to his opponent—to what Rodionov called "the completely groundless demands made by that scum."

At the end, Ivonin delivered judgment. He was unsparing about Spassky, castigating his attitude both to work and to ideology:

> All his requests and wishes were fulfilled. Today we can only regret that these possibilities were not exploited in full and to the end. . . . Spassky's words—that the match was a holiday and that there must be an honest fight—can be called idealism. This was not a holiday, but a very fierce struggle. And it is no coincidence that Marshall, Fischer's lawyer, said that victory for Fischer was a question of national and personal pride. Unfortunately, Comrade Spassky did not make such declarations.

A sense of disillusionment pervaded the meeting. The defeat had been a warning. Like so much else in the USSR, the Soviet chess machine appeared to be rusting away. The first problem was the new champion. Baturinskii thought that "the struggle which we must wage for the world championship will be very difficult. If Fischer made so many demands when he was a challenger, then how will he behave now that he has won the world championship?" So the comrades must work harder and more systematically, and trainers must realize that they were in the service of the state, not independent actors.

Petrosian weighed in on the slothfulness of the elite players: "Our grandmasters have begun to work less." Ivonin had tough words for the disunity among chess players, putting it down to the long monopoly of the world title. "It seems to me that in the past few years, several people have been attacked by the worm of parasitism in chess and a refusal to undertake a lot of research work." There were problems of excessive secrecy and internal struggles that weakened the Soviet Union's external performance.

The Sports Committee itself did not escape censure. In words of foreboding, another deputy president of the USSR Chess Federation, V. I. Boikov, pointed to a decline in the game's predominance:

```
Why is it that the committee can build
complexes, swimming pools, covered stadiums?
What do chess players get? Old cellars. Big
cities such as Sverdlovsk, Novosibirsk, do not
have a chess club, and a club is a place where
qualified cadres are developed. All the work of
the leading masters has been set adrift. . . .
Russia has over 200 sporting schools, of which
only seven have a chess department, and those
are run by candidate masters instead of
grandmasters. The Physical Training and Sport
publishing house is only planning to bring out
three books this year.
```

The issues so agonizingly raked over at this meeting were followed by action. Ivonin produced a fourteen-point plan, affirmed in a committee decree. The plan included more chess education, a chess library that would include foreign publications, reform of the USSR championship, and proposals to improve the professional players' physical training and nutrition.

Nikolai Krogius, who became head of the USSR Chess

Organization, says that in the long run the impact of Spassky's defeat was beneficial: "The authorities sought to assist young chess players and to develop chess in the country as a whole. Many children's chess schools were opened, the publication of chess literature was increased, the system for staging USSR championships was reorganized, greater attention was paid to the leading young chess players headed by Karpov. It sounds paradoxical, but Fischer's victory in reality had a markedly positive influence in raising the status of chess in the USSR."

As for Spassky, he was not allowed to play abroad, he says, for nine months—a bad thing, "as after a defeat you need to play, since you have a lot of energy that needs releasing." The extra 200 roubles a month he had been granted when preparing his title defense was cut, but he was still comparatively well off on his grandmaster's stipend.

It could so easily have been worse for him. Early in the cold war, when the Soviet Union was newly taking part in international competitions, the Politburo's impatience with poor performances led to their moving a General Appolonov from the Interior Ministry to the Sports Committee. Failure abroad brought a telegram from the general to the offender ordering an immediate improvement. Somehow, the athletes then found extra strength. And in 1974, the then interior minister Nikolai Shchelokov, promoted to the rank of general by Brezhnev, visited the Karpov-Korchnoi match (the winner to meet Fischer in the world championship). According to Baturinskii, he asked, "Who went with Spassky to Reykjavik?" On being told, he commented, "If it were up to me, I would put them all in jail."

⁙

No matter how wounding the postmortem, Spassky's career at the top was far from over. He had returned from his defeat with his basic will to compete undiminished, though he told Ivonin that he wanted to consider his position now that he was an ordinary grandmaster. He had decided not to enter the USSR championship, but he intended to play in a big tournament the next year. And indeed, the next year he recaptured the Soviet title. In 1974, in the Candidates round, he beat American grandmaster Robert

Byrne without losing a single game, though he failed to reach the Candidates final for the chance to settle scores with Fischer.

He was still motivated in part by a desire to surprise and tease. On one occasion, this threatened to cost him his passport when an application to go abroad took him in front of the Foreign Travel Commission of Party worthies. Assessing his political reliability, they asked about the situation in Angola. At the time, Portuguese forces were battling with Marxist rebels. Soviet newspapers gave the war many column inches, celebrating the victory of the people over the "colonizers." Perhaps to shock, Spassky replied that he did not have the time to follow developments in Angola. The commission was duly shocked and refused him a passport. The Sports Committee had to step in to reverse the decision.

After his loss of the world title, professional crisis and divorce had coincided again, and in September 1975, Spassky married for the third time. He met Marina Shcherbacheva—a French citizen—at the apartment of a French diplomat; she worked in the commercial section of the French embassy in Moscow. Her grandfather was General Shcherbachev, who had commanded the Tsar's armies on the Romanian front in 1916–1917. Later, the general emigrated to France.

Spassky might have been a king in Russia (or an ex-king), but like every other Soviet citizen who wanted to marry a Westerner and live abroad, he faced obstruction from the authorities. Marina came under pressure to leave the country but refused. After Spassky moved into her Moscow apartment, the two of them were put under surveillance, and in August 1975, Spassky's own apartment was mysteriously robbed and all his personal possessions disappeared (including the camera Fischer had given him). From around this time, his Western visitors were liable to be searched on leaving the country.

The story has a happy ending. A Franco-Soviet summit was scheduled, and the Soviets wanted to avoid bad publicity. Spassky also profited from Brezhnev's signing of the 1975 Helsinki Agreement: its sections on human rights encouraged the free movement of peoples and contained provisions on facilitating binational marriages. The chess establishment saw that the ex-champion was determined to go, but they wanted to keep their ties to him; he certainly did not want a clean break from them. So with some help from Ivonin, says the former deputy minister, and some publicity in the Western press, Spassky and the authorities came to an arrangement. He left the Soviet Union with Marina in September 1976, moving to Paris on a visitor's visa, regularly renewed, while he kept his Soviet passport. Among his peers in Moscow, Spassky's departure reinforced the view that he saw himself as set apart from Soviet society. His son, Vasili, felt it prudent to change his surname to his mother's maiden name, Soloviev, to safeguard his application to become a student of journalism.

The year 1977 saw Spassky again in the Candidates round. Back in Reykjavik, to the delight of the Icelanders, he beat the Czechoslovak grandmaster Vlastimil Hort, and he followed this up with a win over the Hungarian grandmaster Lajos Portisch in Switzerland. In a profound irony, he then represented the Soviet Union against the despised Viktor Korchnoi, who had defected from the USSR in 1976 by walking into a police station in Amsterdam to claim political asylum. From his self-exile, Spassky accepted the Sports Committee's offer of full support. At his request, the committee sent Bondarevskii to join him in Belgrade, and Ivonin even went to give moral support. Spassky lost, 10.5 to 7.5. But in spite of the result, his waging a form of psychological war showed that he might have learned something from Fischer.

Korchnoi was already under strain: he was subjected to a sustained campaign of vitriol in the Soviet press, while Soviet players boycotted tournaments in which he appeared. His family was still in the Soviet Union. After game nine, and 6.5 to 2.5 down, Spassky appeared on the stage only to make his move, darting back behind the scenes. Korchnoi complained that it was like playing a ghost.

Spassky also put on a silver sun visor, swinging it as he came and went. In this poisonous atmosphere, with notes of protest and recrimination going back and forth, Spassky addressed an open letter to "chess players," defending his actions and claiming anarchy had broken out. The match had passed into a phase in which, "expressed by the words of Fedor Dostoyevsky, 'Everything is allowed.'" Spassky had refused to put his name to a letter condemning Korchnoi's defection, but after the match he felt it right to attack him in terms of which Pavlov would have approved. Korchnoi "had lost his moral principles, and thus his future both morally and in chess is insignificant."

Spassky's defeat did not signal the end of his involvement in world-class chess. He again played in the Candidates round in 1980; this time Portisch had his revenge, beating Spassky on a tie break. Spassky's last appearance in the world championship cycle was in 1985, and he continued to participate in the Olympiads and the World Cup until 1989.

Settled in France, Spassky seems to have had the best of all his worlds, a happy marriage, as much competitive chess as he desires, and freedom in his daily life from the Soviet system.

Today, he lives among other Russian émigrés in the tranquil eighteenth-century town of Meudon, on the edge of the French capital and famous as the home of the sculptor Rodin. Often asked to serve as an "ambassador" for chess, he travels extensively in Russia as well as other parts of the world. In his apartment, the chessboard is set up, but the tennis racket too is close to hand.

He bears no malice toward Fischer, telling the *Irish Times* in 2000, "Ever since my youth at about twenty-two, twenty-three years of age, I had a good impression of Bobby. He was always very honest and said exactly what he thought."

⁙

After becoming champion, Fischer stayed put in Iceland for another two weeks, whiling away the days with Palsson, swimming, bowling, and, of course, absorbed in his chessboard. On 15 September, he exchanged the calm of Iceland for the commotion of New York. The following week, there was a lavish reception at City Hall hosted by Republican mayor John Lindsay, who saluted Fischer as "the Grandest Master of them all," while Sebastian Leone, the president of the borough of Brooklyn, hailed his fellow resident as the world champion of "a truly Brooklyn sport—the sport of intellectuals." A large poster read WELCOME, BOBBY FISCHER, WORLD CHESS CHAMPION. Displayed among the official plaudits was evidence of local government frugality—the sign's reverse side greeted earlier conquering heroes, the crew of *Apollo 16,* who had returned to earth on 27 April, six days after landing on the moon.

The officials had shared a question with chess organizers worldwide: Would Fischer show up at the proceedings at all? According to an anonymous aide quoted in the press, when Fischer had been offered the key to the city he responded, "I live here, what do I need a key for?" In the event, the celebrations found him in an unusually relaxed state of mind. So eager was he to sign autographs that he mistook several hovering journalists for groupies, grabbing their pens. And when he gave his speech, he even made a joke: "I want to deny a vicious rumor that's been going around—I think it was started by Moscow. It's not true that Henry Kissinger phoned me during the night to tell me the moves." Comfortingly for those who relied on Fischer for dinner party horror stories, some things remained constant. He banned cameras from the reception, and only after some discussion was the press allowed in.

His future and the future of world championship chess alike seemed assured. An editorial in *The New York Times* commented, "The Fischer era of chess has begun, and it promises a brilliance and excitement the ancient game has never known before." Fischer stated that he would not shrink from defending his title; on the contrary, he would regularly take on challengers. Few expected him to be knocked off his throne for a decade or more. One exception was his former second, Larry Evans: "I just had the feeling he would never play competitive chess again."

There was a widespread consensus that Fischer would soon enter the multimillionaires' club. Almost immediately after the match, entrepreneur and bridge fanatic Ira G. Corn, with whose financial backing the U.S. bridge team had won the world championship in 1970 and 1971, proposed a Fischer-Spassky rematch. Talks were held over a possible simultaneous display in London's Albert Hall. Lucrative tournament offers arrived daily, from Qatar to South Africa, from the Philippine president Ferdinand Marcos to the Shah of Iran.

Promoters and producers, financiers and backers, were soon

reminded of Fischer's allergic reaction to contracts. A frustrated Paul Marshall remembers that megacontracts were drawn up, but "although he wanted the money, he wouldn't make written commitments, and you can't get the money without such commitments."

Warner Brothers had the idea of making a Christmas LP in which Fischer would record some basic chess lessons. Two producers had been dispatched to Iceland during the match to try to agree on terms. Fischer was too busy to grant them an audience. Nevertheless, money was considered no object in the LP's preparation—the potential spoils were forecast to be massive. Larry Evans was contracted to assist with the script for a handsome fee. He asked the president of Warner Brothers whether Fischer had actually signed a contract and was told no, but this was a mere formality. All the particulars had been agreed to in principle. Said Evans, "In that case, I'd rather be paid in advance." He was.

A manufacturer offered Fischer over a million dollars to endorse a chess set. Palsson was promised a percentage if he could get his buddy to agree. "I said to Bobby, 'What's wrong with the idea? You wanted chess in every home.' I'm positive I could have persuaded him, but I had to have more time. They needed an answer immediately because it was September and the sets had to be in the shops by Christmas." In the end, this and every other proposal ran aground.

Fischer, meanwhile, made a few TV appearances, including a show with Bob Hope in which the champion delivered responses to well-meaning questions, sometimes sullenly, sometimes with a shy grin, head rolling to one side, eyes fixed to the ground, words drawling from the side of his mouth. At Fischer's invitation, Palsson had accompanied him to the States—taking unpaid leave from the Icelandic police force—with the idea of becoming his minder and fixer, and perhaps finding a shop window to display his own dancing talents. His wife and children stayed behind in Iceland. "Maybe my wife was a little jealous of Bobby because he always wanted to speak to me and took up so much of my time."

Palsson and Fischer stayed with the Marshalls in New York and then moved west to Pasadena. None who knew Fischer would be surprised to hear that Palsson never received a cent in payment. But today, the Icelander has no regrets about going. He was quoted in the press and treated like a star; during the day, while Fischer slept, he was driven around in a limousine lent to them by Bob Hope. At one glamorous reception, the chairman saluted him as Fischer's bodyguard, "without whom, in Fischer's own words, he would never have become world champion." "They all stood up and clapped," says Palsson. "That was America. It was a great feeling. It was the highlight of my life."

Fischer had sworn to Palsson that he would even meet the president—that an invitation had arrived from the White House and that both of them would go. In fact, White House files reveal that the question of a presidential invitation threw the administration into a state of tortuous indecision, producing a stream of conflicting recommendations. A year earlier, after Fischer's victory over Petrosian, a ten-minute photo opportunity had been canvassed. The president should make time, said this first recommendation, as it would "show [his] interest in an intellectual sport for which there are estimated to be, world-wide, 60 million fans." The idea had originated with Leonard Garment, President Nixon's acting special counsel and close confidant. Dr. Kissinger and the National Security Council added their stamp of approval to the proposed appointment. But a note from Garment on 18 January 1972 killed it off:

> From a source I consider reliable, I have a description of Fischer as "incredibly eccentric, possessing strange religious attachments, having a very colorful private life, can be both incredibly rude and charming, unpredictable."

Following Fischer's triumph, the issue returned to the White House agenda. Interestingly, there was even talk of flying in Spassky, too. General Alexander Haig, Nixon's chief of staff, saw "no problems with the president agreeing to meet with Bobby Fischer. There has been widespread international interest in the match, and the meeting would be pleasing, for example, to the Icelanders considering that their president has just met with

Fischer. On the other hand, we do not think it would be appropriate for the president to meet with Boris Spassky."

What happened to the invitation is unclear. Palsson says it was there, but Fischer could not make up his mind about dates. "Bobby knew I wanted to go to the White House. He had to send a guest list, and he said, 'You're top of the list.' I asked when we were going. He was always postponing it." The publicity value to the president diminished with every passing day. Almost thirty years later, an irate Fischer snarled, "I was never invited to the White House. They invited that Olympic Russian gymnast—that little communist Olga Korbut."

Three months in the States were enough for Palsson. His family did not want to relocate to the United States, and he missed them. He told Fischer he was leaving; Icelandic Air paid for his ticket home. Fischer rushed up to his friend at the airport and said, "Are you really leaving me?" In a fit of guilt, the U.S. Chess Federation found $500 to compensate Palsson for his labors; as he had been with Fischer for five months, that worked out at $3 a day.

Within a few months, Fischer had virtually vanished from public view, pausing only to put in a cameo performance toward the end of 1972 at the Fried Chicken tournament. This took place in San Antonio, Texas, and was funded by George Church, who had made a fortune from his fried chicken franchise empire. Some of the best players in the world were there, though Fischer was not invited. One of the organizers said this was because "there was a danger that for his appearance fee Bobby would demand Mr. Church's entire business." However, he was welcomed as an honored guest and flown in on a private jet. Naturally, he was late, holding up a round of games for fifteen minutes.

The tournament culminated in a three-way tie, between the Armenian veteran Tigran Petrosian, the Hungarian veteran Lajos Portisch, and an anemic-looking twenty-one-year-old Russian. Anatoli Karpov was the Soviet authorities' hope for the next generation, though they were worried about his stamina. He weighed only about 106 pounds and looked as if he barely had the strength to lift any piece weightier than a pawn. But he was hugely gifted, mentally tough, and a member of the Botvinnik school of whole-heartedly Soviet chess players. He once said that his three hob-bies were chess, stamp collecting, and Marxism. His chess, like his personality, was sober, practical, and phlegmatic.

In 1974, Karpov took on the Soviet elite one by one in the Candidates round. Having already beaten Lev Polugaievskii and then Boris Spassky (in a closely fought contest), he emerged vic-torious against Viktor Korchnoi, too. Korchnoi had accused the Soviet authorities of favoring the younger man in their head-to-head.

So Karpov was set to challenge Fischer in a match for the world title. The general assembly of the International Chess Federation met during the chess Olympiad of 1974 to agree to the terms of the match. Fischer had fired off a fusillade of 179 demands, all but two of which FIDE immediately conceded. Petrosian grumbled, "These men do everything that Bobby wishes, and he will sit down at the chessboard on the conditions that he dictates to them." Although Ed Edmondson was back on Fischer's team, once again Fred Cramer was the main conduit for Fischer's conditions, one of which was that the arbiter should be banned from engaging in any journalism about the match, even after it was over. A FIDE member was overheard to comment, "Mr. Cramer will not stay quiet even for three minutes, and he wants the match controller to stay silent for his whole life."

There remained, however, two sticking points. Firstly, FIDE had proposed that the winner be the first person to win six games. Fischer insisted that the championship be decided by ten victo-ries, draws not to count, and that the number of games be unlim-ited. Second, Fischer insisted that if the score reached nine wins apiece, the champion (that is, Fischer) should retain the title, meaning the challenger must win by two clear points, an unheard-of advantage for the incumbent. After much haggling be-hind closed doors, the delegates offered a compromise—victory to be achieved by ten wins, up to a maximum of thirty-six games (at which point the player with the most points would be de-clared the winner). Otherwise, they pointed out, the match could be prolonged indefinitely. Fischer instantly dispatched a note: "I have been informed that my proposals have been rejected by a majority of votes. By doing so, FIDE has decided against my participation in the 1975 world championship. I therefore resign my FIDE world championship title."

All was not yet lost. Many people interpreted his resignation as another, familiar display of brinkmanship. The bidding process for the match continued apace, with Manila offering a staggering $5 million, said to be the second largest purse in sporting history (just below the Muhammad Ali–George Foreman "Rumble in the Jungle" in Zaire).

The full FIDE body assembled in March 1975. Now they made one more concession, agreeing to an unlimited number of games. But they refused to countenance Fischer's nine-to-nine rule. Edmondson went to California to plead with the champion. Meanwhile, FIDE announced that if Fischer did not agree by 1 April, he would be deemed to have forfeited the title. The day came and went. On 2 April, a new champion was proclaimed, Anatoli Karpov. In his acceptance speech, he hinted that he was prepared to meet Fischer in an unofficial match, presumably thinking of Manila and the $5 million. He even met Fischer secretly three times, in Japan, Washington, D.C., and Manila, to discuss terms. Eventually, Sergei Pavlov at the Sports Ministry, backed by the Central Committee, turned down the idea. Chief ideologist Mikhail Suslov himself signed its death warrant. He considered it "inexpedient."

Fischer had been the most dormant of champions, not playing a single competitive game for three years. Eager to prove himself worthy of the crown, Karpov went on to be the most active, growing in strength over the following years, winning a series of elite grandmaster tournaments, and stamping his authority on the chess world. He beat Korchnoi twice more, in the Philippine city of Baguio in 1978 (just) and in Merano in Italy in 1981 (convincingly). Garry Kasparov, Karpov's successor as world champion, wrote of Baguio, "It finally erased the memory of Reykjavik and restored the prestige of Soviet chess."

Where was Fischer? For several years, he lived in the bosom of the Worldwide Church of God in Pasadena, where he was called "a co-worker." The church fed him, they gave him comfortable accommodation in Mocking Bird Lane, they even flew him around in a private jet. In return, Fischer handed over around a third ($61,200) of his Icelandic prize money. He was befriended by Harry Sneider, a national weight-lifting champion who trained church students. Almost every evening, he and Fischer would take some form of physical exercise—soccer, basketball, racquetball, swimming, table football. Fischer was now also spending a lot of time listening to Christian preachers on the radio.

There were other people willing to look after him. One was Claudia Mokarow, also a member of the Worldwide Church of God. International master David Levy visited Fischer in 1976. At the time, his host was staying in a large house with no furniture. Levy and Fischer slept on mattresses on the floor. Fischer used Mokarow as a taxi service, Levy remembers, calling her up to take them to and from the restaurants of his choice.

In 1977 Fischer broke with the church, accusing it of being "satanic," and vigorously attacking its methods and leadership. From this point on, the subject of so much chess acclaim became a near total recluse. Those acquaintances with whom he kept in contact were sworn to secrecy. Relations with anyone who spoke about him to the outside world were broken off—for good. So as not to be recognized, he grew a beard and mustache. However, a letter from Fischer to an old chess acquaintance, Bernard Zuckerman, dated 13 May 1978, shows that he was still using Claudia Mokarow as his answering service. He gave her telephone number and told Zuckerman that was where he could leave messages.

Fischer's life now became a fertile ground for rumor, although few rumors could exaggerate the reality. In early 1981, he spent several months in San Francisco playing a series of seventeen speed games against Peter Biyiasas, a Greek-born Canadian grandmaster. (Fischer won them all.) Biyiasas said that Fischer carried around a locked valise full of Chinese and Mexican pills. "If the Commies come to poison me, I don't want to make it easy for them." There were reports that Fischer had replaced all his fillings after coming to believe that the Soviets were capable of using the metal in his teeth to beam in malignant waves.

On the afternoon of 26 May 1981, Fischer was picked up by the police, apparently mistaken for a bank robber, and was thrown behind bars for two days. He later published a pamphlet, graphically depicting the indignities he suffered: "*I Was Tortured in the Pasadena Jailhouse!* by Bobby Fischer, the World Chess Champion."

It appears that Fischer's refusal to cooperate with the authorities and his inability to recall the address at which he was staying were at least part of the problem. Fischer wrote that he was "brutally handcuffed" and that the metal tore into his flesh. When he stopped answering their questions, one officer, Fischer wrote, "grabbed my throat with one hand and started choking me by the neck." Although he never discovered this policeman's name, he wanted him identified. Fischer described him as "hyper-aggressive, like a little dog who barks and snaps a lot and bares his teeth. He is also quite vicious." Fischer declared that he was stripped and left naked in a bare, dank, drafty cell. Through the tiny window, he sought help from passersby, screaming that he was being tortured to death. Nobody came to his rescue.

Fischer's apparent inability to distinguish between the genuinely shocking and the relatively trivial is striking. The hysterical tone remains constant throughout: "Legality is a sham at the jailhouse. There are *No Smoking* signs everywhere, and no smoking is rigidly enforced—for the prisoners. But I noticed a light-skinned colored cop/jailer smoking whenever he pleased."

The text is signed:

Robert D. James (professionally known as Robert J. Fischer or Bobby Fischer, the World Chess Champion)

After this, "Robert J. Fischer, the World Chess Champion," became a wanderer. For a time in the mid-1980s, he lived in Germany. Michael Bezold, then just a schoolboy but later a grandmaster, analyzed with him each day for three months. Fischer was still a nocturnal animal, rising in the afternoon and often eating a huge breakfast of cereal and eggs and bread at five P.M. He was obsessed with "a game in the 1960s, and the question was whether or not to move the pawn to h6. This was the only question. And he said he'd been analyzing this game for more than thirty years, and he couldn't figure out whether it's better to play h6 or not. It was fantastic."

Then suddenly the recluse resurfaced for all the world to see. In 1992, in the midst of the Yugoslav war, exactly two decades after their encounter in Reykjavik, Spassky and Fischer met in a rematch. It was organized by Jezdimir Vasiljevic, a Serbian financier of dubious repute, who proffered $5 million of his bank's money (two-thirds to go to the winner, one-third to the loser) to entice the ex-champions back to the board. Once again, the world's press assembled en masse, tantalized not only by the prospect of a battle between the two old foes, but by a sighting of Fischer. What would he look like after all these years?

The answer was, totally transformed from the lithe, boyish figure he had presented in Reykjavik. Now forty-nine, balding, pudgy, and with a beard mottled the same shade of gray as his suit, he had the air of a university lecturer. Fischer considered this a "World Championship" contest—absurdly, given that he had forfeited the title seventeen years earlier and Spassky was now rated only about one hundredth in the world.

The match, split between Belgrade and the picturesque island resort of Sveti Stefan in Montenegro on the Adriatic Sea, was in many ways a triumph for Fischer's obduracy (as well as his principles), for the rules were those upon which Fischer had insisted in 1974 in the negotiations with FIDE. But his taking part in the match in the middle of the Yugoslav civil war breached UN sanctions: the U.S. Treasury Department bluntly informed him beforehand that he would be in violation of an executive order (number 12810) if the match went ahead—a serious crime carrying a heavy fine and/or a jail sentence.

He ignored the warning. In a press conference, Fischer opened his brown leather suitcase and removed a letter from the Treasury Department. He then spat at it, with precision. Asked about the then top two players in the world, Karpov and Kasparov, he described them as "the lowest dogs around." A U.S. arrest warrant was later issued—it is still valid.

For admirers of the two champions, the rematch was an unedifying spectacle, rather like the sight of two former heavyweight boxers, well past their prime, climbing back into the ring for a last big payday. After game one, the experts were in a state of high excitement—Fischer had won it brilliantly: he looked like the Fischer of old. But it was a form he was to regain in only a couple of games. Although he won convincingly, ten games to Spassky's five, with fifteen draws, the quality of the chess was regarded as somewhat pedestrian. An immensely profitable few weeks for the two adversaries, the episode tarnished the Reykjavik legend as a bad sequel to a movie can sully the original.

Then the nomad was off again. Zita Rajcsanyi, a nineteen-year-old Hungarian chess star, had been instrumental in drawing him into the Spassky rematch and had kept him company in Yugoslavia. But although Fischer spent several years in Budapest in the 1990s, Rajcsanyi married and disappeared from the scene. At some stage, Fischer moved to Tokyo. There are reports of his having a child. Sightings of him became as rare and often no more accurate than those of the Loch Ness monster.

Fischer has descended into an abyss of unreality, the world of Holocaust denial, persecution complexes, and conspiracy theories. In the 1980s he became fixated on the study of anti-Semitic tracts, such as the Tsarist forgery *The Protocols of the Elders of Zion* and Hitler's manifesto, *Mein Kampf*. In the late 1990s, he broadcast occasional interviews, though he performed only on condition that they went out live. This was a risky proposition for station chiefs: Fischer railed about the Jews, usually referring to them as kikes, Jew-bastards, or Yids. He told those with whom he retained any kind of contact that he had a mission to tell the truth. "It's a dirty job, but somebody has to do it. Huh!" As for the attacks on the Pentagon and the World Trade Center on 11 September 2001, "Well, America got what it deserved." That very day, on Philippine radio, he shouted, "Death to the U.S.A.!" (The USCF subsequently passed a motion condemning their only world champion.) An anticommunism had somehow transmuted into an anti-Americanism. In an interview with Icelandic radio, he recommended the country break with the United States and shut down the Keflavik air base. His e-mail address in Japan was us_is_shit.

Fischer's mother and sister have died. His mother took to the grave an astonishing secret: Her son's biological father was not her ex-husband, Gerhardt, but a Hungarian-born physicist, Paul Nemenyi, which whom she began an affair in 1942. Against Nemenyi's wishes, Bobby was never told what the U.S. government must have known. For a quarter of a century, as Bobby was growing up, the FBI tracked Regina closely, suspecting her of being a communist agent. They documented every detail of her life: her political affiliations, her contacts, her movements. They investigated her telephone records and bank account details; they interviewed her neighbors and work colleagues. Dozens of special agents were involved, and scores of informers serviced them with information. Many of the FBI memos are from or to the then director of the FBI, J. Edgar Hoover. Given Bobby's anti-Semitic and anticommunist obsessions, there is a poignant irony to the fact that his parents were communist sympathizers and that he is ethnically Jewish on both sides of his true parentage.*

Does he still play? With the advent of Internet chess, Fischer gossip began to circulate with ever-increasing velocity within the international chess community. On the Internet, many players—especially grandmasters—adopt a pseudonym as their "handle," their Internet name. One reason for this practice is to prevent potential opponents from studying their games and detecting within them certain structures and patterns. There have been insistent tales of Fischer himself dabbling in cyberspace. An astoundingly successful "handle" is observed smashing opponents with consummate ease and the cyberwhispering begins: "Fischer is back." The remarkable readiness with which these stories are embraced is akin to the eager anticipation of religious cult members awaiting a second coming. With his disappearance, the Fischer mystique has become part of chess lore, captured, for example, in the Hollywood film *Searching for Bobby Fischer,* about a father's relationship with his talented son and the pressures of being compared to the former champion.

*See appendix for the full story of the files.

He invented a clock, the Fischer clock, the principal idea of which has rapidly gained currency in the chess community. Like many of Fischer's proposals, its aim is to strip chess of risk as far as possible so that it is the better player who ultimately wins. With the conventional clock, a situation can occur in which a player has only one minute on the clock to make, say, ten moves—in such circumstances silly slip-ups are quite common. On the Fischer clock, each time a player makes a move, he or she is given more time. For instance, the clock may be set to give the mover an extra two minutes after every move. A mad time scramble is thus avoided.

To reenergize chess and to free it from the oppressive body of theoretical knowledge built up over decades, Fischer now advocates random chess, in which the pieces on the back row are shuffled at the beginning of each game. Random chess would force players to clear their minds of preparatory work and think about each game afresh. Fischer dreams of another Spassky rematch—this time at random chess. Spassky told the authors of this book that he would agree to one, "just for fun."

Reykjavik changed chess itself. In the immediate aftermath of the 1972 match, a sudden fascination for the game brought salad days for the chess masters. Publishers sought them out to satisfy the appetite for information: A huge array of books appeared, from those targeted at the complete beginner to those aimed at the already accomplished. There were books on openings, books on the middle game, books on endings. There were books on tactics and books on strategy, books on how to beat the *patzer* and a book on how to beat Fischer. A number of instant books were released on the match. The first, by David Levy and Svetozar Gligoric, was on its way to the printing presses before the result had been officially declared, and went on sale in New York stores within twenty-four hours of the declaration. Gligoric had penned his final sentence immediately after his good friend Lothar Schmid let slip that Spassky had resigned by telephone. The one-hundred-thousand print run sold out rapidly.

The chess phenomenon was such that grandmasters, and even

international masters, could now make a decent living. The prize money shot up for competitions; cash was to be earned from giving simultaneous matches, from writing, from coaching. Edmar Mednis turned professional along with several other top players. "During the first year subsequent to the match, it was as though money were falling from heaven."

Soon after Reykjavik, San Francisco promoter Cyrus Weiss floated the idea of a professional chess major league, in which five teams across the United States would compete against one another in a series of televised matches. At the time, this seemed far from quixotic. Chess was entering the nation's sporting bloodstream. A decade earlier, the U.S. Chess Federation had fewer than 10,000 members. Now there were over 60,000 and the rate of growth appeared to be carrying the numbers into orbit.

A generation of youngsters was stimulated to take up the game. The rise of Britain as a chess powerhouse can be traced back to Reykjavik. Nigel Short, who one day would challenge Garry Kasparov for the title, decided then, at age seven, that he would become a professional.

The match itself inspired the (then) most expensive musical ever staged, *Chess,* written by Tim Rice and the ABBA partnership of Benny Andersson and Björn Ulvaeus. The idea for the musical had occurred to Rice shortly after Fischer's victory: "The good guy was the Russian, who was meant to be the bad guy, and the bad guy was the American, who was meant to be the good guy. It was all very confusing and a perfect illustration of how politics creeps into everything." His lyrics reflected this:

> *The value of events like this need not be stressed*
> *When East and West*
> *Can meet as comrades, ease the tension over drinks*
> *Through sporting links*
> *As long as their man sinks.*

Again, this cold war aspect was singled out by a 1980s British pop group, the critically acclaimed Prefab Sprout, in their song "Cue Fanfare":

The sweetest moment comes at last—the waiting's over,
in shock they stare and cue fanfare.
When Bobby Fischer's plane touches the ground,
he'll take those Russian boys and play them out of town,
playing for blood as grandmasters should.

However, in America, at least, the explosion of interest did not endure as long as the cold war. Although grandmasters have never quite returned to their earlier levels of impoverishment, within a few years the enthusiasm of promoters had begun to subside, and sponsorship money for tournaments to dry up. And just as Fischer had been primarily responsible for the boom, so, by disappearing from the scene, he was principally responsible for the bust.

Apart from Fischer, none of the Western participants benefited materially. Palsson was left financially worse off than before, though his house is rich in bulging scrapbooks. Paul Marshall never received a dime: "I guess being involved in such an intimate way in what turned out to be a world-shatteringly silly event, and the fact that it was good for dinner party conversations for the rest of my life, was probably enough of a fee." Gudmundur Thorarinsson went on to serve as a member of Parliament for two terms—but failed to scale the political heights to which he had hoped the match would take him. Nevertheless, more than three decades on, he is still starry-eyed over the event he brought to Reykjavik: "People say this was the chess match of the century. It was not the chess match of the century. It was the chess match of all time."

Beyond the legend, what we are left with, of course, are the games. As one would expect from a clash between the two preeminent players of the day, several were of extraordinary brilliance, artistic creations that will be with us always. One thinks, for example, of the magnificent game ten, apparently so effortless, so economical, so unshowy—yet so beautiful. There were also some staggering howlers, a function of the inhuman stress affecting both players: Bxh2 in game one (Fischer), Qc2 in game five (Spassky), pawn to b5 in game eight (Spassky), pawn to f6 in game fourteen (Spassky). Works of art are usually the product of a single guiding mind and hand. A chess masterpiece is the product of competing genius: Crass blunders from either side can disqualify a game from true greatness. But Spassky's errors and defeat must not be allowed to obscure the fact that he was one of the finest players of all time. In his career, he could boast match-play victories against some of the totemic chess names of the second half of the twentieth century—Keres, Geller, Tal, Larsen, Korchnoi, and Petrosian.

Fischer, some will maintain, was *the* outstanding player in chess history, though there are powerful advocates too for Lasker, Capablanca, Alekhine, and Kasparov. Many chess players will dismiss such comparisons as meaningless, akin to the futile attempt to grade the supreme musicians of all time. But the manner in which Fischer stormed his way to Reykjavik, his breathtaking dominance at the Palma de Majorca Interzonal, the trouncings of Taimanov, Larsen, and Petrosian—all this was unprecedented. There never has been an era in modern chess during which one player has so overshadowed all others.

ᴧᴧᴧ

Our story is in essence a tragedy. What could have been the feast of chess anticipated by Spassky is as much remembered for the pathologically manipulative behavior of the challenger, the panic of the officials, and the psychological collapse of the champion, as for the quality of the games.

While we may sympathize with the organizers and the manifest and manifold pressures upon them, the game three capitulation to the challenger can be seen as their moral tragedy. Had they not been impelled to give way to Fischer, Spassky might have left Reykjavik early, and as champion. On the other hand, had Spassky himself not been so fixed on playing Fischer, had he been a little less of a free spirit and a little more willing to work with the authorities, he might have left Reykjavik on his own initiative, and as champion.

Fischer's life testifies to F. Scott Fitzgerald's proposition that "there are no second acts in American lives." Achieving his only goal destroyed his raison d'être. Without that goal, he seemed to lose his already weak hold on reality. With nothing more to prove, fear of defeat prevailed over his desire to play. Fischer turned Reykjavik into a battleground, and the match would be the last real chess war he would ever wage.

Boris Spassky went to Reykjavik to celebrate chess. Bobby Fischer went there to fight. His version of the match triumphed. The relics of the combat can be seen in the Icelandic Chess Federation museum, found down a Reykjavik side street, on the first floor of what looks like the run-down offices of a struggling small business. Some photographs and cartoons capture the atmosphere of the event. And there, recently reclaimed from the cellars of the National Museum to which they had been consigned, are the chessboard, signed by the contenders, the chessmen they pushed across it, and the clock started by Lothar Schmid at five P.M. on 11 July 1972 to begin the match of the century.

APPENDIX

We have mentioned Regina Fischer, Bobby's mother, only in passing. The FBI suspected that she was a Soviet agent. The Bureau's files, the fruit of three decades of surveillance, present a fascinating portrait of a woman possessed of extraordinary force of character and unconventional attitudes. They also tell of the secret at the heart of her family.

Regina's parents were of Polish-Jewish origin. Her father, Jacob Wender, was a dress cutter by profession. The family had moved first to Switzerland, where Regina was born on 31 March 1913, and then, when she was only a few months old, to St. Louis in the American Midwest. Her mother, Natalie, died when Regina was ten; Jacob married Ethel Greenberg, with whom Regina did not get along. Jacob and Regina were naturalized as Americans on 12 November 1926.

After graduating from high school in St. Louis, Regina attended Washington University, the University of Arizona, and the University of Denver. In 1932, nineteen years old and without a degree, she went to Berlin to study and to work as a governess. There she fell in love with Gerhardt Fischer, five years her senior; he was also known by another name, Gerardo Liebscher.

In early 1933, the couple made the decision to uproot to Moscow. Regina claimed later they had done so to get married: Of course, with the rise of the Nazi Party in Germany, she might have felt increasingly uncomfortable there. But that Russia was the chosen destination probably indicates the true reason for their leaving Germany. Gerhardt was a communist. He might even have been a Comintern agent.

In any case, they married in Moscow on 4 November 1933 and lived on in the city for five years. Their daughter, Joan, was born there in 1937. Regina studied at the First Moscow Medical Institute. Gerhardt was associated with the Moscow Brain Institute. For some of the time, they occupied apartment 42 at Zemlianoi Val 14/16, in a neighborhood of substantial Stalin-era apartments, with big living rooms and kitchens. Their choice of refuge from Nazi power scarcely offered peace and security; this was the height of the Great Terror. But unlike many other foreign communists who sought sanctuary in the Soviet Union, Gerhardt was not among Stalin's victims.

Toward the end of that five-year period, there is evidence that the marriage might have become rocky. When Regina went to renew her passport at the American embassy on 29 July 1938, she informed a member of staff that she had separated from her husband. But this could well have been a cover-up. It is likely that Gerhardt had left (or been sent) to operate on the Republican side in the Spanish civil war.

Regina departed for France later that year, meeting up with Gerhardt in Paris (whether he arrived in France from the USSR or Spain is unclear). Peace in Europe was looking increasingly uncertain, and Regina was now determined to return to the United States: She did so on 23 January 1939. Gerhardt, who did not have a U.S. passport, stayed on in Europe; he had somehow managed to acquire a Spanish passport, number 5999, evidence of his involvement in civil war Spain. But it remains a mystery why he was denied access to the States when he was married to a U.S. citizen. In any case, on 4 January 1940, he landed in Chile, where he eventually set up a shop selling and installing fluorescent lighting, and dabbled in photographic work.

.ı.ıı.ıı.

Until Bobby was seventeen, Regina was omnipresent in his life. What she almost certainly did not know, and what Bobby could not have known, is that the family was closely monitored by the FBI, which amassed a nine-hundred-page file on her. The dossier reveals that some factual details routinely offered in biographical accounts of Bobby's early life are wrong.

Regina was first brought to the attention of the FBI on 3 October 1942, when she was working as a student instructor at the U.S. Air Force's Radio Instructors' School at St. Louis University. She expected her second child the following March. Regina was financially desperate,

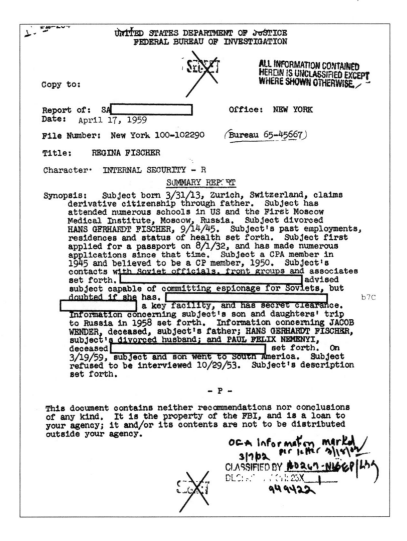

so much so that, through a Jewish charity, she attempted to place her daughter, Joan, with another family.

The arrangement quickly collapsed, the foster mother asking Regina to take Joan back. The woman did not tell Regina that she had contacted the authorities. America was at war. She had discovered some "suspicious" items and documents among belongings Regina had left with Joan and considered that these posed a potential threat to the "national welfare." The suspect possessions included several pages of scribbled "chemical formulas," [sic] as well as a B-2 Cadet camera with a state-of-the-art lens and a collapsible umbrella. There was also a letter from a left-wing friend that included the sentence, "Washington is really a fascinating city, although right now it is getting too hot for comfort." The woman considered it worthy of note that Regina owned "a heavy black rubber apron and two heavy rubber sheets."

So began an operation lasting two decades and costing tens of thousands of U.S. government dollars, though there were perfectly plausible explanations for the items Regina left among Joan's belongings. After returning to the United States, Regina had completed her BA degree at the University of Denver, where she majored in French, German, biology, and chemistry. The last would account for the "chemical formulas" and perhaps the rubber sheet and gloves. As for the camera and collapsible umbrella, her absent husband, Gerhardt, was a professional photographer.

Although the evidence was circumstantial, the FBI came to believe Gerhardt was something more sinister—that he was a Soviet agent. Why did he spend those years in Russia? Why did he have that mysterious Spanish passport? In Chile, had he not joined the Communist Party and fraternized with fellow left-wingers? But most significant of all, in the eyes of the FBI, was a letter also found among Regina's belongings in 1942. It had been posted in June 1941 and was written in a stilted style; the FBI described it as "cryptic" (though English was not Gerhardt's mother tongue). In the letter, Gerhardt explained how he had taken pictures of fishing boats and fishermen at the port of San Antonio about an hour and a half west of the capital, Santiago. The FBI observed that at the same time, three Germans, posing as fishermen at the port, were charged with transmitting espionage information by radio.

If Gerhardt was a Soviet agent, what about his wife? It made no difference to the FBI that Regina was granted a divorce from Gerhardt on 14 September 1945 on the grounds of willful neglect to provide for her and their two children—she had received no financial support since July 1942. (At the time, she was living in Moscow, Idaho. The local paper, the *Daily Idahonian,* had fun with the story—married in Moscow, divorced in Moscow.)

The FBI files contain half a dozen physical descriptions of Regina; one from this period states that she was five feet four, with dark brown hair, dark brown eyes, thick eyebrows, full lips, olive complexion, heavy legs, a low and heavy bust, and a "scruffy" appearance. Her nose features in another description—long and "a little crooked."

According to an informer, in the same year that her divorce came through, Regina was recruited to the Communist Political Association

(CPA) in Oregon. The CPA was described under Executive Order 9835 as a communist and subversive organization that sought to "alter the form of government of the United States by unconstitutional means." President Truman issued Executive Order 9835 on 22 March 1947, initiating a program to seek out any "infiltration of disloyal persons" in the U.S. government. By December 1952, over 6.6 million people had been secretly investigated—no case of espionage was uncovered.

Was Regina an active member of the CPA? The FBI believe she was expelled in 1950 for being "unfaithful." But she was certainly politically engaged, at different times belonging to or associated with a variety of left-wing organizations and causes, from the International Workers Order to American Women for Peace and, much later, the Committee for Non-Violent Action. Over the years, the Bureau accumulated further "incriminating evidence" against her. On 15 May 1945, she contacted a Russian employee at the Soviet Government Purchasing Commission in Portland about the possibility of working as a translator. A plumber notified the FBI that he had once found Regina playing what he described as "communist records" and that she tried to influence him to become a member of the Communist Party. A source "with whom contact is insufficient to judge his reliability" told the FBI that Regina had taken her child (singular) to a communist summer camp. And in a judgment demonstrating the institutional politics of Hoover's FBI, she was accused of exhibiting communist sympathies by picketing an apartment block near her home in a protest against the removal of "a colored family."

The Bureau judged Regina bright and articulate, but also, in the words of one informer, a "real pain in the neck." A source described her as "antagonistic" and "argumentative." It was said that all the tenants in their Brooklyn block disliked the Fischers, and that Regina had a "suit complex," often initiating legal action against the landlord for "imagined grievances."

There was also a psychiatric report. Shortly after Bobby was born, Regina took advantage of a Chicago charity, going to stay in the Sarah Hackett Memorial Home for indigent single women with babies. When she wanted her daughter, Joan, to join her and Bobby—since Joan's fostering had not worked—the charity told her there was no room and that in any event, Joan had a perfectly satisfactory home. (Joan was in St. Louis, perhaps with her grandfather.) Regina smuggled Joan in; the resulting dispute then escalated as Regina tried to rouse the other residents against the managers. She was eventually arrested for disturbing the peace. The judge found her not guilty but ordered a mental health examination. The Municipal Psychiatric Institute diagnosed her as a "stilted (paranoid) personality, querulent [sic] but not psychotic." The report recommended, "If her small children should suffer because of her obstinacy, juvenile court intervention should be initiated."

The FBI investigation was not limited to Regina. Special agents gathered information on Jacob, her father, also a left-winger, as well as her brother, Max, "a known Commie" who had moved to Detroit. Because Regina and Ethel, Jacob's second wife, loathed each other, the FBI approached Ethel for information on her stepdaughter (this was many years after the two women had stopped speaking). On one occasion, in October 1953, the FBI even approached Regina directly—calculating that because she had abandoned the Communist Party, she might be willing to dish the dirt on former comrades. Regina, however, was "uncooperative"; she was prepared to be interviewed, but only with a lawyer present.

In the mid-1950s, the file became relatively inactive. But when, in March 1957, Regina contacted the Soviet embassy about Bobby's trip to Moscow, the case sprang back into life—and with a vengeance. On 21 May 1957, an agent wrote to the director of the FBI:

```
It is to be noted that subject is a well-educated, widely
travelled intelligent woman who has for years been associ-
ated with communists and persons of pro-communist leanings.
In view of the foregoing and in light of her recent contact
of an official of the Soviet Embassy, it is desired that
this case be re-opened and that investigation be instituted
in an effort to determine if subject has in the past or may
presently be engaged in activities inimical to the interest
of the United States.
```

Now her bank accounts were checked, fellow nurses at her hospital were surreptitiously taken to one side and questioned, the make of her car was jotted down (a 1957 Chrysler Sedan), her father's will was examined (Regina inherited a tidy sum—around $40,000), and all previously collated documents were excavated and old sources reinterviewed.

By this stage, Bobby had become a celebrity, and the relationship between him and his mother was placed under the official microscope. The FBI director was reassured that the inquiry was being handled with "the utmost discretion," so as not to arouse Regina's attention. One source told the FBI that Regina could not control her son. She "lives in terror of him [Bobby] but at the same time seems to 'gloat' over his publicity."

Bobby's movements were tracked to and from Moscow via Brussels and Prague. Agents were asked to discover why he was so disgusted with his Soviet hosts. Did they make some kind of communist "approach" to him? After Moscow, and before the Interzonal at Portoroz, an informer described Bobby as "a very sick boy emotionally and in such a mental state at the present time that losing the tournament may cause him to become violent and may cause him to be confined to a mental institution."

In 1959, Bobby and Regina went to Argentina and then Chile. Bobby was playing chess. What was Regina doing? Was she trying to contact her ex-husband? (She may not have known that two years earlier, "Don Gerardo Fischer Liebscher" had remarried, to a Mrs. Renata Sternaux Meyer in Algarrobo in Chile.) The question was considered of such import that on 22 May, Hoover wrote to his counterpart, the director of the Central Intelligence Agency, Allen Dulles, to request assistance and collaboration: "Inasmuch as Mrs. Regina Fischer accompanied her son to South America, it is believed probable that she was with him in Santiago, Chile, during the chess tournament in that city. Accordingly, the possibility exists that Mrs. Fischer may have been in contact with her estranged husband, Gerardo Fischer."

By the end of September 1959, the FBI at last acknowledged its failure to unearth any real subversion: "It appears the only logical investigation remaining would be an interview of the subject, but due to her mental instability, this line of action is not recommended. Therefore, it is recommended that no further investigation be conducted and this case be closed."

In spite of that recommendation, a residual watchfulness continued. In 1960, Regina picketed the White House because the State Department refused the U.S. chess team permission to play in that year's Olympiad in East Germany. Her demonstration provoked many column inches in papers across the nation. A secret service agent reported her movements: She arrived at 10:30 A.M. and departed at 2:33 P.M. She returned to the White House at 4:52 P.M., staying until 5:30 P.M. In the autumn, when Regina moved out of her long-standing Brooklyn home, the FBI dispatched an agent, disguised as a deliveryman, to confirm that she really had settled into her new abode in the Bronx.

During a 1961 "Walk for Peace" from San Francisco to Moscow, sponsored by the Committee for Non-Violent Action, Regina met her second husband, an English left-wing teacher, Cyril Pustan. She relocated to Europe, where the Bureau still took note of her activities: her continued protests in France, West Germany, and Great Britain against the Vietnam War, her attendance in Stockholm on 24 July 1967 at a conference on Vietnam. Finally the FBI gave up, parting company with Regina after nearly a quarter of a century. Regina eventually returned to the United States, where she died of cancer in 1997. (Don Gerardo Fischer Liebscher died on 25 February 1993 in the city of his birth, Berlin.)

Intriguingly, the detailed information in the dossier puts a question mark over Bobby's official parentage: If Gerhardt was his biological father, when did he and Regina conceive their son? Bobby was born in 1943. While Gerhardt and Regina divorced only in 1945, they were physically apart from 1939, though Regina is reported as saying—presumably in an attempt to explain Bobby—that she and Gerhardt had a 1942 rendezvous in Mexico.

Some continuing relationship between them is indicated by Regina's making a move to visit her husband in 1944—though there is no hint as to her motive or intention. She applied for a visa to Chile, but the wartime Department of State returned the forms to her because some details were missing. In May 1945, she presented a statement from the University of Chile offering her a place as a student. She never took this up: the divorce came through four months later. The FBI files contain no evidence that Gerhardt tried to join her in the United States before or after Bobby's birth. What is more, on several occasions she confessed to not having seen her husband since 1939.

If not Gerhardt, who? For reasons never elucidated—always blanked out—there are copious notes on Dr. Paul Felix Nemenyi in the files on Regina. He is described as having a large nose, large knobby fingers, and an awkward, slovenly walk and dress.

Born into a Jewish family in Fiume in Hungary on 5 June 1895, Nemenyi was educated at the Institute of Technology in Budapest and in Berlin. He then held research fellowships in Copenhagen and Imperial College, London. In 1939, he emigrated to the United States. There he worked as a mathematics teacher and later as a mechanical engineer in a highly sensitive post in the Naval Research Laboratory in Washington, D.C. His expertise was in fluid mechanics. He died at a dance in Washington, D.C., on 1 March 1952. The FBI suspected that he too was a communist.

The notes offer an account of the relationship between Regina and Paul that points in one direction only: Nemenyi was Bobby's biological father. A year before Bobby was born, Nemenyi befriended Regina when he was an assistant mathematics professor in Colorado. After Bobby was born, he took a special interest in the child. When Regina moved to Washington with her new baby, it looks as if it was Dr. Nemenyi who found her an apartment to stay in and paid the rent. After she relocated to New York, he paid for Bobby's attendance at Brooklyn Community College and sent Regina $20 a week. He seemed to visit his son often enough for Bobby to become attached to him. At one stage, in 1948, the Bureau discovered Nemenyi telling a social worker that he was very upset about the way Bobby was being brought up, particularly because of the "instability of the mother."

Letters written to and by Nemenyi's son, Peter, who became a civil rights activist, are now available and appear to put the identity of Bobby's biological father beyond doubt. In the month his father died, Peter wrote to Bobby's psychiatrist, Dr. Kline, asking for advice on who should inform Bobby of Nemenyi's death; he assumed the doctor knew that Nemenyi was Bobby Fischer's father. The following month, Regina wrote to Peter complaining that she had no money for food or to repair Bobby's shoes. Bobby had been feverish, but she could not afford a doctor. In an imploring tone, she asked whether Nemenyi had left Bobby any money. She told Peter that Bobby was still expecting Nemenyi's visits; she had not told him of the death.

It seems unlikely that anybody ever told him. If the FBI had not delved so carefully into Regina's life, and if Bobby Fischer, the world chess champion, had not remained an object of fascination for press and public to this day, his family secret would have remained just that.

ACKNOWLEDGMENTS

Fischer-Spassky was an international affair. Necessarily, our research had to be equally wide—and likewise now our expressions of gratitude.

There are those without whom our book could not have been written: to them we offer profound thanks. Though he had a long arranged rendezvous with his autobiography, Boris Spassky unfailingly answered our questions. In Paris, he and Marina also gave us a memorable insight into Russian hospitality. In Germany, the chief arbiter Lothar Schmid set aside several days to take us in detail through the match as well as around the beauties of his ancient home city, Bamberg. Gudmundur Thorarinsson, similarly, could not have been more cordial and helpful and gave us three lengthy interviews. Also in Reykjavik, Freysteinn Johannsson, who was the Icelandic Chess Federation press officer for the match and wrote his own book on it three decades ago, tirelessly tracked down Icelandic facts, names, and telephone numbers. Without him, the book would have taken much longer to write. Saemundur Palsson regaled us with his experiences and warmly entertained us in his home by the sea, as he had the American challenger three decades before.

Viktor Ivonin gave us an unrivaled view of Moscow's part in our story from his remarkable personal records, his archive, and his (not quite) total recall of the Sports Committee and other comrades involved in the match. We would also like to thank Larisa Solovieva for setting aside understandable qualms to share her memories of life with Boris Spassky. From New York, Nikolai Krogius provided us with detailed written responses to our many queries. In Tallinn, Ivo Nei took a break from running Estonian chess at Keres House to recall his role in the match.

Former chess players, administrators, and observers of the match also gave generously of their time and memories: Lev Abramov, Yuri Averbakh, Yuri Balashov, the late Viktor Baturinskii, Yevegeni Bebchuk, Mikhail Beilin, Valeri Chamanin, Naum Dymarskii, Viktor Korchnoi, Aleksandr Nikitin, Aleksandr Roshal, Mark Taimanov, Vera Tikhomirova, Aleksandr Yermakov, and Nikolai Zharikov. Extremely pertinent too were the reflections of Anatoli Dobrynin on the absence of Fischer-Spassky from his White House agenda, Dmitri Vasil'iev on the challenges of his Reykjavik diplomatic posting, and Vitali Yeremenko on fortifying Spassky's inner man. Olga Baturinskaia kindly supported her father during our interview and supplied us with documents and photographs.

This is the appropriate point to mention our Russian researchers and translators. Carl Schreck scoured the Soviet press and chess magazines. Hannah Whitley and Andrew Yorke skillfully translated the dead language of Soviet bureaucracy and interpreted interviews; they also drew on their knowledge of Russian and Russia to offer us insights into the significance of what they read and heard. We are grateful to Tess Stobie for acting as our own Moscow Center, administering our research needs. John would also like to thank Tess and Alastair for their wonderful hospitality.

We must reserve a special place here for Victoria Ivleva-Yorke. Victoria functioned peerlessly as fixer, researcher, and interpreter. No contact was able to resist her combination of charm and insistence; her interest in the story and following up of leads were invaluable.

We have many debts on the other side of the cold war chessboard, the United States. Our thanks are due to Bob Axelrod, Pal Benko, Sid Bernstein, Arthur Bisguier, Robert Byrne, Bill Chase at Cleveland Public Library, Larry Evans, Ralph Ginzburg, Philip Hall, Eliot Hearst, Burt Hochberg, Shelby Lyman, Paul Marshall, the late Edmar Mednis, Hanon Russell, Phil Schewe, Don Schultz, Jim Sherwin, Frank Skoff, Elaine Smith, Harry Sneider, Barb Vandermark, and Josh Waitzkin. On the role of the White House, the U.S. State Department, and the Reykjavik embassy in coping with the match and the troublesome challenger, we are grateful to Gerald Ford, Len Garment, Victor Jackovich, Henry Kissinger, Helmut Sonnenfeldt, and Theodore Tremblay. Franklin Noll trawled through U.S. government records and came up with some pearls.

Taking full advantage of America's justly famed Freedom of Information Act, we asked the FBI if they held a file on Regina Fischer. A year and a half later, two telephone directory–size documents thumped through the letterbox. In the interval, Bureau weeders had pored over the text, and the many blanks spoke of their assiduity. Nevertheless, we are appreciative of the openness of the American system and the efforts in particular of Donna Shackleforth, who so courteously received our regular monthly inquiry after the dossier's whereabouts.

From our experience, the people of Iceland have a claim to be the most naturally courteous and helpful in the world. We have many to acknowledge, all of whom went out of their way to assist us. To demonstrate our regard for their country, we list them alphabetically by first name, as in the Iceland telephone directory: Colin Porter, Dadi Agustsson, Fridrik Olafsson, Fridthor Eydal, Gisli Gestsson, Gunnar Magnusson, Gunnlaugur Josefsson, Gylfi Baldursson, Hilmar Viggoson, Hjalmar Bardarson, Hrannar Arnarson, Karen Thorsteinsdottir, Paul Theodorsson, Ragnar Haraldsson, Saemundur Palsson, Sigfus Sigfusson, Sigmundur Gudbjarnason, Sigurdur Helgason, Steinn Bjornsson, Sverrir Kristinsson, Thrainn Gudmundsson, Tinna Gunnarsdottir, and the late Ulfar Thordarson. Valur Ingimundarson put the match into the wider context of Icelandic politics, and Ingolfur Gislason and Valur Steinarsson carried out research for us in Iceland.

We also want to acknowledge all those who made time to afford us their recollections or professional information and advice: Tony Attwood, Michael Bezold, Dimitri Bjelica, Archie Brown, Henk Chervet, Simon Baron Cohen, Jim Dumighan, Esther Eidinow, Hannah Eidinow, Leonid Finkelstein, Michael Fitzgerald, Svetozar Gligoric, Bill Hartston, Ray Keene, Bent Larsen, David Levy, Lennox Lewis, Helmut Pfleger, Stewart Reuben, Sir Tim Rice, Michael McDonald Ross, Jim Slater, Olexiy Solohubenko, Bob Toner, Wolfgang Unzicker, and Lawrence Warner.

Simona Celotti-Still gave up her spare time to translate many Italian newspaper articles. Hannah Edmonds assisted with German documents and Arlene Gregorius and Joanne Episcopo with Spanish.

We owe a particular debt to grandmaster Daniel King, who offered tremendous encouragement as well as chess advice throughout. Bob Wade gave us the run of his extensive library and furnished us with memories of his research for Fischer.

David would like to thank Charles Eisendrath for bestowing on him the extraordinary privilege of a Michigan Journalism Fellowship and all the fellow journalists who made the sabbatical so immensely pleasurable as well as rewarding; Marzio Mian and Carlos Prieto, who later helped with the book, deserve specific mention. Bill and Betty Ingram made it all possible by agreeing to a house swap; fortunately, their beautiful home in Ann Arbor had an icestorm-resistant roof.

Various chapters of the draft of the manuscript were sent to the following friends, all of whom identified flaws and suggested improvements. We would like to thank Archie Brown, Hannah Edmonds, Esther Eidinow, Sam Eidinow, the omniscient David Franklin, Freysteinn Johannsson, Daniel King, Peter Mangold, David Price, Zina Rohan, Neville Shack, Christopher Tugendhat, Maurice Walsh, Hannah Whitley, and Andrew Yorke.

Finally, we would like to pay tribute—for their support and superb professional skills—to Julian Loose, Charles Boyle, and Angus Cargill at Faber; Jane Beirn and Julia Serebrinsky at Ecco; our copyeditors, Ian Bahrami and Sona Vogel; and Jacqueline Korn at David Higham.

SELECTIVE BIBLIOGRAPHY

A number of books were of particular assistance to us at the outset. On Fischer, especially helpful were Frank Brady's excellent biography and Brad Darrach's fly-on-the-wall account of the match itself. In understanding Soviet chess, the works by D. J. Richards and by Andrew Soltis were invaluable, together with Genna Sosonko's illuminating accounts of leading figures.

Andrew, Christopher, and Oleg Gordievsky. *KGB: The Inside Story.* London: Hodder & Stoughton, 1990.

———. *Instructions from the Centre.* London: Hodder & Stoughton, 1991.

Armitage, S., and G. Maxwell. *Moon Country.* London: Faber, 1996.

Bakhtin, Mikhail. *Problems of Dostoevsky's Poetics.* Caryl Emerson, trans. Minneapolis: University of Minnesota, 1984.

Barnes, Julian. *Letters from London.* London: Picador, 1995.

Berkovich, Felix. *Jewish Chess Masters on Stamps.* London: McFarland & Co., 2000.

Boyd, Brian. *Vladimir Nabokov—The Russian Years.* London: Chatto & Windus, 1990.

Brady, Frank. *Profile of a Prodigy.* Toronto: Dover Publications, 1973.

Brandt, Willy. *People and Politics.* J. Maxwell Brown, trans. London: John Collins, 1978.

Brezhnev, Leonid. *Selected Speeches and Writings.* Oxford: Pergamon Press, 1979.

Brown, Archie, M. Kaser. *The Soviet Union Since the Fall of Khrushchev.* London: Macmillan, 1978.

Brown, Archie. *The Gorbachev Factor*. Oxford: Oxford University Press, 1996.

Buckley, Will. "They Also Serve." *Observer Sport Monthly* 29 (July 2002).

Bulgakov, Mikhail. *The Master and Margarita*. Michael Glenny, trans. London: Harvill Press, 1996.

Bundy, William. *A Tangled Web*. London: I. B. Tauris, 1998.

Burger, Robert. *The Chess of Bobby Fischer*. San Francisco: Hypermodern Press, 1975.

Burton, Robert. *The Anatomy of Melancholy*. Jackson Holbrook, ed. New York: Vintage Books, 1977.

Byrne, Robert, and Ivo Nei. *Both Sides of the Chessboard*. New York: Batsford, 1974.

Cafferty, Bernard. *Boris Spassky: Master of Tactics*. London: Batsford, 1991.

Canetti, Elias. *Auto da Fé*. C. V. Wedgwood, trans. London: Vintage, 2000.

———. *The Torch in My Ear*. New York: Farrar, Straus & Giroux, 1982.

Cockburn, Alexander. *Idle Passion*. London: Weidenfeld & Nicolson, 1975.

Cohen, Warren. *America's Response to China*. New York: Columbia University Press, 2000.

Cradock, Percy. *Know Your Enemy*. London: John Murray, 2002.

Crankshaw, Edward. *Khrushchev's Russia*. Harmondsworth: Penguin, 1959.

Crockatt, Richard. *The Fifty Years War*. London: Routledge, 1995.

Darrach, Brad. "The Deadly Gamesman." *Life* magazine (November 1971).

———. *Bobby Fischer vs. the Rest of the World*. New York: Stein & Day, 1974.

Davies, Norman. *Europe: A History*. Oxford: Oxford University Press, 1996.

Davies, N., M. Pein, and J. Levitt. *Bobby Fischer: The $5,000,000 Comeback*. London: Cadogan Books, 1992.

Dickson, Peter. *Kissinger and the Meaning of History*. Cambridge: Cambridge University Press, 1978.

Dobrynin, Anatoly. *In Confidence*. New York: Random House, 1995.

Dornberg, John. *Brezhnev: The Masks of Power*. London: André Deutsch, 1974.

Dostoyevsky, Fyodor. *Notes from Underground*. Jessie Coulson, trans. London: Penguin, 1972.

———. *The Brothers Karamazov*. David McDuff, trans. London: Penguin, 1993.

————. *The Diary of a Writer.* Boris Brasol, trans. London: Cassel, 1949.

Dudintsev, Vladimir. *Not by Bread Alone.* New York: Dutton, 1957.

Dulles, Allen. *The Craft of Intelligence.* London: Weidenfeld & Nicolson, 1963.

Edmonds, Robin. *Soviet Foreign Policy: The Brezhnev Years.* Oxford: Oxford University Press, 1983.

Edmondson, Ed, and Mikhail Tal. *Chess Scandals.* Oxford: Pergamon Press, 1981.

Eissenstat, Bernard, ed. *The Soviet Union: The Seventies and Beyond.* London: D. C. Heath & Co., 1975.

Eliot, T. S. *The Waste Land.* London: Faber & Faber, 1972.

Ellison, James Whitfield. *Master Prim.* Boston: Little, Brown & Co., 1968.

Euwe, Max. *Bobby Fischer and His Predecessors.* London: Bell & Sons, 1976.

Euwe, Max, and Jan Timman. *Fischer World Champion.* Alkmaarl: New in Chess, 2002.

Fanger, Donald. *Dostoevsky and Romantic Realism.* Cambridge: Harvard University Press, 1965.

Fauber, R. E. *Impact of Genius.* Seattle: International Chess Enterprises, 1992.

Fine, Reuben. *Bobby Fischer's Conquest of the World's Chess Championship.* New York: McKay, 1973.

Fischer, Robert. *My 60 Memorable Games.* London: Faber, 1972.

Fox, Mike, and Richard James. *The Complete Chess Addict.* London: Faber & Faber, 1987.

Friedman, Norman. *The Fifty-Year War.* Annapolis: Naval Institute Press, 2000.

Gaddis, John Lewis. *The United States and the End of the Cold War.* Oxford: Oxford University Press, 1992.

Garson, Robert. *The United States and China Since 1949.* London: Pinter, 1994.

Garthoff, Raymond. *Détente and Confrontation.* Washington: Brookings Institution, 1985.

Ginzburg, Ralph. "Portrait of a Genius as a Young Chess Master." *Harper's* magazine (January 1962).

Glavnic, Thomas, trans. John Brownjohn, *Carl Haffner's Love of the Draw.* London: Harvill, 1998.

Gligoric, Svetozar. *Fischer vs. Spassky.* New York: Simon & Schuster, 1972.

Goldhill, Simon. *Reading Greek Tragedy.* Cambridge: Cambridge University Press, 1986.

Golombek, Harry. *The Inside Story of the World Championship*. London: Times Newspapers Ltd., 1973.

Grossman, Vasily. *Life and Fate*. Robert Chandler, trans. London: Harvill, 1985.

Haldeman, H. R. with Joseph DiMona. *The Ends of Power*. London: Jackson, 1978.

Hartston, William. *Karpov v. Korchnoi*. London: Fontana Paperbacks, 1981.

———. *The Kings of Chess*. London: Pavilion Books Ltd., 1985.

———. *Chess: The Making of the Musical*. London: Pavilion Books Ltd., 1986.

Hartston, W., and P. Wason. *The Psychology of Chess*. London: Batsford, 1983.

Harwood, Graeme. *Caïssa's Web*. London: Latimer, 1975.

Hersh, Seymour. *Kissinger: The Price of Power*. London: Faber & Faber, 1983.

Hingley, Ronald. *The Russian Mind*. London: Bodley Head, 1977.

Ho, Allan, and Dmitry Feofanov. *Shostakovich Reconsidered*. London: Toccata Press, 1998.

Hochberg, Burt. *The 64-Square Looking Glass*. New York: Random House, 1992.

Ilf, Ilia, and Evgenii Petrov. *The Twelve Chairs*. John H. C. Richardson, trans. New York: Random House, 1961.

International Institute for Strategic Studies. *Strategic Survey*, 1969, 1970, 1971, 1972. London.

Isaacson, Walter. *Kissinger: A Biography*. London: Faber & Faber, 1992.

Jones, Malcolm. *Dostoyevsky After Bakhtin*. Cambridge: Cambridge University Press, 1990.

Johnson, Paul. *A History of the American People*. London: Weidenfeld & Nicolson, 1997.

Kahn, Herman. *Thinking About the Unthinkable*. London: Weidenfeld & Nicolson, 1962.

Karpov, Anatoly. *Chess at the Top*. Oxford: Pergamon Press, 1984.

Karpov, A., and A. Roshal. *Chess Is My Life*. Oxford: Pergamon Press, 1980.

Keene, Ray. *Korchnoi vs. Spassky*. London: George Allen & Unwin, 1977.

———. *Karpov-Kochnoi*. London: Batsford, 1978.

———. *Massacre in Merano*. London: Batsford, 1981.

———. *The Return of a Legend*. London: Batsford, 1992.

Khrushchev, Nikita. *Krushchev Remembers: The Last Testament*. Strobe Talbott, trans. London: André Deutsch, 1974.

King, D., and D. Trelford. *Kasparov v. Short.* Cadogan Chess, 1993.

King, Daniel. *Kasparov v. Deep Blue.* Batsford, 1997.

Kissinger, Henry. *American Foreign Policy.* London: Weidenfeld & Nicolson, 1969.

———. *The White House Years.* Weidenfeld & Nicolson and Michael Joseph, 1979.

———. *Diplomacy.* New York: Simon & Schuster, 1979.

Kochan, Lionel, and Richard Abraham. *The Making of Modern Russia.* Harmondsworth: Penguin, 1983.

Korchnoi, Viktor. *Chess Is My Life.* London: Batsford, 1977.

Kotov, Alexander. *Train Like a Grandmaster.* London: Batsford, 1981.

Krogius, Nikolai. *Psychology in Chess.* London: RHM Press, 1976.

Kurlansky, Mark. *Cod.* London: Jonathan Cape, 1998.

Lacy, Terry. *Iceland: Ring of Seasons.* Ann Arbor: University of Michigan Press, 1998.

Lafeber, Walter. *America, Russia, and the Cold War 1945–1980.* New York: John Wiley & Sons, 1980.

Lawson, Dominic. *The Inner Game.* London: Macmillan, 1993.

Laxness, Halldor. *The Atom Station.* Magnus Magnusson, trans. Sag Harbor, NY: Second Chance Press, 1982.

Levy, David, and Stewart Reuben. *The Chess Scene.* London: Faber & Faber, 1974.

Litwak, Robert. *Détente and the Nixon Doctrine.* Cambridge: Cambridge University Press, 1984.

Mandelstam, Osip. *The Collected Critical Prose and Letters.* Jane Gary Harris, ed. London: Collins Harvill, 1991.

Mann, James. *About Face.* New York: Alfred A. Knopf, 1999.

Mednis, Edmar. *How to Beat Bobby Fischer.* Toronto: Bantam, 1975.

Medvedev, Zhores. *The Medvedev Papers.* Vera Rich, trans. London: Macmillan, 1971.

Merridale, Catherine. *Night of Stone.* London: Granta, 2000.

Middleton, Thomas. T. H. Howard Hill, ed. *A Game of Chess.* Manchester: Manchester University Press, 1993.

———. *Women Beware Women.* J. R. Mulryne, ed. London: Methuen, 1973.

Mitchell, Edwin, ed. *The Art of Playing Chess.* New York: privately printed, 1936.

Mitrokhin, Vasily, ed. *KGB Lexicon.* London: Frank Cass, 2002.

Moran, P. *World Chess Championship.* London: Batsford, 1986.

Nabokov, Vladimir. *The Defence.* London: Weidenfeld & Nicolson, 1964.

Nixon, Richard. *The Memoirs of Richard Nixon.* London: Sidgwick & Jackson, 1978.

Nye, Joseph, ed. *The Making of America's Soviet Policy.* New Haven: Yale University Press, 1984.

Orwell, George. *Nineteen Eighty-Four.* London: Martin Secker & Warburg, 1987.

Pachman, Ludek. *Memoirs of Ludek Pachman.* London: Faber, 1975.

Pandolfini, Bruce. *Bobby Fischer's Outrageous Chess Moves.* New York: Simon & Schuster, 1985.

Pasternak, Boris. *Doctor Zhivago.* Max Hayward and Manya Harari, trans. London: Collins, 1958.

Peace, Richard. *Dostoyevsky: An Examination of the Major Novels.* Cambridge: Cambridge University Press, 1971.

Petrosian, Tigran. *The Games of Tigran Petrosian,* vol. 2. Oxford: Pergamon Press, 1991.

Pfleger, H., and G. Treppner. *The Mechanics of the Mind.* Marlborough: Crowood Press, 1988.

Plaskett, James. *The Sicilian Taimanov.* Brighton: Chess Press, 1997.

Plisetsky, Dmitri, and Sergei Voronkov. *Russians Versus Fischer.* Moscow: JACO Ltd., trans. Chess World Ltd., 1994.

Poundstone, William. *Prisoner's Dilemma.* Oxford: Oxford University Press, 1993.

Rein, Evgeny. *Selected Poems.* Valentina Polukhina, ed. Robert Reid et al, trans. Northumberland: Blood Axe Books, 2001.

Riasanovsky, Nicholas. *A History of Russia.* New York: Oxford University Press, 1984.

Richards, D. J. *Soviet Chess.* Oxford: Clarendon Press, 1965.

Roberts, R. *Fischer Spassky: The New York Times Report.* London: Bantam Books, 1972.

Rothberg, Abraham. *The Heirs of Stalin.* Ithaca: Cornell University Press, 1972.

Russell, Bertrand. *Common Sense and Nuclear Warfare.* London: George Allen & Unwin, 1959.

Saidy, A., and N. Lessing. *The World of Chess.* New York: Ridge Press, 1984.

Salzmann, Jerome. *The Chess Reader.* 1949.

Schonberg, Harold. "Chess at the Summit." *Harper's* magazine (July 1972).

———. *Grandmasters of Chess.* London: Fontana, 1975.

Schultz, Don. *Chessdon.* Boca Raton: Chessdon Publishing, 1999.

Smith, Hedrick. *The Russians.* New York: Quadrangle, 1976.

Soltis, Andrew. *Soviet Chess*. London: McFarland & Co., 2000.

Sosonko, Genna. *Russian Silhouettes*. Alkmaar: New in Chess, 2001.

Spassky, Boris, and Jan van Reek. *Grand Strategy*. Alkmaar: New in Chess, 2002.

Speelman, Jon. *Analysing the Endgame*. London: Batsford, 1988.

Steiner, George. *Fields of Force*. New York: Viking Press, 1974.

Stites, Richard. *Soviet Popular Culture*. Cambridge: Cambridge University Press, 1992.

Taimanov, Mark. *Ia byl zhertvoi Fishera [I was Fischer's victim]*. Shakhforum, Saint Petersburg, 1993.

Tal, Mikhail. *The Life and Games of Mikhail Tal*. London: Cadogan, 1997.

Tevis, Walter. *The Queen's Gambit*. London: Heinemann, 1983.

Wade, Bob. *Sousse 1967*. Chess Player.

Waitzkin, Fred. *Searching for Bobby Fischer*. New York: Random House, 1983.

Waterman, Andrew. *The Poetry of Chess*. London: Anvil Press Poetry Ltd., 1981.

Wilson, Fred, ed. *A Picture History of Chess*. New York: Dover Publications, 1981.

Wright, Esmond. *The American Dream*. Oxford: Blackwell, 1996.

Zweig, Stefan. *The Royal Game*. London: Cassell, 1945.

We plundered the archives of many newspapers, especially *Corriere della Sera, The New York Times, The Washington Post,* the *Guardian,* the *Daily Telegraph,* the *Los Angeles Times,* and *The Times* (London). In Moscow, the archives of the Russian Foreign Ministry, *Izvestia, Pravda, Vecherniaia Moskva, Shakhmati v SSSR,* and *64* were essential reading. We are grateful to the London Library and the Wisconsin Historical Society.

INDEX